DOCUMENTS OF MODERN HISTORY

General Editors:

A. G. Dickens
Director, Institute of Historical Research, University of London

Alun Davies
Professor of Modern History, University College of Swansea

ERASMUS

edited by

Richard L. DeMolen

Fellow of the Folger Shakespeare Library

Edward Arnold

© Richard L. DeMolen 1973

First published 1973 by
Edward Arnold (Publishers) Ltd.
25 Hill Street, London W1X 8LL

Cloth edition ISBN: 0 7131 5705 4
Paper edition ISBN: 0 7131 5706 2

Printed in Great Britain by
The Camelot Press Ltd., London and Southampton

CONTENTS

ABBREVIATIONS

Allen   *Opus Epistolarum Des. Erasmi Roterodami*, ed. P. S.
                Allen. 11 vols. (Oxford: Clarendon Press, 1906–47).
Born   *Institutio Principis Christiani*, 1516, or *The Education of
                a Christian Prince*, tr. Lester K. Born (New York:
                Columbia University Press, 1936).
Drummond   *Erasmus: His Life and Character as Shown in His
                Correspondence and Works* by Robert B. Drummond.
                2 vols. (London: Smith, Elder, & Co., 1873).
Emerton   *Desiderius Erasmus of Rotterdam* by Ephraim Emerton
                (New York: G. P. Putnam's Sons, 1899).
Froude   *Life and Letters of Erasmus* by J. A. Froude (New York:
                Charles Scribner's Sons, 1925).
Himelick I   *Enchiridion Militis Christiani*, 1503 and 1518, or *The
                Handbook of the Christian Soldier*, tr. Raymond
                Himelick (Bloomington: Indiana University Press,
                1963).
Himelick II   *Erasmus and the Seamless Coat of Jesus . . . with Selections
                from the Letters and Ecclesiastes*, tr. and ed. Raymond
                Himelick (Lafayette, Indiana: Purdue University
                Studies, 1971).
Hudson   *Moriae Encomium*, 1511, or *The Praise of Folly*, tr.
                Hoyt H. Hudson (Princeton, N.J.: Princeton
                University Press, 1941).
Huizinga   *Erasmus of Rotterdam* by Johann Huizinga. Letters of
                Erasmus, tr. Barbara Flower (London: Phaidon Press,
                1952).
King and Rix   *De Duplici Copia Verborum ac Rerum*, 1512, or *On
                Copia of Words and Ideas*, tr. Donald B. King and
                H. David Rix (Milwaukee: Marquette University
                Press, 1963).
Mangan   *Life, Character & Influence of Desiderius Erasmus of
                Rotterdam* by John J. Mangan. 2 vols. (New York:
                Macmillan, 1927).

Nichols *The Epistles of Erasmus From His Earliest Letters to His Fifty-First Year*, tr. and ed. Francis M. Nichols. 3 vols. (London: Longmans, 1901).

Olin *Desiderius Erasmus, Christian Humanism and the Reformation: Selected Writings*, tr. and ed. John C. Olin (New York: Harper Torchbooks, 1965).

Paynell *Querela Pacis*, 1517, or *The Complaint of Peace*, tr. Thomas Paynell (1559) (New York: Scholars' Facsimiles & Reprints, 1946).

Phillips *Adagiorum Collectanea*, 1500; 1508–1536, or *The Adages of Erasmus: A Study with Translations* by Margaret M. Phillips (Cambridge: University Press, 1964).

Rouschausse *Erasmus and Fisher: Their Correspondence, 1511–1524*, tr. Jean Rouschausse (Paris: Librairie Philosophique J. Vrin, 1968).

Thompson *Familiorum Colloquiorum Formulae*, 1518; 1519–1533, or *The Colloquies of Erasmus*, tr. and ed. Craig R. Thompson (Chicago: University of Chicago Press, 1965).

PREFACE

This English anthology of Desiderius Erasmus is offered as a companion volume to one on Martin Luther, edited by E. G. Rupp and Benjamin Drewery, which appeared earlier in the Documents of Modern History series. Erasmus was in large measure the foil of Luther. By adhering to the authority of the Roman Catholic Church, he became, albeit reluctantly, the spokesman for orthodoxy. In this capacity, he directly challenged the course of the Reformation and sacrificed his reputation as the Prince of Humanists in order to effect a more humane world order; but his protests only served to enhance the importance of Luther's revolt. Condemned by extremists on both sides and dismayed by the reception which his own programme of reform, *philosophia Christi*, had received at the hands of Christendom's monarchs, Erasmus in the end emerged as the battle-scarred warrior.

The following extracts from Erasmus' letters and works attempt to present his life and ideas in chronological sequence. Because of space limitations, the documents are necessarily abridged. Nevertheless, they capture the flavour of Erasmus' mind by permitting his words to tell a story of their own. In order to preserve still further the spirit of Erasmus, the editor has limited the length of his introductions and notes.

Finally, a word of appreciation. The editor is grateful to Professor Albert Hyma of the University of Michigan for introducing him to the erudition and charisma of Desiderius Erasmus. It is to him on the occasion of his eightieth birthday, 18 March 1973, that this book is dedicated. *Alumnus olim, aeternum amicus.*

The Folger Shakespeare Library   R. L. D.
Washington, D.C.

PART I *The Young Erasmus (1469–99)*

The exact year of Erasmus' birth remains unknown. Most probably he was born in 1469 during the night of 27/28 October.[1] Erasmus himself asserted (c. 2 April 1524) that he was born in 1466; but the validity of this statement is doubtful. On weighing the available evidence, it seems that a 1469 birth agrees more closely than a 1466 birth with the undisputed Bockenberg MS., which states unequivocally that Erasmus entered the monastery at Steyn in 1487, and Erasmus' letter to Servatius Rogerus, which states that Erasmus was about seventeen years old when he went to Steyn.[2]

Sensitive by nature, Erasmus had good reason for tampering with the year of his birth. He was anxious to make it appear as though his father, Gerard, had not as yet been ordained to the priesthood when his mother, Margaret, gave birth to him in Rotterdam. To admit to his illegitimacy was sacrifice enough; to acknowledge his 'priestly paternity' was beyond endurance.

Erasmus was the second of two sons, having been born three years after his brother, Peter. At the age of four, Erasmus began school at Gouda under Peter Winckel, a parish curate. Following five years of elementary instruction, he went to Deventer and came under the dual influence of the *Devotio Moderna*

---

[1] 'Compendium Vitae Erasmi Roterodami' (c. 2 April 1524) in *Opus Epistolarum Des. Erasmi Roterodami*, ed. P. S. Allen (Oxford, 1906) I, p. 47. For a discussion of the controversy surrounding the year of Erasmus' birth, see Ernst-Wilhelm Kohls, 'Das Geburtsjahr des Erasmus,' *Theologische Zeitschrift* [Faculty of Theology of the University of Basel], XXII (1966), pp. 95–121, A. C. F. Koch, *The Year of Erasmus' Birth and Other Contributions to the Chronology of His Life* (Utrecht, 1969), and Regnerus R. Post, 'Quelques Précisions sur L'Année de la Naissance D'Erasme (1469) et sur son Education,' *Bibliothèque d'Humanisme et Renaissance*, XXVI (1964), pp. 489–509. Kohls, Koch, and Post argue respectively for 1466, 1467, and 1469.

[2] P. C. Bockenberg (1548–1617) MS., Allen I, p. 584; letter to Servatius Rogerus (8 July 1514), Allen I, p. 566.

and the spirit of Humanism. For it was at Deventer that he first encountered the Brethren of the Common Life and met, albeit briefly, the much admired Rudolph Agricola, the Petrarch of the North.

After the death of their parents, Erasmus and Peter left Deventer with the intention of matriculating at the university. But their guardians, headed by Peter Winckel, refused permission. In the face of a meagre inheritance and stubborn determination, Erasmus and Peter reluctantly entered a minor seminary conducted by the Brethren of the Common Life at 's Hertogenbosch in order to prepare for the religious life. Peter was the first to acquiesce. He joined the reformed order of St. Augustine at Delft.

Sheer exhaustion, coupled with 'fraternal betrayal' and a dismal review of his finances, convinced Erasmus to follow the advice of a former classmate, Cornelius of Woerden, and to enter the monastery of the Canons Regular of St. Augustine at Steyn in 1487. Without vocation or inclination, Erasmus professed solemn vows and was ordained a priest on 25 April 1492. But his monastic life was simply a veneer. It was only a matter of time before he would lay it aside. Ultimately, ordination brought a relaxation of discipline and gave him access to Henry of Bergen, the Bishop of Cambrai. Erasmus wasted no time in arranging for his release from monastic confinement. Henceforth he would exercise his priesthood in the secretarial service of the Bishop of Cambrai, whose usefulness was matched by personal ambition.

Disillusioned by the dreariness of his secretaryship and the vacuity of his residence, Erasmus soon petitioned the bishop for permission to study in Paris. He succeeded and took up residence at the College of Montaigu in 1495. Here he pursued the bachelor and doctor of divinity degrees (Erasmus finally secured the doctor of divinity degree from the University of Turin in 1506), amid the freedom of exchange which the student's life conferred. For four years, he studied scholastic philosophy and theology, partly sustained by the Bishop of Cambrai's patronage and by tutorial stipends. But his heart was neither in scholasticism nor teaching. Having mastered classical Latin at Steyn, Erasmus preferred to cultivate the literati in an effort to unite Europe behind the 'humanitatis literas.' Erasmus' change of direction now required a change of patrons, and Lord Mountjoy's England provided a heavy harvest.

A   BIRTH AND PARENTAGE

Writing in 1524 Erasmus stubbornly maintained that he was born on 27 October 1466, the only son of an unwed couple.

He [Erasmus] was born in Rotterdam on the vigil of Simon and Jude. His age is about fifty-seven years [i.e. 27 October 1466]. His mother was named Margaret and the daughter of a certain physician Peter. She was from Zevenbergen. . . . His father was named Gerard. The latter secretly had an affair with Margaret, in the expectation of marriage. And some say that they exchanged words of betrothal. The parents and brothers of Gerard were indignant about this. . . . It seemed to all that from so large a number one should be consecrated to God. You know the feelings of the old. And the brothers wished to hold on to the property and to have a hospitable retreat for themselves. Gerard, seeing himself completely barred from marriage by the solid opposition of all, did what the desperate do; he secretly fled, and on his journey he sent his parents and brothers a letter inscribed with clasped hands and with the sentence, 'Farewell, I shall never see you again.'

Meanwhile, his intended wife was left with child. The boy was raised at his grandmother's. Gerard went to Rome. There he supported himself adequately as a scribe, for the art of printing was not yet in use. Moreover, he had a very fine hand. And he lived like a young man. He soon applied himself to liberal studies. He gained an excellent knowledge of Greek and Latin. And he even made unusual progress in the study of law. For Rome then bloomed marvellously with learned men. He heard Guarino. He copied all the authors with his own hand. When his parents learned that he was at Rome, they wrote to him that the girl he had sought to marry was dead. Believing this, out of grief he became a priest, and he applied his whole mind to religion. When he returned home he discovered the deception. However, she never afterwards wished to marry, nor did he ever touch her again. . . . [Basel.]

Erasmus, 'Compendium Vitae' (c. 2 April 1524). Olin, pp. 23–4. Allen I, pp. 47–8

1   Nationality

Erasmus was born in Rotterdam, the Netherlands, of Dutch parents.

. . . The Batavi were a German tribe, part of the Catti, who migrated owing to internal dissensions and occupied the extreme tip of the coast of Gaul, then unoccupied, and also at the same time an island situated between two stretches of water, washed by the ocean in front and by the river Rhine at the back and sides. As a people they were strong fighters, with much experience in the Germanic wars, but also powerful through their wealth, so that the Roman military power could not be exhausted while these people were allies of the Empire and contributed to it both arms and men; how generously, Cornelius Tacitus tells us in his book XX. Most scholars agree, and the guess seems uncontradicted, that this island mentioned by Tacitus is what we now call Holland, a country I must always praise and venerate, since to her I owe my life's beginning. And I would that I could bring as much honour to her, as I have little regret in being her son! For as to that accusation of boorishness which Martial levels against her, and Lucan's charge of savagery, I think that either they have nothing to do with us at all, or both can be turned into praise. For which people has not been uncultured at one time? And when was the Roman people more praiseworthy than when they knew no arts except farming and fighting? If anyone argues that the criticisms levelled at the Batavi long ago still hold good today, what better tribute could be paid to my dear Holland, than to have it said that she recoils from Martial's pleasantries, which he himself calls vile? If only all Christians had 'Dutch ears,' so that they would not take in the pestilential jests of that poet, or at least not be infected by them, if understood. If you call that rusticity, we freely admit the impeachment, in company with the virtuous Spartans, the primitive Sabines, the noble Catos. But Lucan, I imagine, calls the Batavi 'savage' much as Virgil calls the Romans 'sharp.'

If you look at the manners of everyday life, there is no race more open to humanity and kindness, or less given to wildness or ferocious behaviour. It is a straightforward nature, without treachery or deceit, and not prone to any serious vices, except that it is a little given to pleasure, especially to feasting. The reason for this is, I think, the wonderful supply of everything which can tempt one to enjoyment; due partly to the ease of importing goods (since the country stands at the mouth of two noble rivers, the Rhine and the Meuse, and is washed on one side by the sea), and partly to the native fertility of the region, intersected as it is by navigable rivers full of fish, and abounding in rich pastures. And there is a plentiful supply of birds from the marshes and heaths. They say that there is no other country which holds so many towns in a small space, not large towns it is true, but incredibly civilised. As for domestic furniture, Holland is unsurpassed in neatness and elegance—or so say those merchants who travel over most of the globe. In no country are there more people who have a tincture of learning than in Holland. If there are few deeply learned scholars, especially in the classics, this may be due to the luxury of life there, or it may be that they think more of moral excellence, than of excellence in scholarship. For it is certain, and many things go to prove it, that they are not wanting in intellectual power, though I myself have it only in a modest degree, not to say scanty—like the rest of my endowments.

> Erasmus, 'Auris Batava' (1508). Phillips, pp. 210–11

Erasmus to Peter Manius, c. 1 October 1520

. . . In the first place it seems to me to make little difference where a man is born, and I think it a vain sort of glorification when a city or a nation boasts of producing a man who has become great through his own exertions and not by the help of his native land. Far more properly may that country boast which has made him great than that which brought him forth. So far I speak as if there were anything in me in which my country might take pride. It is enough for me if she be not ashamed of me—though indeed Aristotle does not wholly disapprove that kind of pride which may add a spur to the pursuit of a worthy aim.

If there were any of this kind of pride in me I should wish that not France and Germany alone should claim me, but that each and every nation and city might go into the strife for Erasmus. It would be a useful error which should incite so many to worthy effort. Whether I am a Batavian or no is not even yet quite clear to me. I cannot deny that I am a Hollander, born in that region which, if we may trust the map-makers, lies rather towards France than towards Germany; although it is beyond a doubt that that whole region is on the borderland between the two. . . .

> Emerton, pp. 1–2. Allen IV, pp. 353–4

B SCHOOLDAYS AND GUARDIANSHIP (1473–87)

Erasmus addressed a letter to Lambert Grunnius, an imaginary papal secretary, in c. August of 1516, in which he recounted his earliest educational experiences. He disguised his identity and that of his brother Peter by choosing two fictitious names: 'Florentius' for Erasmus and 'Antonius' for Peter.

Erasmus to Lambertus Grunnius, c. August 1516
. . .Two brothers there were, Florentius [i.e. Erasmus], and his elder, Antonius [i.e. Peter]. While they were still boys they lost their mother; and their father, dying soon after, left a property, small indeed, but which would have abundantly sufficed for finishing their education, had not the rapacity of their relations, who surrounded the dying man, made that little less. For of the ready money which he had about him at that time not a penny was left. What remained in real estate, however, or was secured to them in writing, and hence not so easily to be seized by the claws of these harpies, would have been sufficient for their education in the liberal arts, had not a great part of it been lost by the carelessness of their guardians. You well know how few people there are who are conscientiously vigilant in other people's affairs. Their guardians, however, had set their minds on having them brought up in a monastery, esteeming it a marvel of parental kindness on their part if they thus provided them with a maintenance. Towards this, already so inclined by their own wish, they were urged by a certain prior [i.e. Peter Winckel], an arrogant man, who enjoyed a considerable reputation for piety, especially in that under him, as schoolmaster, they had learned in childhood the first rudiments of grammar. This latter was generally held to be a man of pious and upright life: that is, he was free from gambling, impurity, extravagance, drunkenness, and other infamous vices; but he was a man wholly selfish and amazingly penurious, nor pre-eminent in anything in popular opinion, nor even approving literary attainments, save such as he himself had scantily and with great difficulty acquired. For when Florentius [Erasmus], now a boy of fourteen, wrote him a somewhat elegantly couched letter, he replied severely that if he wrote him such a letter again he must add thereto a commentary; for it was his own custom to write plainly and 'to the point,' for such was the word he used. He seems to have had an idea, such as I have known many men to have,

that if he could gain any disciple to the monastic life he was offering to God a most acceptable sacrifice; and he used boastingly to relate how many youths he had been the means of adding each year to the Orders of Francis, Dominic, Benedict, Augustine, or Bridget.

Hence, when they were ready for the schools, which they call universities (for they were now sufficiently versed in grammar, and had learned the greater part of the *Dialectics* of Peter of Spain), yet fearing that they might there drink in something of a worldly spirit and refuse the yoke, he saw to it that they were put out of the way into a company of those who are commonly called *Fratres Collationarii* [i.e. the Brethren of the Common Life at 's Hertogenbosch], who having nested themselves in everywhere, make a regular business of hunting up boys to be trained. Their chief care, should they see any youth of unusually high spirit and quick disposition (of which nature are almost all very fertile minds), is to break his spirit and humble him by blows, threats, scoldings, and other devices, which they call 'breaking in'; and thus to fit him for the monastic life. For this reason they are much esteemed by the Dominicans and Franciscans; for these latter admit that their Orders would very soon perish, did not some such seminary as the above feed them. For it is from such cohorts that they select young soldiers. True, I think they have among them some not ill-disposed men; but since they suffer from a lack of the best authors, and live in their own obscurity, spending their lives in the observance of rites and ceremonies; and since they measure themselves by themselves and not by others, compelled as they are to spend a good part of the day in prayer and their customary tasks, I do not see how it is possible for them thoroughly to instruct youth. Certainly the fact speaks for itself, since nowhere else are young men sent forth worse taught or worse trained. The boys lost more than two years with them: at least it was loss of time for the younger, who was somewhat more learned than his teachers in those very branches which they professed to teach. One of the instructors was such that Florentius [i.e. Erasmus] declares he never saw a more ignorant or a more vainglorious monster. And such as he are the men who are often set over boys; for they are not chosen by the vote of the learned, but at the pleasure of the head of the Order, who frequently is uneducated. There was one, however, who always seemed to be delighted with the character of Florentius [i.e. Erasmus]; and when it became a question of his return home, this monk began in private conversations to urge him to join their Order, mentioning many of the advantages by which boys are wont to be attracted. Would that the thing had been done;

for either the love of piety would have detained him willingly among them, or, if the affair had so shaped itself, it would have been lawful for him to return to his former state of freedom. For this body of men, who are motivated by an individual sense of virtue, and a vestige of early religion, are not bound by irrevocable vows. And truly, if the opinion of spiritual men were of more avail than the decrees of the thick-headed, there would henceforth be no irrevocable vow beyond baptismal vows, especially in view of the present malice, or weakness, of mortals. While this monk, therefore, was plying him with frequent exhortations, adding from time to time blandishments, small presents, and finally caresses, the boy, in a manner not at all boyish, answered him that he did not yet understand either this kind of life, or even himself, and that as soon as he was a little older he would seriously consider the matter. Thereupon this man, who was not altogether stupid or bad, gave him up; but I have known some of his fraternity who, not only by harshness or flattery, but also by terrible adjurations, have tried to prevail on rich and noble youths not yet past their fourteenth year to join their Order without the knowledge of their parents. What is kidnapping if this is not?

When, therefore, Antonius [i.e. Peter] and Florentius [i.e. Erasmus] had returned home, the guardians, who had not used the best judgment with regard to their inheritance, small as it was, began to treat about their entering a monastery, partly that they might the more quickly be relieved of their care, and partly that the schoolmaster, who alone was administering the estate (for one, seized by the plague, had died quite suddenly without giving any account of his stewardship, and the third, who was a banker, took very little interest in their care), considered that he would make a most pleasing offering to God, were he to present these two lambs. When Florentius [i.e. Erasmus] perceived that they were acting as if they already had the necessary willingness of their wards, he conferred with his brother, who was three years older than himself, while he was barely fifteen; and asked him if it was really his desire and intention to be bound by obligations from which he could never after free himself. He confessed candidly enough that he was not led on by a love of religion, but was constrained by the fear of their guardians. 'What,' said Florentius [i.e. Erasmus], 'could be more senseless than your action, if from foolish modesty and the fear of men by whom you will certainly not be beaten, you consign yourself to a kind of life of which you know nothing, but out of which you cannot stir a foot when once entered?' Hereupon Antonius [i.e. Peter] began to excuse himself by alleging their small pecuniary resources, little originally, but now much lessened by the negligence of their guardians. 'There is no reason for fear,' said Florentius [i.e. Erasmus], 'we will scrape together what remains, and having gathered up a little sum we will seek some university; friends are not lacking; and besides, many are supported by their own industry that have not a penny at all. Moreover, God helps those whose intentions are noble.'

This reply so appealed to Antonius [i.e. Peter] that he in turn enlarged on the many possible chances of help that had not occurred to his younger brother. Therefore it was settled between them that they would postpone to a later period the monastic question; and that, after they had spent three or four years in those schools, they would be better able, by their years and their knowledge of the world, to discern what would be most beneficial for them. This decision was equally pleasing to them both; but the elder brother was still troubled as to the reply to be given to the guardians, who, all unaware of the intentions of their wards, were working on the monastic problem seriously and sedulously. So a formal reply was concocted between them, of which Antonius [i.e. Peter] approved indeed, but stipulated that the younger should be the spokesman to make reply for both, since he himself was more timid in speech, and somewhat less skilful. So Florentius [i.e. Erasmus] accepted the terms, stipulating only that his brother should be firm; 'for if,' he said, 'you should fail me after I had given our answer, the whole tragedy would fall on my head. Change your mind at once if you think that threats or flattery will move you to yield; for believe me, this is no jesting matter.' Antonius [i.e. Peter] took a solemn oath and pledged his faith that he would stand by his word.

A few days after came the aforesaid guardian; and having enlarged on his kindness towards his wards, as well as on his remarkable care and attention to their interests, he began to felicitate them on having found for them both a place with those monks who are called *Canons Regular* [of the rule of St. Augustine]. Hereupon, the boy Florentius [i.e. Erasmus], responding for both as per agreement, returned thanks to him for his kindness and zeal. For the rest, he said, it did not seem wise to his brother and himself, inexperienced as they then were in both years and worldly affairs, to join any Order, not yet knowing their own minds, and being wholly unacquainted with the nature of what they might be undertaking. They had never yet visited a monastery; nor had they been able to learn what kind of being a monk might be; so that it seemed more satisfactory to them to spend a few years in honourable study, after which this question could receive more mature consideration. Thus the matter would turn out very happily.

This far from boyish reply ought to have been received by the guardian with an embrace, had he been a truly kind man, or one filled with evangelical prudence. Yea, rather I should say, that if he had observed that the youths were too ardent, he should have checked them, nor suffered them to yield to a momentary feeling. But instead, he flushed up with anger, as if he had been struck a blow; so that this man, otherwise of a gentle disposition, was now so filled with impotent rage, that only shame restrained his hands. With exceeding scorn he called Florentius [i.e. Erasmus] an idle rascal, and accused him of having no sense (you recognise the voice of the monks); he resigned his guardianship, and refused to be responsible for them any longer with those tradesmen from whom they bought their provisions. He insisted that there was nothing left, and that they must look around and get food where they could. With these and many other cruel and cutting reproaches he assailed the younger, forcing him (for he was still a boy) to tears; but they did not drive him from his purpose. 'We accept,' he said, 'your resignation as our guardian, and release you from all future care of us.' Then they departed.

When the guardian saw that threats and reproaches had availed him nothing, he called in his brother the banker, who was said to be a man of pleasing address and persuasive speech. The meeting took place in a pleasure garden; the boys were told to be seated, and refreshments were offered them. After some friendly anecdotes, the main question was entered upon, but treated from an entirely different standpoint. Very gently they lied about the wonderful happiness of living in the Order aforesaid, pointed out to them the great expectations that might be realised, and then added their entreaties. Why not? Softened by these means, the elder brother began to weaken, evidently forgetful of the oath which he had more than once taken to be firm. None the less did the younger persist in his determination. In a word, the faithless Antonius [i.e. Peter], after betraying his brother, accepted the yoke, having first stolen all their ready money—no new habit of his. For him the affair turned out well; for he was a man of dull mind, but lusty body; selfish, cunning, and artful; a thief, a drunkard, and a voluptuary; in short, so different from his brother, that one might imagine him to be a changeling. He was always his brother's evil genius. Not long afterwards he played the part among his companions that Iscariot played among the Apostles. When, however, he saw his brother miserably entrapped, his conscience stung him, and he deplored bitterly that he had ruined him by drawing him into the snare. You have here the confession of a Judas; would that he had followed his example and hanged himself, before he had committed such an unfraternal deed! Florentius [i.e. Erasmus], like all who are apt of study, was unsophisticated and careless about everyday matters, and displayed a wonderful simplicity in these things. You will find many with beardless chins who are mature in cunning; but he had a mind for nothing but his studies. His whole bent was in that direction; and by the force of his nature he was borne thither, having lived in school from his early childhood. Of delicate constitution, yet not unfit for mental activity, he had just entered on his sixteenth year. . . . [London.]

Mangan, I, pp. 11–15. Allen II. pp. 294–9

C MONASTIC LIFE: THE CHOICE OF A VOCATION

In his letter to Lambert Grunnius, Erasmus argued that he was forced into the monastery by his guardians and by his impoverished finances.

Erasmus to Lambertus Grunnius, August 1516

. . . Not to be too tedious, no artifice was left untried against the mind of a simple boy left destitute by the treachery of his brother, and broken in health; nor was he watched with less care, zeal, and vigilance than if an opulent city was to be taken; of such importance did it seem to these worse than Pharisees to bury alive one breathing, living youth. There were among them some who used to sound the praises of their own Orders with such intense partisanship that they fell out with each other, and made a laughing-stock of their Christian profession. Since the boy was in advance of his years in talent, learning, and eloquence, each hoped that he might obtain him as a distinguished ornament to his own community. That was their kind of piety, their kind of zeal. . . .

Florentius [i.e. Erasmus] in the meantime was caught between the door and the wall, as the proverb has it. While he thus stood uncertain, looking everywhere for some divinity to appear and point out a way of safety, he happened to visit a certain community near the town where he lived, and found there one Cantelius with whom he had been brought up from infancy. This man was older by some years, having a cunning mind, ever bent on self, yet of high spirit. It was not so much piety as good eating and a love of ease that had allured him to a monastic life. He was a glib fellow and exceedingly lazy, had made but little progress in learning, but was somewhat skilled in singing, for which he had been trained in his early years. Having sought in vain to make his fortune in Italy, and his parents continually complaining of their poverty and their large family, he sought the protection of the cowl, which had this to be said in its favour, that it very conveniently lends itself to the sustaining of many children who would otherwise perish. When Cantelius perceived from his conversation what remarkable progress in learning Florentius [i.e. Erasmus] had made, thinking at once of his own interests, he began with incredible affection (for his nature was mercurial) to exhort him to follow the same kind of life that he himself did, sketching in words a beautiful picture of his own Order, emphasising its blessed tranquillity, liberty, and concord. But why should I go on? It was a brotherhood of angels. He repeatedly dwelt on the abundance of books that were to be had there, and what opportunity for study; for he well knew the bait by which the mind of the boy might be caught. In short, if you had heard this man, you would have said that the place was not a monastery, but the mead of the Muses. Florentius [i.e. Erasmus] loved this Cantelius with intense boyish ardour, due to the candour of his nature (especially since he had found him again beyond his expectation after so long a time), as is customary with those of his years, who are likely to conceive violent affections for certain acquaintances. For he had not yet learned to judge men's minds, but from his own feelings estimated others. Cantelius left no stone unturned, trying in every way to subject the boy's mind to his own purposes by his enchanting words; but the boy remained firm. After that conversation Florentius [i.e. Erasmus] was exposed to a still greater attack from the others; for they had rigged up more powerful battering-rams. They urged to him the desperate condition of his finances, the enmity of all his friends, and finally starvation (than which no kind of death is more cruel) if he did not renounce the world. For such is the term they use, calling by a term of reproach the world—those whom Christ with His own blood has redeemed from the world; and claiming as peculiar to monks that which is common to all Christians. After being for a long time rather annoyed than shaken by them, he returned to Cantelius, merely for another pleasant chat. The latter now used the greatest efforts, in order that he might have Florentius [i.e. Erasmus] as a private and gratuitous teacher. Florentius on his side was inclined to friendships, and glad to oblige his close friends.

At last, when there was no cessation of these importunities, and no ray of hope left him, he betook himself to the monastery, which was not the one intended for him by his guardian, but the one where he had accidentally found his old friend. . . .

Mangan I, pp. 16–18. Allen II, pp. 300–301

1 The Religious Life at Steyn

Erasmus described his life in the monastery in his letter to Grunnius. He repeated the argument that he had been compelled to enter the religious life and was kept there by 'flattery and kindness'.

Erasmus to Lambertus Grunnius, August 1516
. . . Now this place [the monastery of the Augustinian Canons Regular at Steyn] was so unsanitary and unhealthy that it was scarcely fit for raising cattle, much less for his [i.e. Erasmus] delicate little body; but such tender years as his had not yet learned to discriminate in matters of food, climate, or locality. Besides, he had not betaken himself thither with the intention of joining the Order, but only that he might for a little while escape the clacking tongues, until time itself might bring forth something better. Meanwhile Cantelius eagerly enjoyed his good fortune, taking advantage of the good nature and simplicity of his companion. For Florentius frequently and secretly by night would read to him a whole comedy of Terence, so that in a few months, as a result of their secret nocturnal sessions, they had finished the principal authors, but with great risk to the boy's delicate constitution. That, however, was nothing to Cantelius, who, having stumbled on this good fortune, rejoiced inwardly; for he loved no one whole-heartedly except himself. And lest Florentius might draw back from what he had begun, there was nothing which was not permitted him: the welcome society of his equals pleased him; he took part in singing, playing, and the capping of verses; he was not compelled to fast; he was not awakened for nocturns; no one warned or reproved him; everyone favoured and smiled on him. Thus were several months spent without serious reflection; but, when the day was at hand when

he must put off the secular and put on the religious habit, Florentius [i.e. Erasmus] came to his senses, and began ... to treat about his freedom. Once more were harsh threats used, once more was the desperate state of his finances pointed out to him unless he continued in what was well begun. Nor did Cantelius, who disliked the idea of losing his nightly unpaid instructor, fail to do his part vigorously. I ask you, was not this doing violence to a boy who was by nature simple, inexperienced, and unreflecting? But why do I delay? In spite of his objections, the habit was thrown over his shoulders, though they knew that his determination was still unchanged. After this was done, his boyish heart was again cajoled by flattery and kindness. Thus again nearly a whole year passed away in play and thoughtlessness. But he had by now discovered that this kind of life was good for neither mind nor body; for to his mind nothing was sweet but study. Here, however, study had neither honour nor use. In other respects he was not averse to piety; but he was not particularly charmed with their hymns and ceremonies, in which almost their whole life consists. In such communities it is generally the brothers who are dull, half-witted, illiterate, and fonder of their stomachs than of their books, who are pushed forward for such purposes. If any remarkable talent appears amongst them, any youth who has a natural taste for learning, he is repressed lest he rise above the rest. And yet these men require a strong hand over them; and it generally happens that the dullest and the most wicked, if he be sturdy of body, gets on best in the pack. ...

But I do not intend to attack these Orders: providing this or that kind of life is suitable to this or that man, or even necessary, let the vow be irrevocable; but the holier and more exacting the life, then the more circumspectly, the more slowly, and the more seriously ought it to be embraced, and sufficiently early if just previous to forty. Other vows are not binding, unless it is evident there is a sound mind, clear intelligence, and an absence of fear or apprehension. And is this the state of affairs when a lad is pushed, objecting loudly, into the trap by allurements, threats, deceit, or any other means of terrifying him? It is not here a question of the fear that influences a strong man; but it is a question of deceiving and intimidating a simple and unsophisticated boy; and many there are in whom dwells an inborn simplicity, both of age and of personal character. If the signs of virility are present, it makes no difference; the vow holds, and it holds to that extent that the wife at the very altar must be abandoned. Oh, what laws!

In this way Florentius [i.e. Erasmus], the victim of so many machinations, was forced into the religious state, ever struggling and loudly protesting against it still; but his conscience was free; and it seems to me that he is no more held by his vow than if he were to give his word to pirates threatening him with death. . . .

Mangan I, pp. 18–19, 26. Allen I, pp. 301–2, 309–10

Erasmus to Servatius Rogerus, 8 July 1514

. . . The opinion of men is so various (as each bird has his own song), that it is impossible to satisfy everybody. I at any rate am disposed to follow whatever course is best; God is my witness. For if I gave way at one time to the emotions of youth, that has been corrected by age and experience. It was never my intention to change either my mode of life or my dress, not because I approved of them, but to avoid scandal. For you know that it was by the pertinacity of my guardians and the importunate exhortations of others, I was driven rather than persuaded to that kind of life; and that I was afterwards kept to it by the reproaches of Cornelius of Woerden as well as by a sort of shame, although I had found it was not at all suitable for me.

Different persons have different aptitudes. By my bodily constitution I was always impatient of fasting, and when once awake, I could not sleep again for some hours. My mind was absorbed in the pursuit of Letters, for which in that profession there is no use; so that I do not doubt that, if my life had been free, I might have been counted, not only among the happy part of mankind, but even among the good. When, however, I saw that I was quite unfit for the kind of life which I had undertaken, not voluntarily but by compulsion, nevertheless since it is regarded by the public opinion of our age as an act of impiety for a man to abandon the calling which he has once adopted, I had made up my mind to accept with patience this part of my unhappiness as well as others. For you know how unfortunate I have been in many respects, but I think this more grievous than anything else, that I was thrust into that kind of life from which I was more averse both in mind and body; in mind, because I shrank from ceremonies and was fond of liberty; in body, because even if I had like the plan of life ever so much, my constitution was not adapted for such trials.

Some one will perhaps object that I had my year of probation, as they call it, and was of ripe age. Ridiculous! to expect that a lad in his seventeenth year, especially one brought up in study, should know himself, a great thing even in an old man! Though indeed for my own part I

did not approve the life from the first, much less after I had tasted it, but
was ensnared by the reasons I have mentioned. . . . Hammes Castle.

Nichols II, pp. 141-2. Allen I, pp. 565-6

D   AN ACTIVE APOSTOLATE (1493-9)

Following his ordination to the priesthood in 1492, Erasmus actively sought a
way to express his vocation without leaving the Austin Canons.

1   The Secretaryship (1493-5)

Erasmus served as Latin secretary to the Bishop of Cambrai. He accepted the
position in an effort to escape the confinement and routine of monastic life.

Erasmus to James Batt, c. summer 1495
. . . My dearest Batt, I leave the whole matter to your prudent discretion
but again and again I warn you not to hazard my interests by any
inopportune solicitations. First you must take care to counsel with
your Erasmus; then, if my application to learning, my recommenda-
tions, or my writings are worth anything, I will in turn furnish all
needful to equip you for the task. That my letter pleased the Lord of
Bergen [the Bishop of Cambrai] is good to hear; but it was not written
only to please him, but to induce him to grant my request. What
chance there is of that you neglected to state. I have besought you
with what vehemence I could, and now again I beseech, I beg, and
I implore you, dear Batt, to exercise the greatest care in this affair,
which is so near to my heart. To that end read my letters so diligently
that you may feel nothing therein was thoughtlessly, though possibly
confusedly, expressed. Farewell. [Brussels or Mechlin?]

Mangan I, p. 53. Allen I, pp. 144-5

Erasmus to Nicholas Werner, 13 September 1496
. . . The Bishop of Cambrai is a wonderful friend to me. He promises
liberally, but to tell the plain truth he does not send liberally. . . . Paris,
from my library.

Nichols I, p. 118. Allen I, p. 160

2   University Studies in Paris (1495-9)

Erasmus spent four years studying for a doctorate in theology. He helped to support himself by tutoring the sons of wealthy Englishmen who were living in Paris.

Fisherman. Thirty years ago I lived in Paris in a college named from vinegar [i.e. the Collège Montaigu within the University of Paris].

Butcher. I hear a word of wisdom! What's that you say? A salt fish-monger in a college so sour? No wonder, then, if he's so full of theological controversies! For, as I hear, the very walls there lean towards theology.

Fisherman. It's as you say, yet so far as I'm concerned I carried little away from there except a body plagued by the worst humours, plus a most generous supply of lice.—But to continue what I began. That college was then ruled by Jean Standonck, a man whose intentions were beyond reproach but whom you would have found entirely lacking in judgment. Because he remembered his own youth, which had been spent in bitter poverty, he took special account of impoverished students. For that he deserves much credit. And had he relieved the poverty of young men enough to provide a decent support for honest studies, while making sure they did not have too soft a life, he would have merited praise. But this he tried to do by means of bedding so hard, diet so coarse and scanty, sleepless nights and labours so burdensome, that within a year he had succeeded in killing many very capable, gifted, promising students; and others, some of whom I knew, he reduced to blindness, nervous breakdowns, or leprosy. Not a single student, in fact, was out of danger. . . .

> Erasmus 'A Fish Diet', in *Colloquia Familiaria*
> (Basel, 1526). Thompson, pp. 351–2

Erasmus to Nicholas Werner, 13 September 1496
. . . I have lately fallen in with some Englishmen, all of noble birth and high rank. Very lately a young man in priest's orders joined the party. He had abundance of money, and had refused the offer of a bishopric, because he was aware of his deficiency in learning. Nevertheless within a year he is to be again invited to that dignity by the King, although without any bishopric he possesses two thousand crowns a year. When he heard of my knowledge of Letters, he began to exhibit an incredible regard and respect for me; for he lived some little time

in my household. He offered me a hundred crowns, if I would instruct him for a year. He offered me a benefice within a few months; and he offered to lend me three hundred crowns, if I needed it to maintain my position, until I should repay it out of the benefice. . . . I have turned my back on an ample fortune and still more ample expectations. I have disregarded entreaties backed with tears. I am telling you what has really happened without any exaggeration. The English now understand that I care nothing for all the wealth of England. Neither is it without consideration that I refused and still refuse these offers. I will not by any bribe be led away from sacred studies. I have come here to learn, not to teach or to heap up money. Indeed I intend to apply, God willing, for a doctorate in theology. . . . Paris.

Nichols I, pp. 117–18. Allen I, pp. 158–60

Erasmus to Thomas Grey, August 1497
. . . What if you saw Erasmus sit gaping among those blessed Scotists, while Gryllard is lecturing from his lofty chair? If you observed his contracted brow, his staring eyes, his anxious face, you would say he was another man. They assert that the mysteries of this science cannot be comprehended by one who has any commerce at all with the Muses or with the Graces. If you have touched good letters, you must unlearn what you have learnt; if you have drunk of Helicon, you must get rid of the draught. I do my best to speak nothing in true Latin, nothing elegant or witty, and I seem to make some progress. There is hope that they will acknowledge Erasmus some time or other. But what, you will say, is the upshot of all this? It is that you are not henceforth to expect anything from Erasmus that would savour of his ancient studies or character. Remembering amongst whom I live, with whom I daily sit, you must look out for another comrade. . . . Paris.

Nichols I, p. 144. Allen I, p. 192

. . . Sweet Grey, do not mistake me. I would not have you construe this as directed against theology itself, which, as you know, I have always regarded with special reverence. I have only amused myself in making game of some pseudo-theologians of our time, whose brains are rotten, their language barbarous, their intellects dull, their learning a bed of thorns, their manners rough, their life hypocritical, their talk full of venom, and their hearts as black as ink. . . . Paris.

Nichols I, p. 144. Allen I, pp. 192–3

3   Erasmus as Tutor

In addition to tutoring young Englishmen in Paris, Erasmus offered advice to many young men about their studies through correspondence. One such student was Christian Northoff, a young merchant of Lübeck.

Erasmus to Christian Northoff, c. spring 1497
. . . Avoid nocturnal lucubrations and studies at unseasonable times. They exhaust the mind and seriously affect the health. The dawn, beloved of the Muses, is the fit time for study. After dinner either play, or walk, or take part in cheerful conversation. Possibly even among these amusements some room may be found for improvement. Take as much food as is required, not for your pleasure, but for your health. Before supper take a short walk, and after supper do the same. Before going to bed read something exquisite and worth remembering, of which you will be thinking when overcome by sleep, and for which you will ask yourself again when you wake. Let this maxim of Pliny rest always in your mind: All your time is lost which you do not impart to study. Remember that nothing is more fugitive than youth, which, when once it has flown away, never returns. But I am beginning to preach, after promising to be nothing but a guide. Follow, sweetest Christian, the plan I have traced, or any better that you can. Farewell. [Paris.]

Nichols I, p. 110. Allen I, p. 173

4   Erasmus' Exodus from Paris

Erasmus became disenchanted with the heavy emphasis on scholastic thought at the University of Paris. He was anxious to study Sacred Scripture.

Erasmus to Arnold Bostius, c. April 1498
I have been grievously sick for a month and a half with a nightly fever, of a low kind, but one that recurs daily and has almost put an end to me. I am not yet free from the sickness, and yet I am a little recovered; not yet alive, though some hope of life has dawned upon me. You ask me to communicate to you the purpose of my mind. Take this for one thing; the world has long lost its attraction for me. I pass sentence on all my hopes. I wish for nothing but that leisure may be given me, in which I may live wholly to God, bewail the sins of my thoughtless age, busy myself with the holy Scriptures, and read

or write something. I cannot do this in a college or retreat, as I am in extremely delicate health. . . . I had resolved to go to Italy this year, and to work at theology for some months at Bologna, and take a doctor's degree there; and afterwards to visit Rome in the year of Jubilee. This done, I intend to return to my country and settle there. But I fear we shall not be able to carry the plan out as we wish. In the first place I am afraid my health would not bear so long a journey, and the heat of that country. And then I call to mind that one cannot travel to Italy nor live there without great cost; and besides, a considerable sum is required for procuring the title [of doctor of theology]. The Bishop of Cambrai gives sparingly. He is decidedly more generous with his affection than his presents, and extends his promises further than his performances. . . . [Paris.]

Nichols I, pp. 159–60. Allen I, p. 202

Erasmus to William Herman, 14 December 1498
. . . What was the meaning of that letter of yours in which you seemed to find fault with my conduct? Would you know, then, how Erasmus lives here? He lives—nay, I know not if he can be said to live; but if so he lives in the greatest wretchedness, and quite worn out by calamities of every kind; surrounded by plots, deserted by his friends, the sport of fortune. Nevertheless, he lives in perfect innocence. I know you will scarcely believe me. You are thinking of the Erasmus of old times, and of my liberty, and all my brilliant prospects. But if I could only speak to you I could easily convince you. If you wish, then, to form a correct idea of Erasmus, imagine no light-headed reveller or debauchee, but one plunged in affliction, perpetually weeping, hateful to himself, who now neither wishes to live nor is permitted to die; in short, one entirely miserable—not, however, through any fault of his own, but from the unkindness of fortune, and cherishing also the warmest possible affection for you. Paris.

Drummond, I, p. 40. Allen I, pp. 217–18

Erasmus to James Batt, 29 November 1498
It is no secret to me, most excellent Batt, how disappointed you are that I have not come immediately, especially as things have turned out so much better than either of us ventured to hope. But when you have heard my reasons, you will cease to wonder, and you will find that I

have consulted for you no less than for myself. I can hardly tell you how much pleasure your letter has given me. I am already picturing to myself the joy of our meeting; with what freedom we shall chat together, on what intimate terms we shall live with the Muses! How I long to escape from this odious slavery! . . . Paris.

Drummond I, p. 45. Allen I, p. 208

PART II *The Peripatetic Erasmus (1499–1521)*

A ENGLAND

1 First Impressions: 1499

Erasmus loved England even though 'he hated the wild waves and the still wilder sailors' which harassed it. In all he visited England on six occasions. His first visit was at the request of Lord Mountjoy. After a few weeks at the country estate of Mountjoy's father-in-law, Erasmus moved to Mountjoy's home at Greenwich. Here he met the young Thomas More who was to help him enormously (see Erasmus' 1499 description of More, then twenty-one, in Nichols I, pp. 212–13). Later on he journeyed to Eltham Palace and was presented to the children of Henry VII. Touched by Prince Henry's (later Henry VIII) request for a poem, Erasmus penned one which was later published in the first edition of the *Adages* (1500). By autumn, Erasmus was at Oxford, living in St. Mary's College, the Augustinian House of Studies. Next to More, Erasmus' best friend in England was John Colet, to whom he was introduced in October of 1499. Erasmus was most impressed by Colet's lectures on St. Paul's Epistles. If Colet brought about any change in Erasmus it may have been to turn him from patristic to biblical studies and to intensify his desire to master Greek.

Erasmus to Faustus Andrelinus, England summer 1499

. . . We too have made progress in England. The Erasmus you once knew is now become almost a sportsman, no bad rider, a courtier of some practice, bows with politeness, smiles with grace, and all this in spite of himself. If you are wise, you too will fly over here. Why should a man with a nose like yours grow to old age with nothing but French filth about him? But you will say, your gout detains you. The devil take your gout, if he will only leave *you*! Nevertheless, did you but know the blessings of Britain, you would clap wings to your feet, and run hither; and if the gout stopped you, would wish yourself a Daedalus. . . .

Nichols I, p. 203. Allen I, p. 238

Erasmus to John Colet. Oxford October 1499

. . . I am better pleased that you should be led astray by your kindness, than that you should form a strict and impartial judgment of me. Nevertheless that you may not complain of unknown wares having been foisted upon you by a false recommendation, and may choose before you love, I will write you my own description, and shall do so all the better as I am better known to myself than to anyone else. You will find in me a man of slender fortune, or rather of none at all, averse from ambition, most inclined to love, little skilled indeed in Letters, but a most warm admirer of them; one that religiously venerates goodness in others and thinks nothing of his own; who is ready to yield to all in learning, to none in honesty; simple, open, free, equally ignorant of simulation and dissimulation; of a character humble but sound; sparing in speech; a person in short from whom, except character, you have nothing to expect. If you, Colet, can love such a man, if you deem him worthy of your friendship, then reckon Erasmus as much your own property as anything you possess.

Your England is delightful to me for many reasons, but most of all because it abounds in that which pleases me more than anything else, I mean in men most proficient in Good Letters, among whom by general consent I reckon you the chief. Such is your learning, that without the commendation of high character, you deserve to be universally admired, and such the holiness of your life, that you cannot but be an object of love, respect, and veneration to every one.

How can I express to you how much I have been touched and charmed with that style of yours, so placid, sedate, unaffected, flowing out of the abundance of the heart like a limpid fountain, everywhere equal and like itself, open, simple, full of modesty, and having nothing anywhere rough, distorted, or out of place, so that I seem to recognise in your letter a sort of likeness of your character? You speak what you wish, and wish what you speak. Words born in the heart and not on the lips spontaneously follow the thought, instead of the thought following the utterance. In short, by some happy facility, you pour forth without any trouble what another person could scarcely express with the greatest pains. But I must abstain from praising you, at least before yourself, that I may not throw a stumbling-block in the way of our new friendship. I know how unwilling those are to be praised, who alone deserve it. Farewell.

Nichols I, pp. 207–8. Allen I, pp. 244–5

Erasmus to William Blount, Lord Mountjoy. Oxford November 1499
If you and your noble lady and kind father-in-law and the rest of the family are well, we have every reason to rejoice. Here we are better and better every day. Indeed I cannot tell you how your country wins upon me, partly owing to habit, which softens every asperity, and partly to the kindness of Colet and prior [Richard] Charnock, than whose characters nothing can be imagined more sweet and amiable. With these two friends I would not refuse to live in farthest Scythia! What Horace writes, that even the vulgar sometimes see true, I learn from experience. You know it is a vulgar saying, The worse things begin, the better they end. What could be more ill-omened, if I may say so, than that arrival of ours was? Now things turn out more lucky every day. I have got rid of all that weariness with which you formerly saw me suffering. I only implore you, that as you kept up my spirit when it failed, you will maintain your own, now that mine is not wanting. . . .

Send my money carefully sealed with your ring. I am now much in debt to the Prior in more ways than one. He attends to my wants both kindly and promptly. And as he has been very liberal, it is right that we should be grateful and readily repay what he has so readily given. I hold that good friends, like rare furniture, should be sparingly used. . . .

Nichols I, pp. 213–14. Allen I, pp. 266–7

Erasmus to John Colet. Oxford October 1499
. . . But to turn to your epistle, that the boy who brought it may not go back empty. In your dislike of that sort of neoteric divines, who grow old in mere subtleties and sophistical cavillings, your opinion is entirely my own. In our day, Theology, which ought to be at the head of all literature, is mainly studied by persons who from their dullness and lack of sense are scarcely fit for any literature at all. This I say, not of learned and honest professors of Theology, to whom I look up with the greatest respect, but of that sordid and supercilious crowd of divines, who think nothing of any learning but their own. In offering to do battle, my dear Colet, with this indomitable race of men for the restoration of genuine theology to its pristine brightness and dignity, you have undertaken a pious work as regards theology itself,

and a most wholesome one in the interest of all studies, and especially of this flourishing University of Oxford. But, to say true, it is a work involving much difficulty and much ill-will. The difficulty your erudition and energy will surmount, the ill-will your magnanimity will overlook. Among the divines themselves there are not a few who are willing and able to help your noble endeavours. Every one indeed will give you his hand, since there are not any of the doctors in this famous School, who have not listened attentively to the lectures on the Pauline Epistles which you have delivered during these last three years. And in this I do not know which most deserves praise, the modesty of those who, being themselves authorised teachers, do not shrink from appearing as hearers of one much their junior and not furnished with any doctor's degree, or the singular erudition, eloquence, and integrity of the man they have thought worthy of this honour.

I do not wonder at your taking such a burden on your shoulders, for you may be equal to it. I do wonder at your inviting so insignificant a person as me to be partner in so noble an office. You exhort me, or rather you urge me with reproaches, to endeavour to kindle the studies of this University—chilled, as you write, during these winter months— by commenting on the ancient Moses or the eloquent Isaiah, in the same way as you have done on St. Paul. But I, who have learned to converse with myself, and know how scanty my equipment is, can neither claim the learning required for such a task, nor do I think that I possess the strength of mind to sustain the jealousy of so many men, who would be eager to maintain their own ground: the campaign is one that demands, not a tiro, but a practised general. Neither should you call me immodest in declining a position which it would be most immodest for me to accept. You are not acting wisely, Colet, in demanding water from a stone, as Plautus says. With what countenance shall I teach what I have never learned? How am I to warm the coldness of others, while I am shivering myself? I should deem myself more rash than rashness itself if I tried my strength at present in so great an enterprise, and, according to the Greek proverb trained myself as a potter by setting to work on an amphora.

But you say you expected of me some work of this kind, and complain that you have been disappointed. In that case you must find fault with yourself, not with me. We have not disappointed you, for we never either promised or held out any prospect of such a thing. It is you that have deceived yourself, by not believing what I said truly of my own character. Neither again did I come here to teach poetry or rhetoric. These studies ceased to be agreeable to me when they ceased to be necessary. I decline this task, because it is below my purpose, as I do the other, because it is above my strength. As to the one your reproach is undeserved, because I never proposed to myself the profession of what is called secular literature; and to the other you exhort me in vain, because I am conscious of my own unfitness for it. And if I were ever so fit, it could not be, as I am returning before long to Paris. In the meantime, being detained partly by the winter season and partly because there is difficulty in leaving England on account of the flight of some duke [Edmund de la Pole, earl of Suffolk], I betook myself to this learned University, to spend a month or two with men like you, rather than with those gold-chained courtiers.

However, I am so far from opposing your glorious and sacred endeavours, that, not being yet a suitable fellow-labourer, I will promise my earnest encouragement and sympathy. And further when I am conscious of the needful strength, I will put myself on your side, and will make an earnest, if not a successful, effort in defence of Theology. Meantime nothing could be more delightful to me than to discuss daily between ourselves, either by word of mouth or by letter, some subject of sacred literature. . . .

Nichols I, pp. 220-3. Allen I, pp. 246-9

Erasmus to Robert Fisher. London, 5 December 1499
. . . But how do you like our England, you will say. Believe me, my Robert, when I answer that I never liked anything so much before. I find the climate both pleasant and wholesome; and I have met with so much kindness, and so much learning, not hackneyed and trivial, but deep, accurate, ancient, Latin and Greek, that but for the curiosity of seeing it, I do not now so much care for Italy. When I hear Colet, I seem to be listening to Plato himself. In Grocyn who does not marvel at such a perfect round of learning? What can be more acute, profound, and delicate than the judgment of Linacre? What has Nature ever created more gentle, more sweet, more happy than the genius of Thomas More? I need not go through the list. It is marvellous how general and abundant is the harvest of ancient learning in this country, to which you ought all the sooner to return. My lord has so kind a remembrance of you, that he speaks of no one more often or with more pleasure. . . .

Nichols I, p. 226. Allen I, pp. 273-4

2 Second Visit: 1505-6

On his second visit to England, Erasmus sought 'important advice from sensible people'. He talked with More, Colet, and the eminent classicists, Thomas Linacre and William Grocyn. He also accepted a professorship at Cambridge, where he was expected to lecture on St. Paul's Epistle to the Romans. Instead he assisted More in the translation of Lucian's *Dialogues* (1506). His sudden departure from London was in response to an offer from Henry VII's physician (Giovanni Boerio) to serve as guardian to his sons on their journey to Italy. But in point of fact Erasmus left England when it became apparent that Henry VII was not going to give him a benefice.

Erasmus to Servatius Rogerus. London 1505?
I wrote to you long before leaving Paris, and I suppose you have received that letter, though I somewhat fear it may be lost, such is the carelessness of couriers. Therefore, if there has been by accident any default, we must mend it by taking pains to write often. It is a long business to explain what object we have had in retiring to England, especially as we were formerly despoiled of our money here, and some hopes appeared just now to be held out, at home, which were not to be scorned. But I beg you to believe that I have not come back to England without serious reasons, or without the advice of prudent counsellors. The success of the matter is in higher hands; although the gain we have sought is not an increase of fortune but of learning. I have now been spending some months with my lord Mountjoy, who made a great point of calling me back to England, not without the general agreement of the learned of this country. For there are in London five or six men who are accurate scholars in both tongues, such as I think even Italy itself does not at present possess. I do not set any value on myself; but it seems there is not one of these that does not make much of my capacity and learning. And if it were in any circumstances allowable to boast, I might at any rate be pleased to have gained the approbation of those whose pre-eminence in letters the most envious and the most hostile cannot deny. But for myself I think nothing settled, unless I have the approval of Christ, on whose single vote all our felicity depends. . . .

Nichols I, pp. 388-9. Allen I, pp. 414-15

Erasmus to Francis Theodoric. London 1505?
You will do me a great favour, dearest friend, if you will help in collecting, as far as possible, the letters which I have written to various

persons with more than usual care—as I have an idea of publishing one book of Epistles—especially those of which I sent many to Cornelius of Gouda, a great many to my William, and some to Servatius. Scrape together what you can and from wherever you can, but do not send them except by the person I direct.

I do beseech you, my Francis, by our mutual love, and by your happiness, for which I care no less than for my own, that you will apply yourself with all your heart to Sacred Literature. Pore over the old interpreters. Believe me we shall come this way to God's blessing, or we shall never come at all, although I do not doubt you are already doing what I advise. . . .

Nichols I, p. 390. Allen I, pp. 415-16

Erasmus to Servatius Rogerus. London, 1 April 1506
I have already addressed several letters to you, to which I am surprised that you have not returned a word in answer. I am still in London, most welcome, as it seems, to the greatest and most learned of the whole country. The king of England has promised me a benefice; but the prince's arrival has caused the matter to be put off. I am continually turning the question over in my mind: how I can appropriate what is left of my life (I know not how much it may be), all to piety, all to Christ. I see that a man's life, even if it be a long life, is fleeting and transient, and that my own constitution is delicate, its strength not a little impaired by the toil of study, and somewhat by my misfortunes. I see that in learning there is no issue, and so it comes to pass, that we seem to be beginning afresh every day. I have therefore resolved to be content with my mediocrity, especially now that I have mastered a sufficiency of Greek, and to apply myself to meditation and preparation for death. I ought to have done so long ago, and been frugal of my years, my most precious possession, when it was at its best. But though frugality may be late in its influence, what remains must be the more thriftily used, the less and the more worthless it is. . . .

Nichols I, pp. 398-9. Allen I, pp. 420-21

Erasmus to Richard Whitford. London environs, 1 May 1506
For several years, dearest Richard, I have been entirely occupied with Greek literature; but lately, in order to resume my intimacy with Latin, I have begun to declaim in that language. In so doing I have yielded to the influence of Thomas More, whose eloquence, as you know, is such, that he could persuade even an enemy to do whatever

he pleased, while my own affection for the man is so great that if he bade me dance a hornpipe, I should do at once just as he bade me. He is writing on the same subject, and in such a way as to thresh out and sift every part of it. For I do not think, unless the vehemence of my love leads me astray, that Nature ever formed a mind more present, ready, sharpsighted and subtle, or in a word more absolutely furnished with every kind of faculty than his. Add to this a power of expression equal to his intellect, a singular cheerfulness of character and an abundance of wit, but only of the candid sort; and you miss nothing that should be found in a perfect advocate. I have therefore not undertaken this task with any idea of either surpassing or matching such an artist, but only to break a lance as it were in this tourney of wits with the sweetest of all my friends, with whom I am always pleased to join in any employment, grave or gay. I have done this all the more willingly because I very much wish this sort of exercise to be introduced into our schools, where it would be of the greatest utility. For in the want of this practice I find the reason why at this time, while there are many eloquent writers, there are so few scholars, who do not appear almost mute, whenever an orator is required; where as if in pursuance both of the authority of Cicero and Fabius and of the examples of the ancients, we were diligently practised from boyhood in such exercises, there would not, surely, be such poverty of speech, such pitiable hesitation, such shameful stammering as we witness even in those who publicly profess the art of oratory.

You will read my declamation with the thought that it has been the amusement of a very few days, not a serious composition. I advise you also to compare it with More's, and so determine whether there is any difference of style between those, whom you used to declare to be so much alike in genius, character, tastes and studies, that no twin brothers could be found more closely resembling one another. I am sure you love them both alike, and are in turn equally dear to both. . . .

Nichols I, pp. 406–7. Allen I, pp. 422–3

3 Third Visit: 1509–14

Erasmus was encouraged to return to England by Lord Mountjoy in 1509. En route he composed his biting satire, *Praise of Folly*, in honour of More. 'It is a witty sermon, an earnest satire, a joke with an ethical purpose.' *Folly* was first published at Paris in the spring of 1511, and won immediate popularity. At Cambridge, Erasmus lectured on Greek and renewed his friendship with John Fisher, who was serving as chancellor. Moreover, he added to his *Adages*,

translated more of Lucian, edited Seneca and Cato, translated Plutarch and
St. Basil, and edited the letters of St. Jerome. He also began the translation of
the New Testament from Greek into Latin. Finally, for Colet, who had re-
founded St. Paul's School in London, he wrote *A Method of Study* (1511, 1514)[1]
and *On Fluency* (1512).[2] Erasmus was fortunate to have found such worthy
patrons as Mountjoy, Colet, Archbishop William Warham, Thomas Cardinal
Wolsey, Bishop Richard Foxe, and Bishop John Fisher, but he frequently com-
plained of their frugality and his own frailness.

Erasmus to Thomas More outside London, 9 June 1510
When of late days I was returning from Italy to England, being
unwilling to waste the whole time that I had to spend on horseback
in illiterate talk, I sometimes preferred either to think over some of our
common studies, or to enjoy the recollection of the friends, no less
amiable than learned, that I had left here. Of these, my More, you
were among the first I called to mind, being wont to enjoy the remembrance of you in your absence, as I had, when you were present,
enjoyed your company, than which I protest I have never met with
anything more delightful in my life. Therefore, since at any rate
something had to be done, and the occasion did not seem suited for
serious meditation, I chose to amuse myself with the Praise of Folly.
What Pallas, you will say, put that idea into your head? Well, the
first thing that struck me was your surname of More, which is just
as near the name of *Moria* or Folly, as you are far from the thing, from
which by general acclamation you are remote indeed. In the next
place I surmised that this playful production of our genius would find
special favour with you, disposed as you are to take pleasure in jests
of this kind—jests which, I trust, are neither ignorant nor quite insipid
—and generally in society, to play the part of a sort of Democritus;
although for that matter, while from the unusual clearness of your mind
you differ widely from the vulgar, still such is your incredible sweetness
and good nature, that you are able to be on terms of fellowship with
all mankind, and are delighted at all hours to be so. You will therefore
not only willingly receive this little declamation as a memento of your
comrade, but will adopt and protect it, as dedicated to you and become
not mine but yours. For censors will perhaps be found who may
complain that these trifles are in some parts more frivolous than becomes
a theologian, and in others more aggressive than consists with Christian
modesty, and will exclaim that we are bringing back the old comedy,

[1] *De ratione studii.*
[2] *De duplici copia verborum ac rerum (On copia of words and ideas).*

or the satire of Lucian, and seizing everything by the teeth. But those who are offended by the levity and drollery of the subject should consider, that this is no new precedent of mine, the same thing having been done over and over again by great authors; that many ages ago Homer made sport with the Batrachomyomachia, Maro with his Gnat and Salad, Ovid with his Nut; that Polycrates and his corrector, Isocrates, eulogized Busiris, Glauco injustice, Favorinus lauded Thersites and the ague, Synesius baldness, Lucian the fly and the parasitic art; that Seneca wrote a ludicrous apotheosis of the emperor Claudius, Plutarch the dialogue of Gryllus with Ulysses, Lucian and Apuleius both chose the Ass for a subject, and an author mentioned by Jerome the testament of the pig, Grunnius Corocotta.

Therefore these gentlemen, if they please, may suppose me to have been playing a rubber of bowls for my own recreation, or, if they like it better, to have been riding a hobby horse. For when we allow every department of life to have its own amusements, how unfair would it be to deny to study any relaxation at all; especially if the proposed pastime may lead to something serious, and ridiculous subjects be so treated that a reader not altogether thickheaded may derive more profit from them than from some solemn or brilliant arguments found elsewhere; as when one author in a studied oration eulogises rhetoric or philosophy, another writes the praises of some prince, advocates a war against the Turks, predicts future events, or invents fresh quibbles about things of no importance at all. For as nothing is more trifling than to treat serious questions frivolously, so nothing is more amusing than to treat trifles in such a way as to show yourself anything but a trifler. Of my work it is for others to judge, but unless I am altogether deceived by self-esteem, we have praised Folly not quite foolishly.

To reply to the imputation of mordacity, I would observe that genius has always enjoyed the liberty of ridiculing in witty terms the common life of mankind, provided only the licence did not pass into fury. And this makes me more surprised at the nicety of people's ears in the present day, which can scarcely bear anything but solemn titles. Indeed you may find some so perversely religious, that they will rather tolerate the gravest insults directed against Christ than suffer a pope or prince to be aspersed with the slightest jest, especially if the matter affects the loaves and fishes.

But whether a writer censures the lives of men without reflecting on anyone by name, I would ask whether he does not appear as a teacher and adviser rather than a detractor. And pray, how many names can I accuse myself of mentioning? Besides, he who passes over no class of mankind is evidently angry with no individual, but with every vice; and therefore if any one shall be found to cry out that he is hit, he will either betray his consciousness, or at any rate his fear. St. Jerome used this kind of writing with much more freedom and bitterness, sometimes not sparing to mention names; while we altogether avoid names and so temper our pen, that the intelligent reader may easily see that we have sought rather to amuse than to wound. For we have not followed Juvenal's example, nor made acquaintance anywhere with the hidden sink of wickedness, but have endeavoured to pass under review not so much what is shocking as what is ridiculous. Finally, if there is anyone not appeased by these arguments, he may at any rate recollect that it is an honour to be blamed by Folly, and as we have made her the speaker, we were bound to preserve the consistency of the character. But what need have I to suggest such arguments to an accomplished advocate like you, who are able to plead with the greatest skill even causes that are not the best. Farewell, most eloquent More, and defend your *Moria* with all your might. . . .

However mortal folk may commonly speak of me (for I am not ignorant how ill the name of Folly sounds, even to the greatest fools), I am she—the only she, I may say—whose divine influence makes gods and men rejoice. One great and sufficient proof of this is that the instant I stepped up to speak to this crowded assembly, all faces at once brightened with a fresh and unwonted cheerfulness, all of you suddenly unbent your brows, and with frolic and affectionate smiles you applauded; so that as I look upon all present about me, you seem flushed with nectar, like gods in Homer, not without some nepenthe, also; whereas a moment ago you were sitting moody and depressed, as if you had come out of the cave of Trophonius. Just as it commonly happens, when the sun first shows his splendid golden face to the earth or when, after a bitter winter, young spring breathes mild west winds, that a new face comes over everything, new colour and a sort of youthfulness appear; so at the mere sight of me, you straightway take on another aspect. And thus what great orators elsewhere can hardly bring about in a long, carefully planned speech, I have done in a moment, with nothing but my looks.

As to why I appear, today, in this unaccustomed garb, you shall now hear, if only you will not begrudge lending your ears to my discourse—not those ears, to be sure, which you carry to sermons, but those which you are accustomed to prick up for mountebanks in the marketplace, for clowns and jesters, the ears which, in the old days, our friend Midas inclined to the god Pan. It is my pleasure for a little while to play the rhetorician before you, yet not one of the tribe of those who nowadays cram certain pedantic trifles into the heads of schoolboys, and teach a more than womanish obstinacy in disputing; no, I emulate those ancients who, to avoid the unpopular name of philosophers, preferred to be called Sophists. Their study was to celebrate in eulogies the virtues of gods and of heroic men. Such a eulogy, therefore, you shall hear, but not of Hercules or Solon; rather of my own self—to wit, Folly.

Nor do I have any use for those wiseacres who preach that it is most foolish and insolent for a person to praise himself. Yet let it be as foolish as they would have it, if only they will grant that it is proper: and what is more suitable than that Folly herself should be the trumpeter of her praises? 'She is her own flute-player.' Who, indeed, could portray me better than can I myself? Unless it could so happen that I am better known to some one else than I am to myself. On the whole, however, I deem that what I am doing is much more decent than what a host of our best people, and scholars even, do continually. With a certain perverse modesty they are wont to convey instructions to some sycophantic speaker or prattling poet whom they have engaged at a fee; and then they hear back from him their praises, that is to say, some pure fiction. The blushing listener, meanwhile, spreads his plumes like a peacock, and bridles, while the brazen adulator searches among the gods to find a parallel for this good-for-nothing, and proposes him as the complete exemplar of all virtues—from which the man himself knows that he is farther away than twice infinity. Thus the flatterer adorns a crow with other birds' feathers, washes the Ethiopian white, and, in sum, makes an elephant out of a gnat. Lastly, I follow the familiar proverb of the folk, to the effect that he rightly praises himself who never meets anyone else who will praise him. Here, by the way, I wonder at the ingratitude, or perhaps the negligence, of men: although all of them studiously cherish me and freely acknowledge my benefits, not a one has emerged so far in all the ages to celebrate the praises of Folly in a grateful oration. In the meantime, there has been no lack of those who at great expense of lamp-oil and of sleep have extolled, in elegant eulogies, Busiruses, Phalarises, quartan fevers, flies, baldness, and pests of that sort. . . .

. . . You would never believe what sport and entertainment your mortal manikins provide daily for the gods. These gods, you know, set aside their sober forenoon hours for composing quarrels and giving ear to prayers. But after that, when they are well moistened with nectar and have no desire for the transaction of business, they seek out some promontory of heaven and, sitting there with faces bent downward, they watch what mortal men are adoring. There is no show like it. Good God, what a theatre! How various the action of fools! (I may say that now and then I take a seat alongside the gods of the poets.) Here is a fellow dying for love of a sweet young thing, and the less he is loved in return the more helplessly he is in love. This one marries a dowry, not a wife. This one prostitutes his own wife. The jealousy of another keeps watch like Argus. Here is a man in mourning, but mercy me, what fool things he says and does! Hiring mourners as if they were actors, to play a comedy of grief! Another man squeezes out a tear at the tomb of his mother-in-law. This one spends on his belly whatever he can scrape together by hook or crook, but presently he will be just as hungry again. Another finds nothing better than sleep and idleness. There are those who get themselves into a stew, working at what is other people's business, while they neglect their own. There is also the broker, who accounts himself rich on other people's money, but is on the way to bankruptcy. Another thinks that the happy life consists in living like a pauper in order that his heir may be wealthy. Another, for the sake of a small and uncertain profit, sails the seven seas, exposing his life, which no money could pay for, to the hazard of waves and winds. This one prefers seeking riches in war to passing a safe and quiet life at home. Some decide that they can most conveniently attain to wealth by courting and fawning upon childless old men. There are even those who prefer to do the same to rich old women. Both kinds furnish rare sport to the gods who are spectators, because they are usually cheated by the parties they set out to catch.

But the most foolish and sordid of all are your merchants, in that they carry on the most sordid business of all and this by the most sordid methods; for on occasion they lie, they perjure themselves, they steal, they cheat, they impose on the public. Yet they make themselves men of importance—because they have gold rings on their fingers. Nor do they lack for flattering friars who admire them and call them Right Honourable in public, with the purpose, surely, that some little driblet from the ill-gotten gains may flow to themselves. Elsewhere you will see certain Pythagoreans, in whose eyes all things are common —to such a degree, in fact, that whatever they light upon that is lying around loose they carry off with a tranquil spirit, as if it passed to them by inheritance. There are others who are rich only in wishes; they build beautiful air-castles and conceive that doing so is enough for happiness. Some delight in passing for wealthy men away from home,

though they starve meanly enough in their own houses. One man
hastens to put into circulation what money he has; his neighbour
hoards his up through thick and thin. This one pushes forward as a
candidate for public honours; that one finds his pleasure by his fireside.
A good many people bring suits which are destined never to end;
once and again they eagerly strive to outdo each other—in enriching
the judge who sets the postponements and the advocate who colludes
with him. One burns with zeal for revolutions; another is toiling upon
his Grand Scheme. This man leaves wife and children at home and
sets on a pilgrimage to Jerusalem, Rome, or the shrine of St. James,
where he has no particular business. In sum, if you might look down
from the moon, as Menippus did of old, upon the numberless agitations
among mortal men, you would think you were seeing a swarm of
flies or gnats, quarrelling among themselves, waging wars, setting
snares for each other, robbing, sporting, wantoning, being born,
growing old, and dying. And one can scarce believe what commotions
and what tragedies this animalcule, little as he is and so soon to perish,
sets agoing. For sometimes a trivial war or a spell of the plague will
sweep off and utterly wipe out thousands of them at once. . . .

> Preface to the *Moriae Encomium*, Nichols II,
> pp. 1–4. Allen I, pp. 460–62

Erasmus to Colet. London, 29 April 1512
. . . He is no friend to England that will not do his best to aid such an
enterprise. For myself, being well aware how much I owe to England
generally, and how greatly I am obliged to you privately, I thought it
my duty to bestow some small literary present to assist in the furniture
of your school. I have determined therefore to place its name upon these
two commentaries *de copia*, as a work that is suitable for boys and will,
unless I am mistaken, be not unprofitable to them; but it is for others
to judge of the learning and utility of my labours. This credit, however,
I may claim, that the subject is one that has been first thought out and
expounded by me. Julius Pollux, an ancient author writing in Greek,
arranged under several heads the words relating to a variety of subjects
and collected some heaps of synonyms and cognate expressions; but
who does not see how far the scheme of this work is different from
ours? Neither do I care to notice the class to which Isidorus, Marius
and Philiscus belong, writers so far removed from copiousness that
they cannot even, once and away, express what they mean in Latin.

We have endeavoured to indicate some principles and to show as it
were the sources of Copiousness, so that we might come by degrees

from generals to particulars; though I admit with regret that the work has not been carried out with due care. I was therefore not much disposed to publish it; but having found that some persons had a plot against these commentaries, which have narrowly escaped publication in a most inaccurate form, I was forced to correct them as best I could and bring them out into the light, since in the choice of evils that appeared to be the less. . . .

Nichols II, pp. 66–7. Allen I, pp. 511–12

Erasmus to Peter Gillis. London, autumn 1512
. . . I have put in shape the work on Proverbs and so enriched it as to make it quite a different book, and, if I am not mistaken, a much better one, though it was not so very bad before. There is therefore no reason for his [Josse Badius] fearing the editions of other printers. It had been arranged with Francis the bookseller that I should entrust him with the copy; but he went away without taking leave of me. I shall be happy to accept the price fixed in his letter, not being much concerned about the profit. Let him so prepare everything that the work may issue from his press in such a form as not to be easily rivalled.

I shall finish the correction of the New Testament; I shall finish Jerome's Epistles; and if I have leisure, I shall emend Seneca. It may be that I shall myself visit you after Easter. If I am not permitted to do this, I will send the Proverbs first, when I have a sure messenger to send them by. I am a little anxious about his providing Greek type enough for this work, which is half Greek. He must therefore take the utmost pains to get everything ready, and had better practise himself a little in Greek reading, which will be of use in bringing out other books. Do not let him send the money here, nor the books, before I write to him fully what I wish. I do not see that the Dialogues of Lucian which I sent him are coming out. I see some of them have been printed at Louvain, about which I want information. I have translated several books of Plutarch, which I will let him have when corrected. I received Badius' last letter by an Englishman. He says in it that the *Moria* has been printed by him, which nevertheless I have not seen here. . . .

Nichols II, p. 119. Allen I, pp. 517–18

Erasmus, On Copia of Words and Ideas (1512)
. . . Now in order that studious youth may apply itself to this study with an eager disposition, we shall make clear in a few words for what things it is of use. First of all then, this training in varying speech will be useful in every way for attaining good style, which is a matter

of no little moment. In particular, however, it will be useful in avoiding tautology, that is, repetition of the same word or expression, a vice not only unseemly but also offensive. It not infrequently happens that we have to say the same thing several times, in which case, if destitute of copia, we will either be at a loss or, like the cuckoo, croak out the same words repeatedly, and be unable to give different shape or form to the thought. And thus betraying our want of eloquence we will appear ridiculous ourselves and utterly exhaust our wretched audience with weariness. Worse than tautology is *homologia*, as Quintilian says, which does not lighten tedium with any charm of variety, and is wholly monotonous. Moreover, who is so patient a listener that he would even for a short time put up with a speech unvarying throughout? Variety everywhere has such force that nothing at all is so polished as not to seem rough when lacking its excellence. Nature herself especially rejoices in variety; in such a great throng of things she has left nothing anywhere not painted with some wonderful artifice of variety. And just as the eye is held more by a varying scene, in the same way the mind always eagerly examines whatever it sees as new. And if all things continually present themselves to the mind without variation, it will at once turn away in disgust. Thus the whole profit of a speech is lost. This great fault he will shun easily who is prepared to turn the same thought into many forms, as the famous Proteus is said to have changed his form. And in truth this training will contribute greatly to skill in extemporaneous speaking or writing; it will assure that we will not frequently hesitate in bewilderment or keep shamefully silent. Nor will it be difficult, with so many formulas prepared in readiness for action, to aptly divert even a rashly begun speech in any desired direction. Besides, in interpreting authors, in translating books from a foreign language, in writing verse, it will give us no little help, since in such matters, unless we are trained in the principles of copia, we shall often find ourselves either confused or crude, or even silent.

King and Rix, pp. 16–17

Erasmus to Anthony of Bergen. London, 14 March 1514
Most honourable Father, I heard by the report of the Bishop of Durham and of Andreas Ammonius, the king's secretary, of your interest in me and of your truly fatherly love, and am all the more impatient to be restored to my country, if only such a fortune be provided for us by our prince as will suffice to maintain our leisure. Not that I dislike England, or am discontented with my patrons. I have a great number

of friends here, and many of the bishops show me no ordinary favour. Indeed the Archbishop of Canterbury treats me with so much kindness and affection that if he were my brother or my father, he could not deal more lovingly with me. By his gift I have a considerable pension from a benefice which I resigned, and this second Maecenas adds an equal amount out of his own purse. Further assistance is provided by the generosity of noblemen, and this would be much greater if I cared to press my claims. But preparations for war are quickly changing the genius of the island. Prices are rising every day and liberality is decreasing. It is only natural that men so frequently taxed should be sparing in their gifts. And not long ago, in consequence of the scarcity of wine, I was nearly killed by stone, contracted out of the wretched liquor that I was forced to drink. Moreover, while every island is in some degree a place of banishment, we are now confined more closely than ever by war, insomuch that it is difficult even to get a letter sent out. And I see that some great disturbances are arising, the issues of which are uncertain. I trust it may please God mercifully to allay this tempest in the Christian world.

I often wonder what thing it is that drives, I will not say Christians, but men, to such a degree of madness as to rush with so much pains, so much cost, so much risk, to the destruction of one another. For what are we doing all our lives but making war? The brute beasts do not all engage in war but only some wild kinds; and those do not fight among themselves, but with animals of a different species. They fight too with their natural arms, and not like us with machines, upon which we expend an ingenuity worthy of devils.

For us, who glory in the name of Christ, of a master who taught and exhibited nothing but gentleness, who are members of one body, and are one flesh, quickened by the same spirit, fed by the same sacraments, attached to the same Head, called to the same immortality, hoping for that highest communion, that as Christ and the Father are one, so we may be one with him, can anything in the world be of so great concern, as to provoke us to war, a thing so calamitious and so hateful, that even when it is most righteous, no truly good man can approve it. Think, I beseech you, who are those employed in it. Cut-throats, gamblers, whoremongers, the meanest hireling soldiers, to whom a little gain is dearer than life—these are your best warriors, when what they once did at their peril, they do now for gain and with applause. This scum of mankind must be received into your fields and into your cities, in order that you may wage war; in fact you make yourself a slave to them in your anxiety to be revenged on others.

Consider too how many crimes are committed under pretext of war, when as they say: in the midst of arms, laws are silent; how many thefts, how many acts of sacrilege, how many rapes, how many other abuses which one is ashamed even to name; and this moral contagion cannot but last for many years, even when the war is over. And if you count the cost, you will see how, even if you conquer, you lose much more than you gain. What kingdom can you set against the lives and blood of so many thousand men? And yet the greatest amount of the mischief affects those who have no part in the fighting. The advantages of peace reach everybody; while in war for the most part even the conqueror weeps; and it is followed by such a train of calamities that there is good reason in the fiction of poets, the War comes to us from Hell and is sent by the Furies. I say nothing of the revolutions of states, which cannot take place without the most disastrous results.

If the desire of glory tempts us to war, that is no true glory which is mainly sought by wrongful acts. It is much more glorious to found than to overthrow states; but in these days it is the people that builds and maintains cities, and the folly of princes that destroys them. If gain is our object, no war has ended so happily, as not to have brought more evil than good to those engaged in it; and no sovereign damages his enemy in war without first doing a great deal of mischief to his own subjects. And finally, when we see human affairs always changing and confused, like the ebb and flow of Euripus, what is the use of such great efforts to raise an empire, which must presently by some revolution pass to others? With how much blood was the Roman empire raised, and how soon did it begin to fall!

But you will say that the rights of sovereigns must be maintained. It is not for me to speak unadvisedly about the acts of princes. I only know this, that *summum jus*, extreme right, is often *summa injuria*, extreme wrong. There are princes who first decide what they want and then look out for a title with which to cloak their proceedings. And in such great changes of human affairs, among so many treaties that have been made and abandoned, who, I ask you, need lack a title?

But suppose there is a real dispute, to whom some sovereignty belongs, where is the need of bloodshed? It is not a question concerning a nation's welfare, but only whether it is bound to call this or that personage its sovereign. There are popes, there are bishops, there are wise and honourable men, by whom such small matters may be settled, without sowing the seeds of war upon war, and throwing things divine and human alike into confusion. It is the proper function of the Roman pontiff, of the cardinals, of bishops, and of abbots to compose the quarrels of Christian princes, to exert their authority in this field, and show how far the reverence of their office prevails. Julius, a pope not universally admired, had power enough to raise this tempest of war. Will not Leo, a learned, honest and pious pontiff, be able to calm it?

We should also remember that men, and especially Christian men, are free agents; and after they have long prospered under a certain sovereign and still acknowledge his sovereignty, why should everything be upset by a revolution? Long consent creates a sovereign even among heathen nations, much more among Christians, to whom sovereignty is a service, not a lordship; so that if a part of his subjects are taken away, he should be regarded not as injured but relieved from part of his burden.

But suppose, you will say, the other side refuses to yield to the decision of good men; in that case what would you have me do? In the first place, if you are a true Christian, I would have you bear and forbear, disregarding that right of yours, whatever it may be. And in the next place, if you are only a wise man, pray calculate what the vindication of your right will cost you. If the cost is excessive, and it will surely be so, when you assert it by arms, do not then insist upon your title, perhaps, unfounded, after all, at the cost of so much misery to mankind, of so many killed, so many orphans, so many tears. What do you suppose the Turks think when they hear that Christian princes are raging with so much fury against each other, and that only for the title of sovereignty? Italy is now delivered from the French, and what has been the effect of so much bloodshed, but that where a Frenchman was in office before, somone else is in office now? And the country flourished better before than it does now!

If there are any rights which admit of being defended by war, they are rights of a grosser kind, which savour of a Christianity already becoming degenerate and burdened with the wealth of this world; and I know not whether I should sanction such wars; though I see that war is sometimes not disapproved by pious authors, when for the maintenance of the faith, the peace of Christendom is defended against the invasion of barbarians. But why should we dwell on these few human authorities, rather than on those many sayings of Christ, of the apostles, and of the orthodox and most approved Fathers on the subject of peace and the tolerance of evils? What policy is there that may not in some way be defended, especially when the persons who have the conduct of affairs are those whose very crimes are praised by many for the sake of flattery, while no one dares to find fault with their errors? But in the meantime it is not unknown what are the sighs and longings and prayers of reasonable men. But if you look a little closely, you will find that it is generally the private interests of princes that give occasion to war. And I would ask you, do you think it consistent with humanity that the world should be at any moment disturbed by war, when this or that sovereign has some cause or complaint against another, or perhaps pretends to have one.

We may wish the best event but can only wish. For my own part, whatever fortune I have is in England, but I would willingly resign it all on condition that a Christian peace might be established between Christian sovereigns. This object will be no little promoted by your authority, which has much influence with Prince Charles and very much with Maximilian, while it is favourably regarded by the English nobility. I have no doubt you have already found what heavy losses occur in war-time even through the acts of friends. You will therefore be attending to your own interest if you endeavour to bring this war to an end.

Nichols II, pp. 120-5. Allen I, pp. 551-4

4 Fourth Visit: 1515

In the spring of 1515, Erasmus visited England for the fourth time. He was searching for New Testament manuscripts. While in London, he wrote to Pope Leo X requesting permission to dedicate the first volume of his edition of St. Jerome to him, as well as any future publications. In effect he was asking the Pope for general permission to publish all of his forthcoming studies, without having to obtain prior approval. Though Pope Leo never answered his request, Erasmus dedicated his New Testament, *Novum Instrumentum* (1516), to him anyway. Fortunately for Erasmus, Leo X was generous in his praises. Indeed, as Margaret M. Phillips has noted, 'Erasmus' greatest contribution to his time [now] lay before the world.' Erasmus showed further concern for biblical studies when he defended the Hebraist John Reuchlin against the charge of heresy.

Erasmus to Cardinal Domenico Grimani. London, 31 March 1515
After my first interview with your eminence, which was also my last, I was prevented from paying you another visit (as I had received your command and had myself undertaken to do), not by my negligence but rather by your own singular courtesy and goodness. It was indeed a strange circumstance that the very thing which ought to have led me to return was the sole means of deterring me from doing so.

What strange cause was this? you will say. I will tell you in plain words and frankly, as becomes a German. At that time I had quite determined to go to England, to which I was attracted by the sentiment of old acquaintance, by the ample promises of powerful friends and by the special favour of the most prosperous of kings. I had made this island my adopted country and chosen it for the residence of my old age. I was invited and solicited by frequent letters promising all but mountains of gold. My only fear was that I should change my resolution if I returned to your eminence. In our first talk you had so shaken my purpose, so inflamed my spirit, that I know not what would have happened if I had been longer and more closely with you. I felt the love of the city, which I had hardly shaken off, silently growing upon me afresh. It was plain that if I had not torn myself suddenly from Rome, I should never have left it again. I hurried away from your influence and flew rather than travelled to England. 'And now,' you will say, 'do you repent of your resolve? Are you sorry you did not listen to my loving advice?' In good sooth I have not the trick of lying; and do not always regard the matter in the same way. I cannot but be touched with a longing for Rome, whenever I think of the multitude of advantages which it unites. In the first place the light and publicity of the most frequented of all cities, the most delightful freedom, so many rich libraries, the acquaintance of so many learned persons, so much literary conversation, so many monuments of antiquity; in fine, so many lights of the whole world collected in one place! To come to particulars, when I think of the extraordinary attention shown us by other cardinals, and especially by his Eminence of Nantes, of the marked favour of the Cardinal of Bologna, of the unusual kindness of the Cardinal of St. George, and above all of that most happy colloquy with you—these are things that make it impossible for any fortune, however kind, to relieve my heart of the longing which has been left there by my one taste of Rome.

In England at present, although the fortune I have obtained is not contemptible, and is at any rate greater than my deserts, yet, to confess the truth, it does not answer either to my wishes or the promises of my friends. This has come to pass, not so much by any breach of faith on their part as by the perversity of the times. The king himself, who is the kindest of kings, and who has besides both felt and spoken most favourably of Erasmus (as I was assured partly by a letter of his own to me, and partly by what I was told by many others) has been carried away by the tempest of wars bursting suddenly upon us. With such spirit and zeal did this pious and generous young prince engage in the contest which he thought necessary for maintaining the dignity of the Roman Church. So also William, Lord Mountjoy, the earliest patron of our studies after Henry of Bergen, Bishop of Cambrai, has been so overwhelmed with the burdens of war, that he has given us more love than help. He is a person of ancient lineage and of incredible goodness to men of letters, but, as compared with other barons of this country, is richer in mind than in fortune. I might also find fault with my own laziness, for I am so far from being a good suitor that I have need of the luck of Timotheus, to have my net filled while I sleep.

That I cannot be altogether sorry for having come to England is mainly owing to William, Archbishop of Canterbury, primate of all England, not only in title but by every honourable distinction; a man incomparable in every way, the one ornament and safeguard of the realm, great in wisdom, learning and authority, but greater still in this, that from his singular modesty he is the only person who is not aware of his own greatness. A marvellous sobriety of life; an intellect of supreme dexterity; an active mind that has no taste at all for repose; great experience in affairs, having been long employed in important embassies and in the principal business of former kings. He is consequently not only capable of undertaking more administrative work than several other men could do together but there is still something of him left, which he can devote to the perusal of good authors and to the attachment of private friendship. For besides his episcopal duties, he fills the place of chancellor, that is, supreme judge of the whole kingdom. This prelate treats me with so much distinction and kindness, shows himself in short so admirable a patron that, if he were my father, he could not deal more indulgently, or if my brother, more lovingly with me; and much as I left behind me at Rome in so many excellent cardinals, in so many distinguished bishops, and in so many learned men, I seem to have found it all again in this one personage.

Now that, by the labours of Pope Leo [X], peace is restored to the world, my position in England is much improved. But still my mind is more fascinated by a longing for Rome, when it is everywhere proclaimed by Fame, as it is in itself most probable, that under such a sovereign, whatever is to be found in any country of superior learning or of extraordinary merit will at this time, as if on a given signal, come together to Rome, as its proper theatre. Accordingly, more than two years ago I was prepared to make the journey in company with the Reverend Father John, Bishop of Rochester, a person loaded with every virtue becoming a bishop, and to sum up his praises in brief, most like the Archbishop of Canterbury, whose suffragan he is; but he was suddenly recalled from his mission. Again last year I proceeded as far as Basel under my own auspices. But there I was delayed by a matter which whatever may be thought by others, is in my judgment most important, and important indeed it had need to be, to keep me away from Rome. I have been long endeavouring, at the cost of no ordinary vigils, to bring St. Jerome all to life again, who is so far our greatest Latin theologian, that he may be almost called our only one; but whose works are so corrupted that, while there is no other author equally worth reading, he is the one of all others, that cannot be read, still less understood. I have accordingly in the first place arranged in due order all his works; especially his Epistles, which was the most labourious task; and in the next place I have with the help of old manuscripts and by my own ingenuity corrected the errors with which his language is defaced, or I might rather say effaced. We have added an analysis, and such convenient annotations as will make it possible, that fairly educated persons may read this author without difficulty. For, as it was said of Romulus, that the show he made of his noble feats was no less magnificent than his doing of them, so we may see in St. Jerome a fresh and varied erudition combined with a sort of holy ostentation. The passages in Greek and Hebrew, which were either omitted altogether or inserted in such a fashion that they had better not have been put in at all, we have restored with the utmost care. The spurious additions, which make up a considerable part of the book, we have relegated to a separate volume, in order that nothing may be missed by a reader with more appetite than discernment, and that on the other hand, the most ignorant gabble may no longer be circulated under the name of so incomparable a writer. I had looked forward to Italy as the best place for publishing the book, both on account of the assistance of its libraries and the authority of its name; but I fell in at Basel with some persons who were in training for this very work, and has indeed commenced it already, namely John Froben, by whose skill and at whose cost the affair is principally conducted, and three most learned young brothers of the name of Amerbach, who are well skilled in Hebrew. That language is frequently used by Jerome, and in this department I needed, in Greek phrase, a Theseus, having only tasted Hebrew, as people say, with the tip of my tongue. With these assistants I have attacked the task with Herculean vigour. A huge workshop is kept in a glow, while St. Jerome is being reproduced in a most elegant type, at such an expense of money and labour, that it cost the author less to write his works than it has cost us to restore them. To me the labour has been so great that I have almost died myself in endeavouring to bring Jerome to life again. If I am not mistaken, the work will mount up to ten volumes.

You will perhaps ask, what is your concern in this. In the first place, I knew that your constant zeal for good Letters would lead you both to rejoice in the resuscitation of Jerome and to encourage our endeavours —I might rather say, to encourage Christian piety which will, I hope, gain no little aid from his writings. The undertaking cannot be completed as it ought to be done, without the assistance of many well-furnished libraries. If therefore there is anything either in your own library, which is so richly stored with books of all kinds in every language, or in that of the pope, or of others, it will be worthy of your goodness to impart it for the common advantage of the world. And in the next place, it has occurred to me that it would be very appropriate that this edition of our supreme theologian should come into the reader's hands under the happy auspices of the supreme pontiff, and that the most learned of all writers should be recommended to the world by the name of one whose family has given birth to so many princes of literature. The authority of so excellent a pontiff would add much splendour and dignity to Jerome, and on the other hand, Leo would gain no small accession of glory from the celebrity of the most eminent doctor of the Church.

We shall therefore consecrate the restored Jerome to the pope, especially if our judgment is approved by your suffrage. For otherwise we had all but determined to dedicate it to the Archbishop of Canterbury, to whom we owe everything; although I am quite sure that his feeling towards the See of Rome is such that he will willingly give up to the Roman pontiff whatever honour it might bring. And we will so associate his memory with the praises of Leo, that in this way both the interests of Jerome and the fame of my Maecenas will be best consulted.

We have published, besides several other works, the *Adages* in an emended form, and so enriched that a fourth part of the volume is additional. And next summer we propose to issue our, I trust, not unprofitable annotations on the New Testament, together with the Apostolic Epistles, translated by us in such a way as to make them intelligible. On this task I have, I think, been so employed that my undertaking it after Laurentius Valla and the learned and industrious Jacques Lefèvre may not seem to be altogether labour in vain.

We have in hand a little book on the Education of a Prince, which we have destined for Charles, Archduke of Burgundy, the grandson of Maximilian. When we have completed what I have already mentioned, we shall take up again the Commentaries on St. Paul which have been already begun. For I am resolved to dedicate the remainder of my life to sacred literature and shall not be deterred by any toil, if I am only supported by your favour and that of others like you. For you know how old a story it is, that Envy, more noxious than a serpent, meets every extraordinary effort with a discordant hiss. An example of this we have lately seen to our great sorrow in the case of that eminent man, John Reuchlin. It was time that a man of venerable age should enjoy his noble studies and reap an agreeable harvest from the glorious field of his youthful labours. But I hear that some persons have started up, who being themselves incapable of doing anything excellent, seek fame by a most perverse road. Good Heavens! out of what silly trifles, what frightful tragedies have they raised! To think that such disturbances should have arisen out of a little book, or rather a letter, and that written in German, which he neither published himself nor thought of publishing. If any one should discuss in this ill-natured and harsh way the books of St. Jerome, he will find many things widely differing from the decrees of our divines. In such troubles a person venerable both for years and learning is losing now, I believe, the seventh year, to the great distress and indignation of all the learned, and indeed of the whole of Germany. It is their hope, that by your assistance a man of so much eminence may be restored to the world and to Letters.

Next winter we shall be seen at Rome, if Christ grant his favour, and if the king's majesty and the Archbishop of Canterbury give me leave to go again, which if I cannot obtain from them myself, St. Jerome will do it for me. . . .

Nichols II, pp. 183–90. Allen II, pp. 73–9

Erasmus to Raphael Cardinal Riario. London, 31 March 1515
. . . One matter I had almost forgotten. I do most earnestly beseech and adjure you for the sake of good Letters, which your eminence has always loved, that that distinguished man, Doctor John Reuchlin, may enjoy your protection and good-will in the business in which he is concerned. He is one to whom all Germany is indebted, having been the first to arouse in that country a love of Greek and Hebrew literature; a man of various learning, long known to the Christian world by the books which he has published, and especially favoured by the Emperor Maximilian, one of whose counsellors he is, while among his fellow-citizens he fills the honourable office of triumvir, with a reputa-

tion which has never been soiled. I might add the reverence that is due to years and grey hairs. At his age he might fairly expect to reap the harvest of his honourable studies; and we were looking forward to his producing for the advantage of us all what he had been storing for so many years. Therefore to all good men who know him by his writings, not only in Germany but also in France and England, it appears most unworthy that so distinguished a man should be harassed by such hateful litigation, and that for a thing that in my judgment is more trifling than the ass's shadow, which is the subject of the proverbial jest. Now that by your intercession, our sovereigns have returned to peace, how absurd it is for men of learning to carry on war with books and controversies, and that, while those have their weapons sheathed, these should be stabbing each other with pens dipped in poison.

To many here the memory of Julius II is the more in favour on account of James Wimpefling, a man, like Reuchlin, not only commended for his erudition and holiness, but venerable for his age, whom that pope relieved by his own command from similar disputes and imposed silence on his calumniators. Believe me, he will secure the attachment of numberless mortals, whoever he may be, that shall restore Reuchlin to the Muses and to Letters.

Nichols II, pp. 193–4. Allen II, pp. 72–3

5   Two Final Visits: 1516 and 1517

In 1516 and 1517, Erasmus returned to England for two brief visits. His purpose was wholly legalistic. He sought papal dispensation from the obligation to wear the full religious habit of the Canons Regular of St. Augustine (Austin Canons), and from the required residence at Steyn. It is important to remember, however, that even after the dispensation was formally granted (1517), Erasmus remained a professed member of the Austin Canons to the end of his life. He sought dispensation merely to facilitate his scholarly activities.

Erasmus to Leo X. London, 9 August 1516
I thought I should be abundantly fortunate, most blessed Father, if your Holiness had only not condemned the temerity, or importunity, with which I ventured unbidden to address a letter to the eminence of papal dignity, and, what is more august, to the incomparable majesty of Leo. But this audacity has, I find, turned out most happily for me. Your more than paternal kindness has surpassed both my hopes and my wishes. Without any solicitation, you have sent two briefs, in one

of which you distinguish me and my studies with a testimonial as complete as it is authoritative, and in the other, you recommend me no less lovingly than earnestly to the King's Majesty. It is the highest object to deserve the approbation of the Almighty; and next to this I certainly think it is, to be commended by the oracular voice of the Supreme Pontiff, still more by that of Leo, that is to say, of him who, invested with the highest of all human dignities, graces it in turn by every kind of excellence and learning. If those despatches had reached me in time, as I was then at Basel, no perils of travel could have deterred me from flying to the feet of your Holiness. But having returned to my native land, while advancing years somewhat impede my movements, I am also kept back by the liberality of the government, and tied to home by the extraordinary affection of my country; the most illustrious Prince Charles, King Catholic, the incomparable light and glory of this our age, in whose dominions I was born and by whose father, Philip, I was not only known but loved, having invited me to his court, while I was abroad, with the promise of an annual salary, and that without my either soliciting or expecting it, and immediately upon my return having conferred on me an ample and honourable benefice. On the other hand I have found by the surest proofs how much the King of England's early predilection known for me, how much the goodwill of the most reverend Cardinal of York, and the Archbishop of Canterbury's old interest in my behalf have been increased by the commendation of your Holiness, which was both more agreeable to me and more effectual with them, inasmuch it was not extorted by any asking on my part, but spontaneously bestowed.

Seeing myself therefore so much indebted to your Holiness, I have conceived the wish of becoming still more obliged. Indeed, I shall be glad to owe my whole fortune and the sum of my felicity to Leo alone; and it is to my mind no inconsiderable part of happiness to be indebted without grudging. What my request is, will be orally explained by the Reverend Father, the Bishop of Worcester, the resident envoy of the King of England, at the Court of your Holiness, and will be signified by letter by Andreas Ammonius, your Holiness' nuncio in England. In which matter, I do not doubt I shall experience that goodness which your letter freely promises, and which I am also led to expect from the benevolence of your character, whereby you recall the image of Christ, whose worthy vicegerent you are; especially as the business is of such a nature as not so much to concern my own credit, to which you have a sincere regard, as the general interest of the world, for which your solicitude is ever on the watch. I might have mis-employed the recommendation of the greatest princes to obtain the favour I am seeking, but I prefer to owe whatever benefit it may be to your goodness alone. . . .

The New Testament in Greek and Latin, revised by me, together with our annotations, has been published for some time, under the safeguard of your auspicious name. I do not know whether the work pleases everyone, but I find that up to this time, it has certainly been approved by the most approved and principal theologians, and among the first by that incomparable prelate, Christopher, Bishop of Basel, who witnessed its printing. For by this labour we do not intend to tear up the old and commonly accepted edition, but to emend it in some places where it is corrupt and to make it clear where it is obscure; and this not by the dreams of my own mind, not, as they say, with unwashed hands, but partly by the evidence of the earliest manuscripts and partly by the opinion of those, whose learning and sanctity have been confirmed by the authority of the Church—I mean Jerome, Hilary, Ambrose, Augustine, Chrysostom, and Cyril. Meantime, we are always prepared either to give our reasons, without presumption, for anything which we have rightly taught or to correct, without grudging, any passage where as men we have unwittingly fallen into error. We sent one volume to Rome last winter, still fresh and warm from the press, which I suppose was delivered to your Holiness; and I would send the other now, if I did not know that there is no place in the world where the work is not by this time within reach of everybody. Although the greatest pains have been bestowed upon it, so far as the limit of time allowed by the prince, and the condition of my health admitted, yet I shall never be tired out and will never rest until I have made it so complete and so correct that it may appear not altogether unworthy of the great pontiff and great personage, to whom it is dedicated.

The revised Jerome will be published next September. It will be, I think, an auspicious revival, and is expected with much interest by all the learned. And in future no page will be produced by Erasmus, which will not carry with it some praise of Leo. . . .

Nichols II, pp. 314–17. Allen II, pp. 288–91

Erasmus to Andrew Ammonius. Rochester, 22 August 1516
My John would certainly have had a beating if More had not come just in time to take his part. For as soon as our friend knew that we had pulled up at Rochester, he hurried down to have another look at

Erasmus, whom he seems to fear he will not soon see again. He advised the servant to lead the horse off to the stable, after your spontaneous offer of it. I see you must be more cautiously dealt with, as you take hold of every handle for making a present. I should have sent your gift back, even if More had advised the contrary, had I not been afraid you would suspect, either that I did not like it, or that I was unwilling to be obliged to Ammonius, whereas there is no one to whom I am more willing to be obliged, as there is no one I love more dearly. May I die, Ammonius, if I do not value and love that magnanimity and true friendship of yours, more than all the bustle of a papal fortune. I can never think myself unfortunate so long as such friends are preserved to me.

I am delighted with the horse which is distinguished by its spotless colour, but more commended by the spotless sincerity of its giver. I should have preferred to play the part of robber upon some one else, as my lord of York, Colet or Urswick. But they know better; although the last does promise a splendid horse, and I have no doubt will fulfil his promise—not at the Greek calends but at those of October. . . .

Nichols II, p. 323. Allen II, p. 320

B   FRANCE AND ITALY

1   Parisian Studies: 1500–1501

Erasmus returned to his theological studies at the University of Paris in 1500. In order to sustain himself he edited Cicero's *De Officiis* (1501) and compiled a collection of adages, or classical proverbs, with explanatory notes, which were published in inexpensive editions in June of 1500. The purpose of the *Adages* was to help those who wished to write elegant Latin by providing them with a guide to the subject matter of classical literature, arranged under appropriate headings. He also studied Greek with enormous diligence and much success. It was his intention to apply his knowledge of Greek to a thorough examination of the Greek text of the New Testament. He assumed that these texts were more accurate than the Vulgate edition of the Bible. With a definitive text, theologians would be in a better position to interpret the teachings of Christ.

Erasmus to James Batt. Paris, 12 April 1500

I pray, my dear Batt, that you may be enjoying the health which I lack myself; for ever since I returned to Paris, mine has been delicate. The fatigues which we underwent by land and sea in our winter journey, have been followed not by careful rest, but by constant night-work, so that there has been no cessation, but only a change of labour. And the weather moreover has been both disagreeable in itself and singularly unfavourable to my health. I call to mind that ever since I came to France, no Lent has ever gone by without bringing sickness to me. But of late having removed my lodging, I have been so affected by the change, as to feel manifest symptoms of that nocturnal fever which was so near sending us below two years ago. We are fighting against it with every care and with the aid of doctors, but have scarcely escaped yet, being still in a doubtful condition. And if that fever does get hold on me again, it will be all over, my dear Batt, with your Erasmus. How-ever, we are not in despair, and have confidence in St. Genevieve, whose present help we have more than once experienced, and all the more as we have the advice of William Cop, a most skilful doctor, and not only that, but a faithful friend, and, what is more, a votary of the Muses. . . .

It is my intention as soon as this work is done, to direct all my efforts to finish the Dialogue, and to devote the whole summer to writing books. In the autumn, if possible, I shall go to Italy to take my doctor's degree; I depend upon you to obtain for me the means and the leisure. I have been applying my whole mind to the study of Greek; and as soon as I receive any money I shall first buy Greek authors, and afterwards some clothes. . . .

Nichols I, pp. 234–5; 236. Allen I, pp. 285–8

Erasmus to William Blount, Lord Mountjoy. Paris, June 1500. Preface to the first edition of the Adages (*1500*)

Instead of the epistle for which you modestly ask, your Erasmus sends you a volume, and that of fair proportions. Would it were such as to satisfy either your claims upon me or my affection for you, and to have no reason for fearing your nice and accurate judgment. The work was not written, but dictated, at a time when we were suffering, after our journey, from a slight but daily recurring fever; and this was done behind the doctor's back, who was warning us meantime not to touch a book. Accordingly, laying aside all serious labours, and indulging in a more dainty kind of study, I strolled through the gardens provided by various authors, culling as I went the adages most remarkable for their antiquity and excellence, like so many flowers of various sorts, of which I have made a nosegay. I was induced to undertake the work partly by your own wish, which was seconded by prior Charnock; and partly by the thought, that my labour, if not productive of glory to the author, might at any rate be neither unprofitable nor unpleasing to readers, who, weary of our common and trivial language, were in search of more sprightly and brilliant modes of expression . . .

If any one should think that the examples are too few, we reply, that they are a collection made from the two months' dictation of an invalid, who had other business on hand. If too many, that we have left out not a few. If he should observe that many of them are too bare and naked, let him only wait patiently for the latest handling. We have sent out these pages to make a trial, with small expense and risk, what is likely to be the fate of a new work. Any one that will point out our mistakes, if in kindness, shall receive our thanks, if in malice, shall still be heard; while he who blames what he does not understand, will be met by the Apellean adage. Let the cobbler stick to his last. There are some who will not find in it anything to their taste; it is not written for them. . . .

Nichols I, pp. 243–4. Allen I, pp. 290, 296

Erasmus to James Batt. Paris September 1500

. . . I am eager to leave France as soon as possible, and long to live among my own people. This I find will be more conducive both to my good name and to my health. For now my countrymen at home believe that I choose to be abroad to enjoy greater liberty, while the people here suspect, that I am not wanted at home and live here as a sort of outcast. Lastly, if there were no other, there is this most urgent reason, that I may see you and my William [Blount, Lord Mountjoy] pretty often. The book just printed has no sale here now, because Augustine [Vincent Caminadus] has ceased the interpretation of it, and there is a general flight on account of the plague. And yet, if it is not soon sold, I shall not find a printer for my book on Letters, which I now have in hand. Wherefore, dear Batt, do pray exert all your efforts, all your powers, and all your ingenuity to get this done. . . .

I do wish, my dear Batt, that you knew Greek, both because I find Latin literature incomplete without it, and because it would make our intercourse more agreeable, if we took delight in the same studies. You must put the first elements of that language before your pupil. 'Send them,' you will say. Well, they are sold here and cheaply; but I answer, that I have not a halfpenny. You will guess the rest, what a slavery I undergo, and you know well my impatience of slavery.

However, this state of things must soon end one way or other—I trust well. . . .

Nichols I, pp, 260, 261. Allen I, pp. 300, 301

Erasmus to Faustus Andrelinus. Orleans, 20 November 1500
My boy brought me a message from you that I was a coward, because I had shifted my quarters on account of some fear of plague. An insufferable reproach, if addressed to a Swiss warrior, but hurled at a poet, fond of ease and retirement, it misses its aim. Indeed in cases of this kind, I hold the absence of fear is not so much a sign of courage as of stupidity. When you have to do with an enemy that may be driven back, resisted and conquered by fighting, in that case he who lists may play the hero for me. What are you to do against an evil which can neither be seen nor conquered? There are things which may be escaped, but cannot be overcome. . . .

I know that it is needless for me to ask you to do what you are constantly doing of your own accord, still I will ask you to honour with your recommendation our *Adages*, that abortive production of mine, with a view to its speedy sale. This favour you will accord, not to the work itself, but to our friendship. For I am not so conceited as not to see what the book is. But when you want to get rid of indifferent goods, there is more need of a puffer, the less they are worth; and we shall be all the more obliged to you, if you give your vote in accordance not with your judgment, but with your good will. I might urge, that you have not left it open for yourself to do anything but praise my poor volume, to which you have attributed every merit in a letter which served as an introduction to it. Finally we undertake that this rough-hewn and misshapen production shall be not merely submitted to the file, but taken back to the workshop and entirely remodelled, so as to come out at last in such a form, that you may not repent of your testimony, nor the subject of it be ashamed of your undeserved commendation. In which remodelling we shall hope to have your help, not only as a writer, but as a designer. . . .

Nichols I, p. 275. Allen I, pp. 311-13

Erasmus to James Batt. Orleans, 11 December 1500
. . . Augustine has gone back to Paris, whether as a friend or an enemy, it is not yet clearly made out, and it is not safe to trust either looks or words. However, I hope for the best, for in this matter I had rather appear over-credulous than over-suspicious. It is not only most convenient, but it is necessary for me to move back to Paris in order

to proceed in those Greek studies which I have begun, and to finish the works I have in hand. There are also other reasons, which I do not like trusting to paper. And without some money I can neither sit still here, nor go away, unless indeed after such serious quarrels and even bitter contests you would have me return to Augustine [Vincent Caminadus] as a humble suppliant, thereby showing myself conquered and ready to submit to be gulled by him after his own fashion. I have no objection to take what he will give; for from whom should I more readily accept a service than from one who is under such obligation to me, and who owes all that he is to what I have done for him. But I have quite made up my mind to remain here until you have sent me some little money, so that, when I go back to Paris, I may be at liberty either to accept Augustine's civility, if freely and sincerely offered, or to defy him and take my own part, if he betrays himself in an assumed and pretended goodwill.

However happily this may turn out, still a little money must be scraped together from somewhere, with which I may get clothes, buy the whole works of Jerome (upon whom I am preparing commentaries), as well as Plato, procure Greek books and hire the services of a Greek teacher. How much all these things are necessary to my glory and even to the security of my position, I think you are aware; at any rate I beg you to believe it when I affirm it of my own knowledge. It is incredible, how my heart burns to bring all my poor lucubrations to completion, and at the same time to attain some moderate capacity in Greek. I should then devote myself entirely to the study of Sacred Literature, as for some time I have longed to do. I am now, thank Heaven, in fair health, and hope to remain so. Therefore every nerve must be strained this year, in order that what we are forging may come to light, and also that by our treatment of theological subjects, we may drive our Zoili, of whom there are so many, to hang themselves, as they well deserve. I have threatened long, but either my own want of energy or my health or some unpropitious fatality has stood in the way. Now at last I must rouse my courage and put forth all my strength, and I trust with the aid of Heaven, if I am permitted to live three years, to overwhelm the malignity of the most envious by the lustre of merit. . . .

Nichols I, pp. 282–4. Allen I, pp. 320–21

Erasmus to Greveradus. Paris, 18 December 1500
. . . I have long ardently wished to illustrate with a commentary the Epistles of St. Jerome, and in daring to conceive so great a design,

which no one has hitherto attempted, my heart is inflamed and directed by some divine power. I am moved by the piety of that holy man, of all Christians beyond controversy the most learned and most eloquent; whose writings, though they deserve to be read and learned everywhere and by all, are read by few, admired by fewer still, and understood by scarcely any. Good Heavens! shall the names of Scotus, Albertus, and writers still less polished be shouted in all the schools, and that singular champion, exponent and light of our religion, who deserves to be the one person celebrated—shall he be the only one of whom nothing is said? Many readers are repelled by that abstruse erudition by which he should be especially recommended, and there are few to admire one whom very few understand. But if such an author be illustrated by adequate commentaries, it may be expected that the glory of Jerome will shine forth with a new light.

I am not unaware of the audacity of my project—what a task it will be, in the first place, to clear away the errors, which during so many ages have become established in the text—and in the next place what a mass there is in his works of antiquities, of Greek literature, of history— and then what a style, what a mastery of language, in which he has not only left all Christian authors far behind him, but seems to vie with Cicero himself. For my own part, I may be led astray by my partiality for that holy man, but when I compare the speech of Jerome with that of Cicero, I seem to miss something in the prince of eloquence himself.

Whatever I can supply by nightly labour and constant study, by moderate learning and a mind not altogether dull, shall not be wanting in the service of Jerome. But as in a great war, auxiliary forces are required, so in this important work I see the need of some high guidance and inspiration; and whom I should choose as fittest to furnish me with that, no one can tell better than you. You have always been, as Henry has often told me, a warm and zealous lover of our author, and this is the great pledge, by which a mutual alliance and friendship between us is to be initiated. Come then, excellent sir, reach me your hand, and exalt your mind to take part in so noble an enterprise. The Saint will himself be present and favour the champions of his writings, which cost him so many vigils; and our pious labour will not be deprived of its reward. . . .

Nichols I, pp. 289–90. Allen I, pp. 332–3

Erasmus to Anne of Borsselen (the Lady of Veer). Paris, 27 January 1500–1501
. . . Proceed as you have begun, regard my learning as a suppliant

descending upon you, and imploring your aid, not only in the name of our various fortunes, but also for the love of true theology, that excellent queen, whom the inspired psalmist describes, according to the interpretation of Jerome, as standing on the king's right hand, not mean and ragged as she is now seen in the schools of Sophists, but in vesture of gold, wrought about with diverse colours, to whose rescue from degradation my nightly studies are devoted.

With this object in view, I have long felt the necessity of two things; to visit Italy, so that my little learning may derive an authority from the celebrity of the place, and to take the title of doctor. The one is as absurd as the other. For they do not change their minds, who cross the sea, as Horace says, nor will the shadow of a name make me a whit more learned. But it is no use acting a good play to be hissed by all the audience; and we must put on the lion's skin, to force the conviction of our competence upon the minds of those who judge a man by a title, and not by his books, which indeed they do not understand. With such monsters have I to contend, and the struggle requires another Hercules.

Nichols I, pp. 296–7. Allen I, pp. 344–5

Erasmus to Abbot Anthony of St. Bertin. Paris, 16 March? 1501
My letters, kind Father, must recall to your mind the ass of Æsop; for after having so often experienced your good nature, they have attained so much confidence that they venture to come to your lordship in dishabille, whereas before they shrank from doing so however carefully attired. I should be sorry, however, that you should attribute this neglect to carelessness, and not rather to the literary labours which always occupy me as far as my health admits, and which worry me now without any regard to health at all. For I have by a lucky chance got some Greek works, which I am stealthily transcribing night and day. It may be asked why I am so pleased with the example of Cato the Censor, as to be learning Greek at my age. I answer, Reverend Father, that if I had had this mind when a boy, or rather if the times had been more favourable to me, I should have been the happiest man in the world. As it is, I am determined that it is better to learn late than to be without the knowledge which it is of the utmost importance to possess. We had a taste of this learning a long time ago, but it was only with the tip of the tongue, as they say; and having lately dipped deeper into it, we see, what we have often read in the most weighty authors, that Latin erudition, however ample, is crippled and imperfect without Greek. We have in Latin at best some small streams and turbid

pools, while they have the clearest springs and rivers flowing with gold. I see it is the merest madness to touch with the little finger that principal part of theology, which treats of the divine mysteries, without being furnished with the apparatus of Greek, when those who have translated the sacred books have in their scrupulous interpretation so rendered the Greek phrases that not even that primary meaning which our theologians call 'literal' can be perceived by those who are not Greek scholars. . . .

But what need is there of citing some few and trifling instances out of the multitude of important passages that might be mentioned, when I have on my side the sacred authority of the pontifical council, whose decree is extant in the Decretal Epistles, to the effect that there should be provided in the chief academies (as they were then) persons capable of teaching perfectly the Hebrew, Greek, and Latin languages, inasmuch as they held that without this knowledge sacred literature could not be apprehended, still less discussed. This most wholesome and holy law is now so disregarded that we are satisfied with the merest rudiments of Latin, being persuaded, I suppose, that all theology may be got out of Scotus, as a sort of cornucopia. With this kind of men I do not contend. Every one may please himself for me. . . . For my own part, I choose to follow the path to which St. Jerome, with the noble band of so many ancient Fathers, invites us. I had rather, so help me heaven, lose my senses with them, than be as wise as you please with the herd of neoteric divines! Besides, I am going to attempt an arduous and so to say Phaethontean feat, and that is to restore the books of Jerome, and to illustrate them with a commentary. Having set my mind on this, and seeing the necessity of completing my Greek studies, I determined to employ for several months a Greek teacher; and a thorough Greek he is, always hungry, and charging an exorbitant price for his lessons. . . .

Nichols I, pp. 312–14. Allen I, pp. 351–2

Erasmus to Antony of Luxembourg. Tournehem, 18 July 1501
. . . For the rest, my dear Antony, if we enjoy some degree of health, it is a pleasure to acknowledge it. We are living a happy and agreeable life, both because we enjoy the society of Batt and because we are heart and soul in letters; a life of the gods if we had only a few more books! Owing to this condition of mind to literature, should you not, my dear Antony, think me most ungrateful, if I were out of humour with my studies for not having brought me any profit? Let others be loaded with gold and carried to the height of glory, while my muses

bring me nothing but vigils and envy. Still I shall never turn my back upon them, as long as this mind endures and retains its contempt for fickle fortune. I am not unaware that I have pursued a kind of study which some think strange, others endless, others unprofitable, others even impious; so they seem to the crowd of those who are professors of learning. But I am all the more encouraged, as I am sure of two facts, that the best things have never found favour with the crowd and that this kind of study is most approved by the smallest number, but the most learned. If Jerome was mad or unlearned, it is good to share the folly of such a man; it is good to be numbered in his unlearned flock, rather than in those other divine choirs. And even if we shall fail to reach the goal in this our course, it will not be discreditable to have at any rate striven to attain the very fairest objects. If men do not approve this purpose of mine, God, I think, will both approve and aid it; and some time hence men will approve, or at any rate posterity. . . .

Nichols I, pp. 335–6. Allen I, pp. 369–70

Erasmus to Johann Botzheim, Catalogue of Lucubrations. *Basel, 30 January 1523*

Erasmus discusses the composition of his *Enchiridion* which he wrote at Tournehem in 1501.

The *Enchiridion militis Christiani* was begun by me nearly thirty years ago when staying in the castle of Tournehem, to which we were driven by the plague that depopulated Paris. The work arose out of the following incident. A common friend of mine and of Batt was in the castle, whose wife was a lady of singular piety. The husband was no one's enemy so much as his own, a man of dissolute life, but in other respects an agreeable companion. He had no regard for any divines except me; and his wife, who was much concerned about her husband's salvation, applied to me through Batt to set down some notes in writing, for the purpose of calling him to some sense of religion, without his perceiving that it was done at the instance of his wife. For even with her it was a word and a blow, in soldier fashion. I consented to the request and put down some observations suitable to the occasion. These having met with the approval even of learned persons, and especially of Joannes Vitrarius, a Franciscan friar of great authority in those parts, I finished the work at leisure, after the plague (then raging everywhere) had routed me out of Paris and driven me to Louvain.

Nichols I, pp. 337–8. Allen I, pp. 19–20

Erasmus to Fr. Edmund. Castle of Courtenbourne, autumn 1501
I have retired to this country house of the kind Prince of Courtenbourne,
intending to be quietly occupied these winter months in sacred literature. I wish that under the Warden's leadership, I had been allowed to
have you for a companion. For the rest, it will be like your goodness
to encourage Adrian to supply me with a few books. I want him to
send Augustine and Ambrose on St. Paul; and to beg Origen for a
time from the people at St. Bertin, and be bound for me to return it;
he shall not be disappointed. Moreover, I very much wish, if it can
be done, to have the Homilies of Origen, which the Warden has,
sent with the rest. I should also be glad to welcome Lyranus and any
other writer upon St. Paul. A cart shall be sent on Saturday to carry
everything hither. Meantime you will take care to get the books ready
for that day. . . .

Nichols I, pp. 342–3. Allen I, pp. 375–6

2 Respites: 1504–5, 1506

Erasmus returned to Paris at the end of 1504. It was still the centre of theological
studies and Erasmus wished to devote himself to the study of scripture. Armed
with Valla's *Annotations on the New Testament* (which he had discovered near
Louvain), Erasmus succeeded in editing Valla's neglected notes on the texts of
the gospels, the epistles, and the Book of Revelation. It was published by Josse
Badius at Paris in 1505.

  In June of 1506, Erasmus stopped at Paris on his way to Italy. He brought
with him a supply of finished manuscripts—translations of Lucian and Euripides and a collection of epigrams—which were also published by Badius.

*Erasmus to Christopher Fisher, Doctor of Pontifical Law. Paris, c. March
1505*
When I was hunting last summer in an old library—for no coverts
afford more delightful sport—some game of no common sort fell
unexpectedly into my nets. It was Laurentius Valla's Notes on the
New Testament. I was taken on the spot with the desire to communicate my discovery to all the studious, thinking it churlish to devour
the contents of my bag without saying anything about it. I was somewhat frightened, however, not only by the old prejudice against
Valla's name, but also by an objection, specially applicable to the present
case. But as soon as you had perused the book, you not only confirmed
my opinion by your weighty judgment, but began to advise and even

urge me with reproaches not to be induced by the clamour of a few to deprive the author of the glory which he served, and many thousands of students of so great an advantage, affirming without doubt, that the work would be no less agreeable than useful to healthy and candid minds, while the others with their morbid ideas might be boldly disregarded. In pursuance of your opinion we shall discourse in the present Preface of the purpose and utility of the work, provided that we may premise a few words in confutation of the general prejudice against the name of Laurentius. . . .

We must now come to the considerations that more properly belong to this subject. I imagine there will be some persons, who as soon as they read the title of the work, and before they know anything of its contents, will exclaim loudly against it; and that the most odious outcry will be raised by those who will chiefly benefit by the publication, I mean the theologians. They will call it an intolerable act of temerity, that this grammarian, after harassing all other branches of learning, cannot keep his captious pen even from sacred literature. And yet if Nicolas Lyranus is listened to, while he plays the pedagogue to ancient Jerome, and pulls to pieces many things that have been consecrated by the consent of ages, and that out of the books of the Jews, which though we may admit them to be the source of our received edition, yet for ought I know may be intentionally corrupted, what crime is it in Laurentius, if after collating some ancient and correct Greek copies, he has noted in the New Testament, which is derived from the Greek, some passages which either differ from our version, or seem to be inaptly rendered owing to a passing want of vigilance in the translator, or are expressed more significantly in the Greek; or finally if it appears that something in our text is corrupt? They will say perhaps that Valla being a grammarian has not the same privilege as Nicolas a theologian? I might answer, that Laurentius has been counted by some great authorities as a philosopher and theologian. But after all, when Lyranus discusses a form of expression, is he acting as a theologian or as a grammarian? Indeed, all this translating of Scripture belongs to the grammarian's part; and it is not absurd to suppose Jethro to be in some things wiser than Moses. Neither do I think that Theology, herself, the queen of all sciences, will hold it beneath her dignity to be attended and waited upon by her handmaid, Grammar; which if it be inferior in rank to other sciences, certainly performs a duty which is as necessary as that of any.

If they reply that Theology is too great to be confined by the laws of Grammar, and that all this work of interpretation depends upon the influence of the Holy Spirit, it is truly a new dignity for divines, if they are the only people who are privileged to speak incorrectly. But let them explain first what Jerome means when he writes to Desiderius: It is one thing to be a prophet and another to be an interpreter; in one case the Spirit foretells future events, in the other sentences are understood and translated by erudition and command of language. Again, what is the use of Jerome laying down rules for the translation of the sacred writings, if that faculty comes by inspiration? Lastly, why is Paul said to be more eloquent in Hebrew than in Greek? And if it was possible for the interpreters of the Old Testament to make some mistakes, especially in matters not affecting the faith, why may it not be the same with the New, of which Jerome did not so much make a translation as emend an old one, and that not strictly, leaving words, as he himself testifies, some of which are those principally called in question by Laurentius? Again, shall we ascribe to the Holy Spirit the errors which we ourselves make? Suppose the interpreters translated rightly, still what has been rightly translated may be perverted. Jerome emended, but what he emended is now again corrupted; unless it can be asserted that there is now less presumption among the half-learned, or more skill in languages, and not rather corruption made easier than ever by printing, which propagates a single error in a thousand copies at once.

But, say they, it is not right to make any change in the Holy Scriptures, in which even the points have some mysterious meaning. This only shows how wrong it is to corrupt them, and diligently what has been altered by ignorance ought to be corrected by the learned, but always with that caution and moderation which is due to all books, and above all to the sacred volume.

Again, it is said that Laurentius had no right to take upon himself an office which Jerome undertook at the bidding of Pope Damasus. But their objects were not the same. Jerome substituted a new edition for an old; Laurentius collects his observations in a private commentary, and does not require you to change anything in your book, although the very variety we find in our copies is sufficient evidence that they are not free from errors. And as the fidelity of the old books is to be tested by the Hebrew rolls, so the truth of the new books requires to be measured by the Greek text, according to the authority of Augustine, whose words are cited in the *Decreta* (distinc. ix). In reference to which passage, I think no one is so cruel as not to pity, or so grave as not to laugh at that silly gloss of someone who dreamed that Jerome had asserted in his Epistle to Desiderius, that the Latin copies are more correct than the Greek, and the Greek than the Hebrew—not seeing that Jerome was confirming what he alleged by the suggestion of a proposition plainly absurd, and that the preceding words *aliud est si* have the same meaning as if he had *nisi forte*, 'unless perhaps.' It would have been madness else to translate one Testament from the Hebrew and to emend the other from the Greek, if in both cases the Latin versions were better. . . .

There is another thing I hear some say, that the old interpreters, skilled in the three tongues, have already fully unfolded the matter as far as is necessary. But, first, I had rather see with my own eyes than with those of others; and in the next place, much as they have said, they have left much to be said by posterity. Consider again, that to understand even their explanations, some skill in languages is required. And lastly when you find the old copies in every language corrupted as they are, in what direction are you to turn? Consequently, most learned Christopher, what you often say is as true as truth, that they have neither sense nor shame, who presume to write upon the sacred books, or indeed upon any of the books of the ancients, without being tolerably furnished in both literatures, for it may well happen that while they take the greatest pains to display their learning, they become a laughing-stock to those who have any skill in languages, and all their turmoil is reduced to nothing by the production of a Greek word. And if there are any who have not the leisure to learn Greek thoroughly, they may still obtain no small help by the studies of Valla, who has examined with remarkable sagacity the whole New Testament, adding incidentally not a few observations out of the Psalms, of which the edition in use is derived from the Greek and not from the Hebrew. I conclude that the studious will owe much to Laurentius, and Laurentius will owe much to you, through whom he is presented to the public, and by whose judgment and patronage he will be more commended to good intellects, and better protected against the malevolent. . . .

Nichols I, pp. 380–85. Allen I, pp. 407–12

Erasmus to John Colet. Paris, 12 June 1506
Leaving England and returning to France, I can hardly tell you, with what a mixture of feelings I am affected. It is not easy to decide, whether I am more happy in seeing again the friends I formerly left in France or more sad in leaving those I have lately gained in England. For this I can truly affirm, that there is no entire country which has

bred me so many friends, so sincere, so learned, so devoted, so brilliant, so distinguished by every kind of virtue, as the single city of London; every one of whom has so vied in loving and assisting me that I know not whom I should prefer to another, and am bound to return an equal affection to them all. The parting from those cannot but be painful to me. But again memory brings me comfort; by constantly thinking of them I seem to make them present, and I hope it will soon come to pass that I shall meet them again, not to part until separated by death. To bring this speedily and happily into effect, I am confident —such is your love and partiality for me—that you will exert yourself with my other friends.

It is impossible to say how pleased I am with the disposition of [Giovanni Battista] Boerio's children. No boys could be more modest, more tractable or more industrious in their studies. I trust therefore that they will answer to their father's intentions and my pains, and some day or other bring great credit to Britain. . . .

Nichols I, p. 412. Allen I, p. 428

3 Italy: the Vintage Years, 1506-9

On his arrival in Italy, Erasmus was awarded a doctorate in theology by the University of Turin (1506). The degree recognised Erasmus' important contributions to the study of the Church Fathers and Scripture. But Erasmus' major purpose in travelling to Italy was to master Greek and to secure the services of an Italian printer. Erasmus aimed high and convinced Aldus Manutius, the prince of printers, to publish a revised and enlarged edition of his *Adages* (1508). Erasmus derived much benefit from his association with Aldus, who had gathered about him a score of young humanists.

Erasmus to Augustine Steuchus. Freiburg, 27 March 1531
When I was at Rome, after I had been invited to visit him by [Domenico] Cardinal Grimani, and that, if I am not mistaken, through Peter Bembo, and the invitation had been more than once repeated— so much did I dislike paying court to the great; at last I went to his palace rather from shame than inclination. There was no creature to be seen either in the court or in the vestibule. It was afternoon. I gave my horse to my servant, and mounting the stairs by myself, went into the first reception-room. I saw no one. I went on to the second and third. Just the same. I found no door closed and marvelled at the solitude around me. Coming to the last room, I found one person, keeping watch at an open door. He had the tonsure, and was, I believe, a Greek

physician. I asked him how the cardinal was engaged. He said he was within talking with several gentlemen. I made no reply, and he asked what I wanted. 'To pay my respects to him,' said I, 'if it had been convenient, but as he is not at leisure, I will call again.' As I turned to go, I lingered at a window to look at the view; and the Greek came to me again to inquire whether I wished any message to be taken to the cardinal. 'There is no need,' said I, 'to interrupt his conversation, but I will come back shortly.' At last he asked my name, which I gave him. As soon as he heard it, he went hastily in without my noticing it, and coming out directly, bade me not to go. Without further delay I was fetched in, and the cardinal received me not as a cardinal, and such a cardinal, might receive a person of humble rank, but as he might a colleague. A chair being placed for me, we talked together for more than two hours, and all that time I was not allowed to remove my hat, a marvellous act of courtesy from a man of such rank. In the midst of much learned discourse about literary studies, in which he sufficiently showed that he already intended what I now hear he has done about his library, he began to advise me not to leave Rome, the nursing-mother of intellects. He invited me to share his house and all his fortunes, adding that the climate of Rome being damp and warm would agree with my constitution, especially that part of the city where he had his palace, which had been built by one of the popes, who had chosen it as the most healthy situation that could be found. After much talk on one side and the other, he sent for his nephew, already an archbishop, and a young man of noble character. As I offered to rise, he stopped me, saying that a disciple should stand before his master. At last he showed his library, rich in many tongues. If I had happened to become acquainted with this personage earlier, I should never have left the city, where I found more favour than I deserved. But I had already made up my mind to go, and things had gone so far that it was scarcely open for me to stay. When I told him I had been sent for by the King of England, he ceased to press me. Still he begged me over and over again not to suspect that his promises did not come from his heart, or to judge his character by the ordinary manners of a court. It was with difficulty that I had leave to depart, but when he found that I wished to go, he consented not to detain me longer, stipulating with his last words, that I should pay him one more visit before leaving Rome. Unfortunately I did not go, fearing that I might be overcome by his eloquence and change my mind. I never made a more unlucky choice. But what can you do, when driven by destiny?

Nichols I, pp. 416–3. Allen IX, pp. 206–7

Erasmus to Servatius Rogerus. Bologna, 16 November 1506
Though we write lately from Florence, still as letters are often lost in so long a journey, I will write again today. We have come to Italy principally for the sake of Greek: but in these parts, while wars are hot, studies are chilled, which will make us anxious to fly back all the sooner. We have taken a doctor's degree in Theology, not at all by our own choice but compelled by others. . . .

Nichols I, p. 420. Allen I, p. 433

Erasmus to Aldus Manutius. Bologna, 28 October 1507
There is a wish, most learned Manutius, which has many times occurred to my mind. As not only by your skill and the unrivalled beauty of your topography, but also by intelligence and learning of no common order, you have thrown a vast light upon the literature of Greece and Rome. I should be glad if those merits had brought you in return an adequate profit. For as to fame, there is no doubt that to the furthest posterity the name of Aldus Manutius will fly from mouth to mouth among all that are initiated in the religion of letters. Your memory then, as your character now, will deserve not only admiration but love, because you devote yourself to the restoration and publication of good authors, with the greatest solicitude, but, as I hear, with no proportionate gain. Like Hercules you are employed in labours of the noblest kind, which are of more advantage to others than to yourself. I am told that you are editing Plato in Greek, a book expected with the greatest interest by the learned world. I should like to know what authors you have printed on the subject of medicine. I want you to give us Paulus Aegineta. I wonder what has so long prevented you from publishing the New Testament, a work which, if I guess aright, will be exceedingly welcome even to the great majority of our class, I mean the class of theologians.

I send you two tragedies, which I have translated boldly enough, but whether with corresponding success you will judge for yourself. Thomas Linacre, William Grocyn, William Latimer, and Cuthbert Tunstall, friends of yours as well as mine, approved them highly. You know these men to be too learned to be mistaken in their judgment, and too honest to be tempted to flatter, unless indeed they are a little blinded by their partiality for me. Those Italians also, to whom I have shown my attempt, do not condemn it. Badius has printed the plays, and, as I hear from him, has no reason to regret it, for he has already succeeded in selling all his impressions. But my reputation has been somewhat compromised, the pages being full of misprints. He offers himself to print a new edition to correct the former one, but I am afraid, to use the phrase of Sophocles, that he will mend one mischief with another. I should think my lucubrations secure of immortality, if they came out printed in your type, especially that minute type which is the most elegant of all. In that case the volume will be very small and the matter may be carried out at a trifling cost. If you find it convenient to undertake the business, I propose to supply the corrected copy sent by bearer without any charge, except that you will be so good as to send me a few volumes for presentation to friends.

I should not be afraid of undertaking the work at my own expense and risk, were it not that I shall have to leave Italy in a few months. For the same reason I am anxious to get the thing done as soon as possible. It is scarcely a ten days' business. If you insist on my taking a hundred or two hundred copies for myself, although Mercury (as patron of commerce) is not apt to be very propitious to me, and it will be inconvenient to have a parcel to carry, still I will not refuse to take them, provided you fix a favourable price.

Farewell, most learned Aldus, and pray rank Erasmus among those who heartily wish you well. You will do me a favour by letting me know whether you have in your warehouse any authors not in common use; as those learned Englishmen have charged me to make the inquiry. If on the whole you are not inclined to print the Tragedies, please return the copy to the bearer, to be brought back to me.

Nichols I, pp. 428–30. Allen I, pp. 437–9

Erasmus, 'Festina Lente,' Adages (1508)
. . . When Aldus took up this work [printing], what scholar did not commend him? Which of them did not contribute something to help him, unequal as he was to such a task? How often old manuscripts have come, sent unasked for by Hungarians and Poles, accompanied by a gift of money, so that he might give them to the world with proper attention? What Aldus was striving to do among the Italians—for he himself has met his end, though his firm still enjoys the credit of a beloved name —John Froben is trying to achieve on this side of the Alps with no less energy than Aldus, and not without success, although there is no denying that he makes less money by it. If you ask why, there may be many causes but I think this is one, that there is not the same openness of mind among us as among the Italians, at any rate in the matter of literature. And I am not afraid to say what I know by experience. At the time when I, a Dutchman, was supervising the publication of my book of proverbs in Italy, every one of the scholars who were there

offered me, without being asked, copies of authors which had never been printed, and which they thought I might be able to use. Aldus himself kept nothing back among his treasures. It was the same with John Lascaris, Baptista Egnatius, Marcus Musurus, Frater Urbanus. I experienced the kindness of some whom I did not know either by sight or by name. I brought nothing with me to Venice but the raw material of a future work, as yet confused and undigested, and culled only from well-known authors. It was great audacity on my part that set us both on, myself to write and Aldus to print. We broke the back of the work in nine months, more or less, and meanwhile I had had an encounter with a trouble I had not met before, the stone. Imagine how much of value I should have missed, if the scholars had not furnished me with manuscripts. Among these were the works of Plato in Greek, Plutarch's *Lives* and his *Moralia*, which began publication just as my work was ending; the *Deipnosophistai* of Atheneus, Apthonius, Hermogenes with the commentary, the *Rhetoric* of Aristotle with the notes of Gregory Nazianzen; Aristides together with the notes, the little commentaries on Hesiod and Theocritus, the collection of proverbs which goes under the name of Plutarch, and the other called after Apostolius, which was lent me by Jerome Aleander. There were other less important things, which have either escaped my memory or need not be mentioned here. None of these had hitherto been printed.

Now listen to the fair dealing of a northern friend of mine, one of my closest in fact, and one who is still among the number since we must learn to understand our friends' character and not to hate it. When I was preparing the Venetian edition, I happened to notice among his books a Suidas with proverbs written in the margins. The work was large, and numerous volumes had to be looked through. Wishing to save myself this bit of work, I asked him to lend me the volume just for a few hours, long enough for my boy to copy down the notes in my book. Again and again I asked, to meet with a refusal. When no entreaty prevailed and I could not persuade him, I asked him if he was thinking of editing a book of proverbs himself, in which case I would gladly hand over the work to someone who could do it better. He swore that he had no such idea. Then what makes you act so, said I! At last, as if it were dragged out of him by torture, he admitted the reason: up to now learned men had enjoyed the admiration of the public for possessing such things as these, and now they were becoming public property. *Hinc illae lachrymae*. There are old manuscripts lying in the colleges and monastic houses of Germany, France, and England, but (with the exception of a few places) are the owners going to reveal them of their own accord? Far from it. Even when asked they will conceal them, or deny that they have them, or let them out on hire at exorbitant prices, ten times the worth of the book. The best cared-for manuscripts are damaged in the end by decay or insects, or stolen. Great men are so far from giving support to the world of learning, that they think no money more plainly thrown away than what is spent on such purposes; nothing satisfied them but what brings in a good interest. If the northern princes were to favour good learning as honestly as the Italians, the serpents of Froben would not be so far from the riches of Aldus' dolphins. Aldus, making haste slowly, gained both riches and fame, and deserved both; Froben, holding his staff erect, looking to nothing but usefulness to the public, not losing the simplicity of the dove while he expresses the wisdom of the serpent (better, it is true, in his trade-mark than in his actions)—Froben has amassed less money than fame. . . .

Phillips, pp. 185–7

C   THE LOW COUNTRIES, GERMANY AND SWITZERLAND

1   The Lean Years: 1501-4

During the opening years of the sixteenth century, Erasmus wandered about the Low Countries, driven by fear of the plague and penury. He was also driven by the desire to edit St. Jerome and to learn Greek. Quite by chance, Erasmus responded to a request from a distraught wife and produced a manual on the good life. *The Handbook of the Christian Knight*, *Enchiridion militis Christiani* (1503), encouraged the reader to cultivate those virtues which are in keeping with the spirit of the gospel. As Erasmus expressed it: 'I have tried to give the reader a sort of art of piety, as others have written the theory of certain sciences.'

Erasmus to James Tutor. Tournehem, 17 July 1501
I was preparing, most excellent Tutor, to remove to you straight from Paris, for where could I go with more pleasure? And I had collected a few coins together, so as not to be a burden on your fortunes. But when

I heard there were some symptoms of the disease in your parts, I was forced to set sail in this direction. I visited your parents at Antwerp, excellent people, as is natural, like yourself. I was in Holland nearly two months, not settled, but like the dogs in Egypt, continually running about and drinking. For my part I would rather live among the Phoenicians.

. . . We took ship at a great risk from Dordrecht on the day before Sacrament [the eve of the feast of Corpus Christi]. Staying at Zierikzee some days on my boy's account, who had contracted a fever on the voyage, I was on the point of falling ill myself, if I had not taken flight from Zeeland (from Hell I might well call it) in the greatest haste.

We paid our respects to the bishop. He invents, as usual, fresh excuses for not giving anything. The affairs of the lady of Veer were in such a state that I could not speak to her without great risk, nor come away without serious suspicion. You know the charge against the provost. While he is in prison, the lady is in ward in her own house. Being therefore clear of any hopes from that quarter, for it is a wretched thing to remain in suspense for nothing, I betook myself straight to Batt, in whose company I find great delight. I am reading Greek, but by myself, for Batt has not time to spare, and is fonder of Latin. It is my intention to rest at anchor here for a month or two. After that we shall steer whichever way the winds are favourable. You are waiting all this time to know with what kind courtesy the Reverend Father treats us, now we are near him. I have nothing to write, my dear Tutor, on this head. Euripus has not so many tides as that man's mind. A little before we came, he was so warm that he sent off that bustling fellow, Lewis, to Holland to fetch us, and moreover bestowed two gold pieces for the expense of the journey. But when I came myself, he was so cold that it seemed almost unnatural. I am resolved that I ought not to depend upon these fluctuating admirers. . . .

. . . I am thinking of visiting Italy this autumn, or rather dreaming of it, for there is not a gleam of hope. I hear that Jerome, the bishop of Besançon's brother, is determined to go there, that he appreciates scholars, and has no bad opinion of my ability. If, when I was with you, I had had my wits about me, I should certainly have crept somehow into his acquaintance. . . .

Nichols I, pp. 327–9. Allen I, pp. 362–4

Erasmus to James Tutor. Tournehem 18 July 1501
. . . We wasted more than a month and a half in Holland not without great expense; I say wasted because nothing was ever more thrown

away. Again the illness of my boy detained me several days in Zeeland, not only much to my annoyance, as I was in a hurry to come away, but also with no little danger to my health. I never before found any climate more disagreeable or more unsuitable to my constitution.

Other matters, my sweet Tutor, have turned out much as things generally have done with Erasmus. The prelate of Cambrai is just like himself. The lady of Veer is oppressed by misfortunes and appears to need, rather to be relieved than to be burdened. I am now resting in Batt's embraces and among my books, but am not altogether without you, for Tutor is often present in our conversation. Believe me, if you believe anything at all, I find so much hypocrisy, so much perfidy in friendships, not only those of an ordinary kind but those that are called pyladean, that I am not inclined now to try any new ones. In Batt alone I have experienced an attachment no less constant than sincere. His friendship I do not owe to Fortune, as it is only virtue that brought us together, and I am not afraid that Fortune will deprive me of it. For why should he cease to love me in my affliction, when his love began in my deepest affliction? You, most learned James, as you are like him in name, also reproduce his candour and singleness of heart. My feeling about you both is such that if your faith failed me, which God forbid, I should have no faith in faith itself.

Our health, thank Heaven, is pretty good, and somewhat stronger than when we were with you. We have almost wholly deserted the Roman muses for the Greek, and shall not rest till we have attained a moderate proficiency. I cannot tell you how much I wished to go back to your household, as I thought I should be able, without putting you to expense, to enjoy your society, which has a special charm for me, and to put mine at your disposal. But I was frightened away by the plague, which drove me from Paris and has thrust me into exile here. For what is there ever here to attract me, except Batt, whose society I have not to myself, as he is forced to spend much of his time upon his court service? . . .

If there is any occasion, you will, as usual do your utmost to defend Erasmus' good name and frighten the wolf away with your loudest and bravest bark. I have hunted eagerly for a Greek grammar to buy and send you, but they are sold out, both Constantine's and Urban's. Nicolas Benserad will bear witness to this, whom you may believe without putting him on his oath.

As to my future plans, I sometimes think of going to England again, to spend a month or two in theological study with my friend Colet. For I fully recognise how much advantage I might gain by so doing;

but I am still afraid of those cliffs of evil fame, where I made shipwreck before. I have the same longing to visit Italy as I have always had, but as Plautus says: it is not easy without wings to fly. The plague keeps us away from France. In Holland the climate agrees with me, but I have a distaste for those Epicurean meals. The men are a poor, uncultivated race; study is held in the most hearty contempt; learning meets with no encouragement and abundance of envy. And all my people appear to be silently insisting on my being backed up by authority, and so armed as it were against the arrogance of unlearned men before I return. We are therefore for the present undecided and shall turn our course to the point where favourable winds may invite. . . .

Nichols I, pp. 332–4. Allen I, pp. 366–8

Erasmus to William Herman of Gouda. Louvain, September 1502
We are still at Louvain, kept here, as we were cast here, by the plague. This year Fortune has played fine havoc with us. Batt has been removed by death, or rather by poison. The Bishop of Besançon has also died, of whom I had great hopes. The lady of Veer has been snatched away by a worse than servile marriage. My English lord is cut off from me by the sea. Augustine is called away by his legal studies. France, Britain and Germany are all at the same time closed against me by the plague.

I am pleased with everything at Louvain, only the living is a little coarse, and the prices high; and besides I have no means at all of making money. A readership which was offered by the authorities I refused. I am fully occupied with Greek, and it is not altogether lost labour, for I have advanced so far as to be able to write what I want in Greek tolerably well without preparation. I hear your Apologues have been published, and want you to send me some copies. Also send me back the Greek Fables, as you do not need them now; for we are suffering here from a great scarcity of Greek books. Augustine writes insultingly to me about his Adages, while you do nothing but laugh. . . .

Nichols I, pp. 352–3. Allen I, p. 381

Erasmus, The Enchiridion (*1503*)
. . . In order that you may not be put off from the path of righteousness by the fact that it seems hard and rough—partly because you must give up the pleasurable things of this world and partly because you have everlastingly to cope with three very wily foes in the flesh, the Devil, and the world—keep this third rule always in mind: like Vergil's Aeneas you should shrug off as nothing all the bogy men and fantasies which assail you, so to speak, in the very jaws of hell. If you despise

these empty illusions and scrutinise more carefully and steadily reality itself, you will surely see that no path is easier than the way of Christ, quite apart from the fact that it alone leads to felicity, and disregarding any prospect of reward.

What kind of worldly life can you choose, I ask you, in which there are not sorrows and difficulties in abundance to be suffered and endured? Who but the most ingenuous or foolish does not know that a courtier's life is full of trouble? Good Lord! What a lasting and humiliating bondage one has to serve in these positions, how anxiously he has to curry favour with the prince and court the goodwill of those who can help him or block his path. Over and over again he has to compose his face to suit the occasion and stomach the insults doled out by powerful men.

Again, what kind of evil can you name which the military life is not loaded with? (You can be your own best witness as to both kinds of life, since you have learned about both at your own peril.) Still again, what does the businessman not endure, 'trying to escape ruin by sea, land, or fire.' What a burden of household cares, what vexations do those who try marriage find in it! How much trouble and work and risk in getting into public office! Look where you will, you see a vast swarm of fretful annoyances; mortal life itself is subject to a thousand ills common to just and unjust alike. Now, all of these things will turn into a mountain of benefits if they befall you while you are on the road to Christ; if you are not, they will be that much more distressing, that much more profitless, and yet must be endured.

Consider those who serve this world. In the first place, how many years they puff and sweat and strain, and for what fleeting bagatelles! Finally, with what dubious prospects! And add to this the fact that in the world there is no end at all to care and anxiety; the longer one has exerted himself, the more painfully he is troubled. Then what is the end at last of a life so bedevilled and distracted? Unquestionably, eternal punishment.

Now go and compare this life with the way of virtue, which is not difficult from the start and grows easier with practice, which becomes the delightful road that we travel with steadfast hope towards the highest good. Is it not absolute madness to prefer to purchase, at the same price, everlasting death rather than immortal life? But those people are acting even more demented who choose to go with the grimmest travail to everlasting travail rather than with moderate effort towards endless tranquillity. Even if the path of virtue were vastly more laborious than the way of the world, nevertheless this harshness of effort would be softened by the hope of reward, and we have that divine blessing which turns all gall into honey. In the world care produces care, grief is born of grief. There is no respite or quiet: all around a man, labour and affliction; inside him, a more grievous sickness. The very remedies make things worse. . . .

But come now, suppose the wages and effort to be alike. How much better, even so, to serve under the standards of Christ than the banners of Satan. Indeed, how much better to be knocked about with Christ than to swim in pleasures with the Devil! Furthermore, should one not flee by horse and sail from a master who is not only most abominable but also most cruel and treacherous, who enforces a service so ruinous and extends promises so empty, but which still not infrequently take in deluded wretches?

Or suppose he make good his promises? Again, he exalts men when he pleases only that they may suffer much more at losing what they have so arduously gained. After a merchant has blurred out the distinctions between right and wrong in his passion to accumulate property, after he has exposed his reputation, his life, his soul to a thousand perils —even if the die of fortune has rolled luckily for him—what has he concocted for himself but an occasion for anxious care if he keeps his wealth, or torture if he loses it? But if the die falls unluckily, what is left for him except to become twice miserable: once, because he was frustrated in getting what he hoped for, and, again, because he cannot think without sorrow of such an expense of wasted effort.

No one has pressed on with fixed purpose towards soundness of understanding without achieving it. Just as Christ will not be mocked, by the same token He will not mock us. Reflect that when you flee from the world to Christ, you do not give up anything, if the world has any advantages, but are exchanging trifles for things of importance. Who would not gladly exchange silver for gold, a stone for a gem? If your friends are offended, what of it? You will find more agreeable ones. You will be deprived of pleasures, will you? You will enjoy inward satisfactions sweeter, cleaner, and more certain. You must share your material goods? You will increase in those riches which neither moths destroy nor thieves carry off. You will no longer be important among worldlings? But you have the stamp of approval from Christ, your Creator. You please fewer men? Better ones, though. Your body grows lean, but your soul feasts. Your external sleekness diminishes, but your spiritual comeliness becomes luminous.

And if you will run through the other aspects in this same way, you will find that everyone of these seeming goods to be abandoned in this world is replaced by something of far greater value. Suppose, however, that there are things which, though they cannot be desired without sin, can nevertheless be possessed without it: of this sort would be popular esteem, the goodwill of the people, favour, authority, friends, the honour virtue commands. Now, it commonly happens that those who seek first the kingdom of God are given all these things gratuitously. This is what Christ has promised and what God did for Solomon. Fortune often pursues those who run from it and runs from those who pursue it. Certainly, whatever happens to those who love God, nothing can be unpropitious to one for whom loss is turned into gain, scourging into comfort, insults into glory, pain into pleasure, grief into sweetness, evil into good.

Do you hesitate, then, to enter upon this journey and to give up that other one, when you have comparisons so disparate—better to say, non-existent—as God with Satan, hope with hope, reward with reward, hardship with hardship, comfort with comfort? . . .

Himelick I, pp. 90–4

2   Prince of Humanists: 1514–17

These were among Erasmus' most productive and peripatetic years. He published his Greek text of the New Testament, editions of St. Jerome, Seneca, and Plutarch, and *The Education of a Christian Prince*, *Institutio principis Christiani* (1516). The latter work is a treatise on government in which Erasmus sets forth his belief in the educability of man and his preference for an elective monarchy. Through these works and through the contacts he made at the printing houses of John Froben and John Amerbach, Erasmus established himself as the leader of Europe's literary and theological studies. In pursuit of scholarship, Erasmus travelled widely in Switzerland, Germany and the Low Countries.

Erasmus to Andrew Ammonius. Castle of Hammes (Calais), 8 July 1514
I called more than once at your house for the purpose of bidding a final farewell to the sweetest of all my friends and of enjoying to the last possible moment an association which has been one of the greatest pleasures I have had in my life.

We had a fair passage, though it was an anxious one for me. The sea was calm, the wind favourable, the weather fine, the hour most convenient, for we set sail about seven o'clock. But those sea-robbers had carried off a mail filled with my writings to some other ship. This is a thing they do on purpose in order to steal something, if occasion serves, or, if not, to extort some money by selling you what is your own. Accordingly, believing the labours of so many years to be gone forever, I felt for the time as much grief as any parent for the death of his offspring. In all other matters these fellows treat foreigners just in the same way, so that it would be better to fall into the hands of any Turks than into theirs. I often wonder that such scoundrels are tolerated by the English government to the great annoyance of those who visit the country, and the greatest discredit of the whole island, as every traveller carries home the story of the inhuman reception he has met with, and other people form an estimate of the nation by the acts of these robbers.

I do not know whether I have told you that I paid my respects in person to the king's majesty, who received me with quite a friendly air. Then the Bishop of Lincoln bade me be of the best and surest hope. He said nothing about any present, nor did I venture to hint at it for fear of seeming importunate. The Bishop of Durham, as I took leave, gave me six angels, and that of his own accord, and, if I am not mistaken, for the fourth time. The archbishop took some pains to find an opportunity of adding a like amount, and the Bishop of Rochester gave me a royal. This is the sum total of what I carry away; and I wished you to know it, that it may not be thought I have collected a great amount of money under the pretext of leave-taking.

I am now at the castle of Hammes, where I am to spend a very few days with my lord Mountjoy, and shall then go on to Germany, visiting some friends on the way. If Fortune answers to my wishes and to the promises of others, we shall soon return to England. If not we shall be advised by circumstances. God grant that I may return in safety and find my Ammonius not only safe but enriched with the choicest gifts of Fortune. If any opportunity should arise for promoting the interests of your Erasmus, I have, no doubt, that you will be the same good friend in his absence as you have always hitherto been to him, whether absent or present. . . .

Nichols II, pp. 137-8. Allen I, pp. 563-4

Erasmus to Servatius Rogerus. Castle of Hammes by Calais, 8 July 1514
Most gracious Father, your letter, after having been tossed about by a great many hands, has reached mine at last, now that I have left England. It has indeed given me incredible pleasure inasmuch as it still breathes your old affection for me. I will answer it briefly, writing, as I do, on a journey, and will address myself to the main questions about which you write.

. . . I admit that a really good man will live well in any kind of life;

neither do I deny that I was myself inclined to great vices, but without my nature being so corrupt that I might not have been led aright, if I had had a suitable director, whose religion was Christianity and not a Jewish superstition. Meantime I have looked to see in what kind of life I should be least bad, and I think it is that which I have followed. I have lived among sober persons and in literary pursuits, which have turned my thoughts from many vices. I have been able to pass my time with men who really savour of Christ and by whose conversations I have become a better man.

I do not boast of my books, which perhaps you despise. But many persons confess that they have been made not only more learned but better by reading them. The love of money never affected me. Neither am I in the least degree moved by the vanity of fame. I was never a slave to pleasures, though I did not escape some stain. Drunkenness and intemperance I have always avoided. Whenever I have thought of rejoining your society, I have been reminded of the jealousy of many, the contempt of all, of conversations how cold, how silly, how utterly without any savour of Christ! of feasts how secular!; in fact, of a whole system of life, in which, if you take away what they call the ceremonies, I know not what is left that one would choose. And lastly I have thought of the weakness of my constitution, increased by age and sickness and labours, which would prevent my satisfying you, while I should kill myself. I have been for several years subject to the stone, a serious and fatal disease. For some years I have drunk nothing but wine, and am obliged to be careful in the choice of it on account of my sickness. I cannot be indifferent as to food or climate. For this disease, frequently recurring, makes the strictest regimen necessary; and I know the Dutch climate; I know your mode of living, not to speak of morals. Therefore, if I had returned, I should only have brought trouble to you and death to myself.

But you perhaps think it a great happiness to die among your brethren. That is a sort of persuasion which imposes not only upon you, but on almost all. We rest our religion upon place, dress, food, or some trifling ceremonies. We think it is all over with one who changes a white coat for a black, wears a hat instead of a cowl, or occasionally shifts his locality. I venture to say that the greatest bane of Christian piety has arisen out of these so-called religions, although it was perhaps a pious zeal that first introduced them. The authority of popes, often too easy and indulgent, has come to their aid. For what is more foul or more impious than these religions when they are lax? And if you turn to those that are commended and even most commended, I know not what image of Christ you will find, unless you can so regard some cold Jewish ordinances. It is on these they pride themselves, and on the strength of these they judge and despise others. How much more in accordance with the sentiment of Christ, to regard the whole world as one household, or as it were one convent, to think of all mankind as our brethren or fellow canons, to hold the sacrament of baptism as the highest order of religion, and not to look where a man lives but how well he lives.

You wish me to fix on a permanent residence, a course also suggested by advancing age. And yet the wanderings of Solon and Pythagoras and Plato are commended. The apostles were wanderers, especially Paul. St. Jerome, monk as he was, is now found at Rome, now in Syria, now in Africa or elsewhere, and in old age is still pursuing sacred Letters. I am not to be compared with him, I admit; but I have never changed my place, unless either forced by plague or for the sake of study or health; and wherever I have lived (perhaps I shall speak too arrogantly of myself, but I will say the truth), I have been approved by those most approved and praised by those most praised. And there is no country, whether Spain, or Italy, or England, or Scotland, which has not invited me to its hospitality. If I am not approved by all, which I do not desire, I have found favour at any rate with the highest. At Rome there was not a cardinal that did not receive me as a brother, without my soliciting any such distinction. This was especially the case with the Cardinal of St. George, the Cardinal of Bologna, Cardinal Grimani, the Cardinal of Nantes, and the present pontiff, not to speak of bishops, archdeacons and men of learning. And this honour was not rendered to wealth, which even now I do not possess and do not desire; nor to any overtures of mine, from which I have been always most averse, but only to Letters, which however derided by our countrymen, are worshipped by the Italians. In England there is not a bishop who is not pleased to receive my greeting or who would not welcome me as a guest, or as a member of his household. The king himself shortly before his father's death, when I was in Italy, wrote to me a most loving letter with his own hand. He often speaks of me now with as much respect and affection, as any one could possibly do, and whenever I wait upon him, he receives me with the greatest kindness and regards me with such loving looks, that you may easily see that his sentiments are no less favourable than his words. The queen has tried to get me to be her preceptor; and everybody knows that if I cared to live even a few months at court, I might heap up as many benefices as I liked. But I allow nothing to interfere with my leisure and studious labours.

The Archbishop of Canterbury, primate of all England and chancellor of the kingdom, a good and learned man, treats me with as much kindness as if he were my father or my brother; and that you may understand how sincerely this is meant, he gave me a benefice of about a hundred nobles, which he afterwards, by my wish and on my resignation of the cure, changed to a pension of a hundred crowns. Beside this, he has given me in presents four hundred nobles during these few years, and that without my asking on my part. On one day he gave me a hundred and fifty nobles. From other bishops I have received above a hundred nobles, which have been offered to me with spontaneous liberality. Lord Mountjoy, a baron of this realm and formerly my pupil, gives me yearly a pension of a hundred crowns. And the Bishop of Lincoln, who is now all powerful with the king, makes magnificent promises.

There are two universities here, at Oxford and Cambridge, both of which seek to have me. For I have spent several months at Cambridge teaching Greek and Divinity, but without remuneration, and so I have resolved always to do. There are colleges in which there is so much religion and such a well regulated mode of living that if you saw it you would think less of any monastic rule. At London there is Dr. John Colet, dean of St. Paul's, a man who, uniting the highest learning with admirable piety, exerts a great and general influence. It is well known that he has so much affection for me that there is no one whose society he prefers. I say nothing of a host of other personages, not wishing to annoy you by boasting or by loquacity.

I will now say something about my books. I think you have read the *Enchiridion*, by which not a few confess themselves to have been inflamed to a love of piety. I claim no merit of my own, but rejoice with Christ, if by his gift, through my means, any good has been done. I do not know whether you have seen the Book of Adages, as it has been printed by Aldus. It is not a theological work but one that is useful for every branch of learning, and cost me incalculable nights of toil. I have published a book on copiousness of matter and language which I dedicated to my friend Colet, a useful work for persons preparing to preach, though such studies are scorned by those who despise all good letters. During the last two years, beside other employments, I have corrected the Epistles of Jerome, distinguishing with dagger-marks the spurious additions and illustrating the obscure passages with notes. I have also corrected the New Testament from the collation of ancient Greek manuscripts and annotated more than a thousand places, not without profit to theologians. I have begun a commentary on the Epistles of St. Paul, which I shall finish, when I have published what

I have already mentioned. For I have resolved to give up my life to Sacred Literature. These are the things to which I devote my hours of leisure and of work; persons of consideration say that I have a capacity for them which others have not; for your kind of life I have no capacity. I have associated with many grave and learned persons, both here and in Italy and France, and have never found any who advised me to return to you or considered that to be the better course. Even your own predecessor, Nicholas Werner, of happy memory, was wont to dissuade me from doing so, advising me rather to attach myself to some bishop, and adding that he knew both my disposition and the character of his poor brethren. These were the words he used in the vernacular tongue. In the condition of life in which I am now, I see what to avoid; but what I should rather follow, I do not see.

It now remains for me to satisfy you about my dress. Having formerly used the ordinary canons' dress, when I was at Louvain, I obtained leave from the Bishop of Utrecht to wear, according to the Paris fashion, a linen scapular instead of the entire linen robe and a black cassock instead of the black cloak. When I went to Italy and saw the canons, wherever I travelled, wearing a great black gown with the scapular, I then, in order not to give offence by a variety of dress began to wear a similar costume. Afterwards, a plague occurred at Bologna, where those who attend on the sick wear a white linen scarf hanging from the shoulders and have to avoid meeting other people. Consequently, one day, when I was going to see a learned friend, some rude fellows drew their swords with the intention of attacking me, and would have done so if a lady had not warned them that I was an ecclesiastic. And another day, when I was going to the treasurer's sons, I was met on both sides by people with sticks and most grievous cries. Accordingly under good advice, I put my scapular away and obtained permission from Julius II to wear the religious habit or not as I might think fit, provided I retained the clerical dress, and by his letters he pardoned any error before committed in that respect. Accordingly while I was in Italy, I stuck to the clerical dress, not to create a scandal by making a change.

When I returned to England, I intended to use my accustomed habit; and having sent for a friend of the highest reputation, both for life and learning, I showed him the dress I meant to wear and asked him, whether it would be right in England. He said yes, and I went out in it, but was warned forthwith by other friends that the dress could not be tolerated in England, and I had better put it out of sight. I did so; and as it could not be hidden without giving birth to scandal if found, I put it away in a chest, and up to this time have availed myself of the licence formerly given me by the pope. The Pontifical laws excommunicate anyone who throws aside the religious habit in order to mix more freely among secular persons. In my case, it was put away in Italy by compulsion, to save me from being killed; and afterwards, in England, because it was not tolerated there, when I should have much preferred to wear it. To resume it afresh now would beget more scandal than was created by the original change.

I have explained to you the whole scheme of my life, and what my ideas are. I am quite ready to change even this mode of life, if I see anything better. But I do not see what I can do in Holland. I know I shall not find either the climate or the food agree with me; and I shall draw all eyes upon me. I shall return old and grey to the place I left when young; I shall return an invalid. I shall be exposed to the contempt of the lowest people after being accustomed to be honoured by the greatest. I shall exchange my studies for drinking parties. And whereas you promise your assistance in finding me a place where I may live, as you say, with a good income, I cannot think what that can be, unless you would quarter me upon some convent of nuns, where I should be a servant to women, after having declined to serve archbishops and kings. I do not stick about income, having no anxiety to be rich, but only to have as much fortune as is needed for my health and literary leisure, so that I may not be a burden to anyone. As to these matters, I should like to talk with you in person, for one cannot do so by letter either in comfort or safety. Yours, though sent by the surest messengers, has gone so far astray, that unless I had happened to come to this castle, I should never have seen it, and I received it after it had already been read by many others. Please therefore do not write any secret matter unless you know where I am, and have a very sure messenger. I am now on my way to Germany, that is to Basel, for the purpose of publishing my lucubrations; and in the winter I may perhaps be at Rome. On my way back I will arrange for our having an interview somewhere; but now the summer is almost gone, and the journey before me is long. . . .

Nichols II, pp. 141–50. Allen I, 565–73

Erasmus to William Blount, Lord Mountjoy. Basle, 30 August 1514
Most excellent Maecenas, I stayed with the abbot two days and we had a merry time. He did not forget to make me a present on my departure, and added many kind promises. In fact everything was going on happily, when all of a sudden Fortune gave me a lesson not to trust to any current of events. I had scarcely left an inn about half-way between Rousselaere and Ghent, when my horse shied at some linen spread on

the ground. I was leaning forward to say something to the groom, when the horse took fright a second time and swerving in the other direction, strained the lower part of my spine. The pain was so severe that I could not help screaming aloud. I tried to dismount, but could not. My servant took me in his arms and set me on the ground. I was in the open country with no places of entertainment near, except some that were very cold and rough, and six good miles away from Ghent. I felt the pain become less severe as I walked, but the journey was longer than one could have made on foot, even if sound. Imagine my state of mind. I made a vow to St. Paul that I would complete my Commentary on the Epistle to the Romans if I escaped this danger. Soon after, when I was beginning to despair, I was forced to try whether I could mount my horse, and succeeded better than I had hoped. I went on at a foot pace and found I could bear it. I then told the servant to go on faster, and bore that too, though not without torture. Arrived at Ghent, I dismounted and went into a room, where the pain, after rest, betrayed itself in its full intensity. I could not stand alone nor sit, and when I lay down, could not move in the least. I sent for a doctor and an apothecary, and was altogether in such a condition that I could think of nothing but death. When I had occasion to move in the morning, I found I could stand, move and sit without assistance, and offered my thanks to God and St. Paul; though I still feel the mischief, especially if I turn my body. I have therefore been staying a few days at Ghent, detained by the hospitality of my friends, and not feeling quite secure about the pain.

I have met here the President of Flanders, a person most learned in every kind of literature, and two members of the council, Antonius Clava and Gulielmus Wala, [Robert] Caesar and some others I knew before. I shall now go on to Antwerp, if my health permits; and wherever I am, will let you know about my health. . . .

Nichols II, 151–2. Allen II, 5–6

Erasmus to Ulrich Zasius. Basel, 23 September 1514
Your singular erudition, united with equal eloquence, has become known to me through two most learned and no less eloquent friends, Beatus Rhenanus and Joannes Gallinarius. Your rare humour I see in your letter. For after in one most polished letter a person like yourself, loaded with every commendation of virtue, has deigned to invite us, who are nothing, to your friendship. You presently in another letter deprecate the charge of presumption, because forsooth so small a person has written to so great a personage!

To have done with these affectations, with which in Italy the learned used to please themselves, and to deal as a German with a German in plain truthfulness, I take my measure by my own foot, as the saying is, and know how scanty is my store; so far am I from acknowledging the praises you attribute to me. For the rest I congratulate our Germany, which has long flourished in military renown, but is now made more illustrious by so many persons excelling in every kind of literature; a glory, than which none is truer or more abiding. . . . Nothing could occur to me more gratifying or more honourable than to be admitted into the number of your friends, and I should not have allowed you to take the initiative, if I were not so fixed and bound to this treadmill that I have scarcely leisure to take my meals.

My book of *Adages* is being so enriched that it may be thought another work. Jerome is in hand, and is soon to be printed with our annotations. The New Testament is being prepared, corrected, and illustrated with our scholia. A revised edition of the *Copia* is being brought out, and a book on similes is also to be published. My translations from Plutarch are already printed; and I am preparing with great pains an emended edition of Seneca Annaeus. When you consider that any one of these tasks is enough to require a whole man, and that not an Erasmus but a man of adamant, you may guess how completely I am without a vacant moment. You must therefore pardon me, first for sending so hasty a reply to your polished letter, a plain instance of an Homeric exchange of bronze for gold; and also if I shall in future seem more chary of my letters than you may wish. As soon as I have got myself a little clear of these labours, I shall be happy to encounter my Zasius in regular volumes. . . .

Nichols II, pp. 161–3. Allen II, pp. 25–6

Erasmus to John Sapidus. Basel c. October 1515
. . . As for your vocation, I admit it is laborious, but I utterly deny that it is a tragic, as you call it, or deplorable position. To be a schoolmaster is next to being a king. Do you reckon it a mean employment to imbue the minds of your fellow-citizens in their earliest years with the best Letters and with the love of Christ, and to return them to their country honest and virtuous men? In the opinion of fools it is a humble task, but in fact it is the noblest of occupations. For if even among the heathen it was always an illustrious thing to deserve well of the Commonwealth, no one, I will boldly say, serves it better than the moulder of unfashioned boyhood, provided he be learned and honest, two qualities which are so equally matched in you, that I know not in which you surpass yourself.

As to the diminution of your salary, Christ himself will recompense you abundantly; and goodness is its own ample reward. Neither should your mind be disturbed, when you see so large an income awarded at the public expense to the lazy leisure of individuals, who live for their own pleasure, or wait upon their prince without any advantage to the public; while he who is the common parent of all the children, and in the most necessary of all matters exerts himself to the utmost in the public service, is paid with so poor a salary. Such an office demands an upright and incorruptible man, who would take delight in his pious work, even without any pay, while a high salary and a position of dignity would attract the meanest characters. You will yourself, my Sapidus, add by your accomplishments a dignity to the office, which, if it be of little repute among men, is surely of the highest account with Christ.

There is no reason why you should be jealous of our literary society at Basel. Schlettstadt has also its shrine of the Muses, perhaps a little less frequented. But you have one man in Paul Volz, the Abbot of Haugshofen, whom you may set against a multitude. Good Heavens! what purity of mind, what sincerity of character, what a prudent simplicity, what an ardour for study, and with such accomplishments what an utter absence of pride! Such I conceive to have been the character of those ancient religious leaders, Antony, Hilary, and Jerome. If you number your company, I admit you are few; but if you weigh them, one such man may count for many. Please let him know that I do not forget him. Be sure to remember me also to your sweetest wife. The effectual comfort of your toils, Margaret, fairer than any pearl. . . .

Nicholas II, pp. 235–7. Allen II, pp. 154–5

Erasmus, 'Sileni Alcibiadis,' Adages (1515)
. . . Here then lies the difference between the follower of the world and the follower of Christ: the first admires and chases after the worthless things which strike the eye at once, while the second strives only for the things which are least obvious at a glance and furthest from the physical world, and the rest he passes over altogether, or holds them lightly, judging everything by its inner value. Among the 'good things' (as Aristotle calls them) which are not a natural property of man come first and foremost riches. But with the common people, nay, with almost everyone, the man who has got hold of them by hook or by crook is regarded most highly. The whole world hunts for them over hill and dale. The thing next in order of importance is noble birth, though if nothing else goes with it, it is simply laughable, an empty

name. It is sensible to half-worship a man who can trace his descent from Codrus, King of Athens, or from the Trojan Brutus (was he ever born, I wonder?) or from the Hercules of legend, and call the man obscure who has won fame by his learning and his merit? Is one man to be illustrious because his great-grandfather made a great slaughter in war, and another common, with no statues erected to his name, when he benefited the whole world with the riches of his soul? In the third place come the gifts of the body; anyone who happens to be tall, hardy, handsome, and powerful is included among the number of the lucky ones, but all the same riches come first and birth second—the last thing to be thought of is the mind. If you divide man according to St. Paul into three parts, body, soul, and spirit (I am using his very words), it is true that the common people value highest what is most obvious: the lowest part, condemned by the Apostle. The middle term, which he considers good if it joins forces with the spirit, is approved of by many also. But the spirit, the best part of ourselves, from which springs as from a fountain all our happiness—the spirit by which we are joined to God—they are so far from thinking it precious that they never even ask whether it exists or what it is, although Paul mentions it so often in his teaching. And so we get this utterly reversed estimate of things; what we should particularly honour passes without a word and what we should strive for with all our might is regarded with contempt. Hence gold is more valued than learning, ancient lineage more than virtue, the gifts of the body more than the endowments of the mind; ceremonies are put before true piety, the rules of men before the teaching of Christ, the mask is preferred to the truth, the shadow to the reality, the counterfeit to the genuine, the fleeting to the substantial, the momentary to the eternal. . . .

Phillips, pp. 278-9

Erasmus to Urban Regius. Basel, 24 February 1516
. . . I sincerely congratulate our Germany on the possession of such a truly great prince. Would that there were many like him, to apply their minds to the things which have always been thought worthy of the noblest of mankind. I am already much in his debt, both for his kind, though mistaken, opinion of me and for challenging and inviting me so munificently to accept a position, for which I might well canvass with all my might, if I were only free to offer my services to anyone after having devoted them to the most illustrious Prince Charles, my own sovereign, and that with my liberty (by the vote of

the chief council) excepted, or rather reserved; for if I see that in danger I shall resign everything. At the same time I have not deserted nor do I ever intend to desert my excellent Maecenas, the Archbishop of Canterbury; but being settled on the borders, I hope to be able to satisfy both my countries, the one in which I was born and that into which I have been adopted. If it were otherwise, I should not plead my age as an excuse, although mine is rather decrepitude than age, for I am in my forty-ninth year, not more; but age should be reckoned by strength and not by years. . . .

Nichols II, p. 244. Allen II, pp. 204–5

Erasmus to Prince Charles. Basel, c. March 1516

. . . It is a sound estimate of Plutarch that no one serves the state better than he who imbues the mind of a sovereign with sentiments worthy of one that has to take thought for all; while on the other hand, no one does a greater injury to mankind than he who corrupts a young prince's heart with wrong opinions or desires, and as it were poisons the spring from which his people draw their supplies. The same author takes to task that famous saying of Alexander the Great: 'If I were not Alexander, I would be Diogenes.' The greater his empire, the more need had he of the mind of Diogenes, to be equal to such a strain. But as you, illustrious prince, surpass Alexander in your fortune, so may we hope that you will excel him in wisdom. He won a vast dominion, not without bloodshed, nor long to last. You have been born to the fairest empire and destined to a greater; and the pains which he took to acquire his dominions, you may perhaps have to expend in the voluntary cession of part of yours, which it may be better not to retain. You owe it to Providence that your realm has been acquired without injury to any; your wisdom will best be shown if you can keep it in peace and tranquillity. . . .

Preface to *The Education of a Christian Prince*
(*Institutio Principis Christiani*), Nichols II,
p. 250. Allen II, pp. 206–7

Erasmus to William Budé. Antwerp, c. 19 June 1516

In this work, however, I did what in fact I usually do. I had intended to carry the thing through with a light hand, calling attention to some small details, and just to point out the passages, as it were, with my little finger. Well, when the work was on the verge of publication, I was urged to alter the received version, either by correction or by interpretation. The accession of labour, which I thought would be very light, I found in effect to be extremely heavy. I was then persuaded to add some annotations of a more exhaustive kind. The result, as I need not tell you, was that everything had to be re-arranged. There was this additional trouble; I thought that they had some emended copies at Basel, and when I was disappointed in this expectation, I was forced to correct beforehand the manuscripts which the printers were to use. Another thing: two fairly good scholars had been engaged to correct the press, one a lawyer, the other a theologian, who had besides some knowledge of Hebrew; but they, being unpractised in that employment, could not complete what they had undertaken, and I was obliged to take upon myself the revision of what they call the last proofs. The writing and printing of the book were going on at the same time, a sheet being completed every day. Meanwhile, I could not devote my whole time to this business. Jerome was in the press at the same time and claimed a fair share of my attention. And I was firmly resolved either to die at work or to get clear of that treadmill before Easter. When I came at last to the annotations, I was already wearied out and almost broken down; but I accomplished what I could, considering the limit of time and the state of my health. Some things I purposely passed over and shut my eyes to many points upon which, soon after publication, I held a different opinion. Accordingly, I am preparing a second edition, in which I earnestly beg you to assist. I shall think it a kindness to be even censured by persons like you; but you will beware of one thing, that no scent of the proposed new edition shall reach the public, as we do not want the copies to be left on the printer's hands. I was much pleased with your friendly warning; although I do not quite understand what you mean by the subtleties on which I am fond of dwelling; except that I candidly think all my observations are trifles and often wonder what there is in them that some people so highly praise; for indeed this is done by several persons of importance.

See how hard it is to satisfy the judgment of everybody. Some find fault with me for presumption in touching upon matters of such moment, being myself of so little account. In the *Enchiridion* I ventured to differ widely from our own age, without being deterred by the authority of anyone. In the *Adages*, a fragmentary work, how often do I roam into the fields of philosophy and theology, forgetting, as it may seem, the immediate subject, and take a higher flight than the occasion demands! . . . In the book on the Christian Prince I lay down rules on which no divine has ventured to touch. But perhaps it is to Lucian's *Dialogues* and Euripides' *Tragedies*, which I practised myself in translating, that you apply the term λεπτολογία. Nothing is slighter than my Cato, on which I spent half a day. Still these trifles, however, slight, I certainly prefer to any of the productions of darkness.

For the rest, I am quite aware and do not deny that many minute dissertations occur in my New Testament; for this was required by the nature of the subject. Nevertheless, if anyone will calculate, still more if anyone tries the experiment, what it is to make such translations and notes, he will understand that a complete commentary might have been written with not much greater trouble than it cost us to compose those minute observations. And yet these λεπτολογήματα, such as they are, are received with favour by the gravest theologians who admit they have derived from them a great deal of light; unless perhaps there is nothing but flattery in what is said by so many men of the highest character, whose names I might rehearse and whose letters I could produce, if I did not hate anything like vain-glory.

If, on the other hand, I chose to measure myself by my own foot-rule, I should undertake nothing but what is little and shrink from a burden that is too much for my poor spirit and poor body. And in fact, somehow or other, my mind takes more pleasure in mixing serious thoughts with trifling subjects than in trifling with subjects of importance; and I think nothing more trifling than to shout over those small questions, which make a great many divines think themselves gods; for I may speak the plain truth to you.

With respect to the kind of work I have been about, I think I have surpassed all that have gone before me, if not in learning, at any rate in industry and care. In the emendation of the Psalter by Jerome himself, how many of the notes are almost worthless! And I intend to persevere, if I have only enough of life and strength. I have composed a prelude to the Psalm, *Beatus vir*. I shall go to work on St. Paul. Jerome has come out entirely resuscitated. I have made some translations from Plutarch, in whose works nothing appears to be without weight. Do therefore explain what are the λεπτολογίαι you wish me to avoid. . . .

Nichols II, pp. 281–4, Allen II, pp. 253–5

Erasmus to Peter Gillis. Brussels, 6 October 1516
. . . Would you like to hear something to make you laugh? An honour which those, who make the greatest and most continual efforts to reach it, often fail to attain, has almost lighted upon me in my sleep! The Catholic King has been on the point of making me a bishop. Where? you will say. Not in the furthest Indies—from which, however,

our friend Barbirius, put in charge of those whom he will never see, draws a supply of gold—but among the Sicilians, a people once Greek, and even now lively and gay. But it has been a fortunate mistake and has turned out just as I should wish. It was discovered that the patronage of the See belonged to the pope; and then the king requested the pope as a favour to himself to allow his appointment to stand. All this was going on at Brussels, while I was amusing myself with my writing at Antwerp; and it was on this account that the chancellor had ordered me to be summoned. If I had had any scent of the matter, I should have been still slower in changing my quarters. When I arrived, and those who knew about it congratulated me and wished it might turn out well, I could do nothing but laugh. I thanked my friends, nevertheless, for their kind intention, while I warned them not to put themselves in future to any useless trouble in an affair of this kind, as I was not ready to exchange my leisure for any bishopric, however splendid. There is a dream to amuse you! And yet I was gratified by the disposition shown by so great a sovereign, who does not generally favour any but those whom he knows to be worthy, or at any rate supposes to be so.

I am glad, my sweet Peter, to have relieved you from so much trouble, for I was beginning to pity you and your dear wife. And yet you cannot hold me answerable for all the trouble I gave. Your love was so boundless, that you were never satisfied with the kindnesses you heaped upon me; while your wife, whose first study is to content you, could in this matter scarcely ever do enough. Now that Erasmus is away, you will enjoy her society in greater comfort. How little it is, that separation takes away from us, and even that may be made up by frequent letters, which I hope you will send me, as lively and cheerful as can be; for I shall understand by that, that you are in good health. This is what I have at heart as much as anything; and it is for the most part, believe me, in your own hands.

Most of our diseases proceed from the mind, and you will be less upset by the labours of study, if you regulate your studies by reason. Arrange your library and all your letters and papers in certain settled places. Do not allow yourself to be attracted, now to one author, and now to another, but take one of the best in your hands with no intention of letting him go until you have come to the last page, noting as you go along whatever seems worth remembering. Lay down for yourself a definite scheme of life, determining what you want to do and at what hours, and do not crowd one thing upon another without finishing what you begin first; in this way you will lengthen your day, which is almost totally lost. And whereas you find fault with your memory, you will do well, in my opinion, to make a diary for each year—it is no great trouble to do so—and note down daily, in a word or two, if anything has taken place that you wish not to forget. I have known persons who have found great advantage in this system, one of whom was that excellent prelate, Francis Busleiden, Archbishop of Besançon. Above all things, I beg and entreat you to accustom yourself in the conduct of life to be guided by judgment, and not by impulse. If you have made any mistake, consider at once whether you can set it right in any way or diminish the evil; that you will do better if you do it quietly than in an excited state. If there is any remedy, apply it; if not, what good can come of anger or sorrow, except that you double the evil by your own fault. I beseech you by our friendship to let nothing be more important to you than life and health. If you can keep your fortune without loss of health, do so by all means; if not, you lose more than you gain, when you save your fortune by risking your health or quiet. And, as a last argument, if you do not care enough for yourself, see that you do not ruin two persons by one blow; for we shall never think ourselves safe if you are not safe too, since I look upon you, so help me Heaven, as the better part of myself.

Do not take too much pains about trifling matters. Life is fleeting; health is brittle, and not to be casually squandered. Some things must be disregarded, and the mind raised to what is great. Make Seneca and Plato your familiars; if these are often in converse with you, they will not suffer your mind to sink. It is the characteristic of a truly great mind to overlook some injuries and have no ear or tongue for some people's abuse. Make the experiment, how much more effect is produced by politeness and conciliation than by headlong and uncontrolled passion.

Support your excellent father's old age, as you do, with kind attentions, not only because he is your father, but still more because he is such a father as he is. Enjoy the society of your sincere friends and make the best of those that are feigned.

Live with your good wife in such a way that she may love you not only as a bedfellow, and not only love but respect you. And so confide in her as to make her a partner with yourself, in all the things that relate either to household affairs or to the enjoyment of life. Maintain your authority over your household, but in such a fashion that domestic familiarity may be flavoured with courtesy. As to the bringing up of children, it is useless for me to give any advice, as you have such a model in your own father. You see, sweetest Peter, how I have the best advice for you, while I have little for myself. But it is my affection for you that makes me so silly. . . .

Nichols II, pp. 401–4. Allen II, pp. 356–8

Erasmus, The Education of a Christian Prince (*1516*)

. . . Do not think that the profession of a Christian is a matter to be lightly passed over, entailing no responsibilities, unless, of course, you think the sacrament which you accepted along with everything else at baptism is nothing. And do not think you renounce just for the once the delights of Satan which bring pain to the Christ. He is displeased with all that is foreign to the teachings of the Gospel. You share the Christian sacraments alike with all others—why not its teachings too? You have allied yourself with Christ, and yet will you slide back into the ways of Julius and Alexander the Great? You seek the same reward as the others, yet you will have no concern with His mandates.

But on the other hand, do not think that Christ is found in ceremonies, in doctrine; kept after a fashion, and in constitutions of the Church. Who is truly Christian? Not he who is baptised or anointed, or who attends church. It is rather the man who has embraced Christ in the innermost feelings of his heart and who emulates Him by his pious deeds. Guard against such inner thoughts as these: 'Why is all this addressed to me? I am not a mere subject. I am not a priest. I am not a monk.' Think rather in this fashion: 'I am a Christian and a prince.' It is the part of a true Christian to shun carefully all vulgarity. It is the province of a prince to surpass all in stainless character and wisdom. You compel your subjects to know and obey your laws. With far more energy you should exact of yourself knowledge and obedience to the laws of Christ, your king! You judge it an infamous crime, for which there can be no punishment terrible enough, for one who has sworn allegiance to his king to revolt from him. On what grounds, then, do you grant yourself pardon and consider as a matter of sport and jest the countless times you have broken the laws of Christ, to whom you swore allegiance in your baptism, to whose cause you pledged yourself, by whose sacraments you are bound and pledged?

If these acts are done in earnest, why do we make a farce of them? If they are only sham, why do we vaunt ourselves under the glory of Christ as pretext? There is but one death for all—beggars and kings alike. But the judgment after death is not the same for all. None are dealt with more severely than the powerful. . . .

Born, pp. 153–4

Erasmus, The Education of a Christian Prince (*1516*)

. . . The cardinal principle of a good prince should be not only to preserve the present prosperity of the state but to pass it on more prosperous than when he received it. To use the jargon of the Peripatetics, there are three kinds of 'good': that of the mind, that of the body, and the external good. The prince must be careful not to evaluate them in reverse order and judge the good fortune of his state mainly by the external good, for these latter conditions should only be judged good in so far as they relate to the good of the mind and of the body; that is, in a word, the prince should consider his subjects to be most fortunate not if they are very wealthy or in excellent bodily health, but if they are most honourable and self-controlled, if they have as little taste for greed and quarrelling as could be hoped for, and if they are not at all factious but live in complete accord with one another. He must also beware of being deceived by the false names of the fairest things, for in this deception lies the fountainhead from which springs practically all the evils that abound in the world. It is no true state of happiness in which the people are given over to idleness and wasteful extravagance, any more than it is true liberty for everyone to be allowed to do as he pleases. Neither is it a state of servitude to live according to the letter of just laws. Nor is that a peaceful state in which the populace bows to every whim of the prince; but rather [it is peaceful] when it obeys good laws and a prince who has a keen regard for the authority of the laws. Equity does not lie in giving everyone the same reward, the same rights, the same honour; as a matter of fact, that is sometimes a mark of the greatest unfairness.

A prince who is about to assume control of the state must be advised at once that the main hope of a state lies in the proper education of its youth. This Xenophon wisely taught in his *Cyropaedia*. Pliable youth is amenable to any system of training. Therefore the greatest care should be exercised over public and private schools and over the education of the girls, so that the children may be placed under the best and most trustworthy instructors and may learn the teachings of Christ and that good literature which is beneficial to the state. As a result of this scheme of things, there will be no need for many laws or punishments, for the people will of their own free will follow the course of right.

Education exerts such a powerful influence, as Plato says, that a man who has been trained in the right develops into a sort of divine creature, while on the other hand, a person who has received a perverted training degenerates into a monstrous sort of savage beast. Nothing is of more importance to a prince than to have the best possible subjects. . . .

Born, pp. 212–13

Erasmus, The Paraclesis, *1516*

. . . Indeed, I disagree very much with those who are unwilling that Holy Scripture, translated into the vulgar tongue, be read by the uneducated, as if Christ taught such intricate doctrines that they could scarcely be understood by very few theologians, or as if the strength of the Christian religion consisted in men's ignorance of it. The mysteries of kings, perhaps, are better concealed, but Christ wishes his mysteries published as openly as possible. I would that even the lowliest women read the Gospels and the Pauline Epistles. And I would that they were translated into all languages so that they could be read and understood not only by Scots and Irish but also by Turks and Saracens. Surely the first step is to understand in one way or another. It may be that many will ridicule, but some may be taken captive. Would that, as a result, the farmer sing some portion of them at the plough, the weaver hum some parts of them to the movement of his shuttle, the traveller lighten the weariness of the journey with stories of this kind! Let all the conversations of every Christian be drawn from this source. For in general our daily conversations reveal what we are. Let each one comprehend what he can, let him express what he can. Whoever lags behind, let him not envy him who is ahead; whoever is in the front rank, let him encourage him who follows, not despair of him. Why do we restrict a profession common to all to a few? For it is not fitting, since Baptism is common in an equal degree to all Christians, wherein there is the first profession of Christian philosophy, and since the other sacraments and at length the reward of immortality belong equally to all, that doctrines alone should be reserved for those very few whom today the crowd call theologians or monks, the very persons whom, although they comprise one of the smallest parts of the Christian populace, yet I might wish to be in greater measure what they are styled. For I fear that one may find among the theologians men who are far removed from the title they bear, that is, men who discuss earthly matters, not divine, and that among the monks who profess the poverty of Christ and the contempt of the world you may find something more than worldliness. To me he is truly a theologian who teaches not by skill with intricate syllogisms but by a disposition of mind, by the very expression and the eyes, by his very life that riches should be disdained, that the Christian should not put his trust in the supports of this world but must rely entirely on heaven, that a wrong should not be avenged, that a good should be wished for those wishing ill, that we should deserve well of those deserving ill, that all good men should be loved and cherished equally as members of the same body, that the evil should be tolerated if they cannot be corrected, that those who are stripped of their goods, those who are turned away from possessions, those who mourn are blessed and should not be deplored, and that death should even be desired by the devout, since it is nothing other than a passage to immortality. And if anyone under the inspiration of the spirit of Christ preaches this kind of doctrine, inculcates it, exhorts, incites, and encourages men to it, he indeed is truly a theologian, even if he should be a common labourer or weaver. And if anyone exemplifies this doctrine in his life itself, he is in fact a great doctor. Another, perhaps, even a non-Christian, may discuss more subtly how the angels understand, but to persuade us to lead here an angelic life, free from every stain, this indeed is the duty of the Christian theologian. . . .

Olin, pp. 96–8

Erasmus to Louis Ber. Brussels, 1 January 1516–17
I do not know yet whether you have any reason to congratulate me, but at any rate it is most kind of you to do so, dreaming that I have achieved such a fortune as your love would wish for me. But whatever the value of the prize I have won, if you knew what court I have paid for it, you might well think it strange. If you regard my merits, it may seem great; if my ambition, enough; although I have exchanged the prebend for a pension of less amount, so as not to trench upon my leisure, which is of more importance to me than money. I have good reason to love you, following me as you do in my absence with the same partiality with which you have always welcomed me when with you.

As to envy, that may perhaps be earned by those who profess some brilliant accomplishment, or invade the glory of others by extraordinary erudition, or obtain prominence by supplanting those about them; but what have I to do with envy, who make no profession at all, and having scarcely a moderate share of learning do not stand in anybody's light nor claim either precedence or equality in relation to any mortal being? I only endeavour by my small exertions to promote the general instruction. It has been thought that I express myself in some places with too much heat; but those who think so do not take into account the want of due respect with which sacred literature and the writings of the Fathers are received. While I was pushing on through my work, although my indignation was repeatedly curbed by reason, I could not in every case hide my feelings. But I was afterwards forced to be more restrained by the extreme scrupulosity of some of my friends. For, indeed, if it can be done, I should wish to assist study in such a way as not to offend any mortal being. If I do not always succeed in this, I am comforted by the consciousness of rectitude and by the consideration, that up to this time I have the approval of the most approved persons; and we may well hope that what now satisfies the candid will in time satisfy all. At any rate I trust that I shall never be pleased with anything that is false in learning or religion, even in my own books. . . .

Nichols II, pp. 451–2. Allen II, p. 425

Erasmus to William Budé. Antwerp, 15 February 1516/17

. . . You think that age has made me more frugal in my style. I do not dispute it, neither is it anything wonderful if the same thing happens to me, as we see occurred to Isocrates, to Lysimachus, and to Cicero himself. I trust that the increase of age may have the same effect upon me as it had upon them, and make my speech not only more temperate but better; although if you and I choose to weigh our ages, there is not much difference between them, unless we are, either of us, mistaken in our calculation. For I am now in my fifty-first year, and you, as you write, are not far from your forty-eighth. Although, therefore, I am much more aged than you, I am not so much older. But I will tell you in confidence what it is that makes my style considerably worse. You know how one's style is improved by reading, just as a field is fertilised by manure, and ploughed land is allowed to lie fallow every other year to prevent its becoming barren from constant tillage. But I have now for many years been exhausting this unlucky plot of mine, not naturally fertile, by perpetual cultivation, without relieving it by an intermission or by the cheering influence of reading. For that hasty reading, by which the Adages and the Notes to the New Testament and Jerome were compiled, is so far from invigorating the mind, that there is scarcely anything that is so detrimental both to memory and to intellectual acuteness. Then the very nature of the subject rejects all majesty of expression. You are fortunate yourself in having made choice of a subject which serves as a suitable field or theatre, upon which you may give the world a sample of your rare erudition and eloquence. It has been my lot to deal with the matters I have described, whereas there is absolutely no kind of writing for which I was naturally less fitted. And yet, when once I found myself among them, I had to accommodate myself to the play and to the scene. Some subjects, again, I have undertaken at the request of friends, so that up to this day it has scarcely ever been my lot to perform on my own stage or to minister to my own genius, if any genius at all is mine. . . .

I am amused with what you say about 'gilding' and 'voluntary slavery.' You are either singularly ignorant of my character or very crafty in hiding your knowledge. Up to now it has been seed-time with me; what harvest I shall reap is doubtful. I am still living on my own juice, like a snail or rather like a polypus, feeding myself by gnawing my own arms. But I have had the promise of a salary from the prince's treasury, and one prebend has been already given me, which I have exchanged for an annual pension. But oh, the endless crowd of vultures! And I could be anything sooner than a vulture. If my mind could be diverted from Letters, either my failing health would long have diverted it or the jealousy of ignorant babblers, by whose pertinacity I have been almost stoned. . . .

Nichols II, pp. 484–5; 486–7. Allen II,
pp. 468–9; 472

Erasmus to Martin Dorp. Antwerp, 21 February 1517
With regard to a different kind of studies, I admit that what you write is true, and that a person dissenting does no harm to an author, and even in many cases does good. But in this case, one who dissents does not so much show his own superior learning as that his adversary is not a Christian; and even if he does not intend that himself, still the person attacked is lowered in the opinion of an ignorant public, and a handle is given to the most perverse class of people who are fed or grow great by the misfortune of others. I never had any suspicion of your own intention, but perhaps I had a better knowledge of human character, and considered the circumstances of the case more deeply than you did. If any people are distressed at our agreement, let us do our best, my Dorp, to increase their sorrow; as they do not deserve to be happy who rejoice at the misfortunes of their neighbours. There is no reason for you to be frightened by rumours. No one on earth is less disturbed by them than myself. Those who wish well to Erasmus will readily extend their love to Dorp, if they perceive that you are heartily my friend. I received two letters from More yesterday, and before two days are over, the messenger will take mine in return, in which I will add what you wish. Indeed, I had already written something about the good terms we are on, before I received any hint from you.

I am invited to France by letters from several persons with splendid promises, and that in the king's name; but I am not disposed to trust myself again on the stage. My inclination demands retirement; and the age I have reached, or rather my state of health, also compels me to keep quiet. . . .

Nichols II, pp. 500–1. Allen II, pp. 481–2

Erasmus to Andrew Ammonius. Antwerp, 24 February 1516/17
You will scarcely believe, Ammonius, how nearly I have been burnt here by the jealousy of the theologians. At Louvain they squared at me like prizefighters. It was a conspiracy with Atensis at its head, who is all the more mischievous, as he is an enemy pretending to be a friend. At the same time they were busy with the prince, to unite the pope's authority with his. But at last I went to Louvain myself, and so completely dispersed all this smoke, that I have established a close friendship with the theologians from the greatest to the least; while at court the intrigues have been suppressed by the favour partly of the nobility and partly of the learned, and especially by the aid of the Bishop of Chieti.

I have been long expecting the Oracle of Safety [dispensation from Rome]. If that does not come, Erasmus is as much played out as the last bean, and you have nothing left but to write his epitaph. For my own part, I would rather have made two journeys to Rome than be tortured with long suspense. I do not say this to detract from my obligation to you. I know the delay does not come from any intention of yours, but from my own destiny.

I have put your Jerome into the hands of the booksellers, that I might send him in a more elegant dress; and they, as usual, put one off. But if you have not bought a copy, I will send it still.

Whatever money you order will be ready for you at once; and I shall still never cease to be indebted to you for the whole of this good turn. Only make haste that I may be safe before Easter, and show yourself a veritable Aesculapius. But if any reason shall arise for giving up hope, it will be some morsel of comfort to be relieved at once from suspense; but your genius will not let me despair. . . .

Nichols II, pp. 504–5. Allen II, p. 484

Erasmus to William Latimer. Antwerp, February 1517
. . . As regards the Bishop of Rochester, I am still less in agreement with you. You think it better not to attempt to do anything at all, unless you complete what you begin; and you advise that some expert in Greek learning should be fetched from Italy, who may remain with the bishop until he is grown to maturity in this branch of study. But

as this is more easily desired than done, our conclusion has been that
of the play: we must do what we can. Italy is a long way off and has
not now so many persons distinguished for learning as she had when
you were there. There was the risk too, that instead of the distinguished
scholar we send for, some bungler may arrive. And you are not unaware
of the character of the Italians, nor at what rate even those of small
account expect to be paid for emigrating to barbarous countries; not to
speak of persons who may come with a store of good letters, not always
having morals of equal quality; and in this respect you know how nice
the bishop is. The result will be, that while one looks about to see
whom it is best to send for, while one takes advice about the salary to
be offered, while the travelling arrangements are being made, a great
deal of time is lost. I know it has been wisely and rightly said: 'Deliberate
before you begin, and, after you have done that, do promptly what
you have resolved'; but I observe that many people do nothing but
deliberate until it is too late to carry out their resolution. We all know
the case of men who deliberate whether to marry or not, and then
deliberate what lady they shall choose. Meanwhile time is on the wing,
and before they have made up their minds, they become confirmed
old bachelors.

I am unwilling to suspect you of the common weakness of admiring
nothing but what is brought from afar. To me any learned man is an
Italian, even if he were born in Ireland; any man is a Greek who has
an accurate and happy knowledge of Greek authors, though he does
not wear a beard! For my own part I stand up for the glory of Italy,
if only because I find that country more favourable to me than my
own fatherland; but to speak candidly what I think, if I could get
Linacre or Tunstall for a teacher, not to speak of yourself, I should not
want an Italian. I would, therefore, entreat you to consider whether it is
not unwise, in the first place, to look abroad for what is to be found
at home; and, in the next place, to despise a fairly good instrument of
which we have need, because we cannot get a superfine one; or to
refuse any investment unless the very highest rate of interest is secured.
Did not Grocyn himself, whose example you cite, first learn the rudiments of Greek in England? He afterwards travelled in Italy, and
attended the lectures of the most distinguished professors; but meantime it was an advantage to him to have learned those rudiments,
whoever may have taught them. When the pupil is intelligent, it is an
important step merely to point out the way. I agree with you, that it
is desirable that even the first elements should be taught by a supreme
artist, if it can be done. But if it cannot, it is better to make a beginning

somehow or other than to remain altogether uninstructed, especially
in this kind of study. It is something to be familiar with the letters,
to read the Greek words with felicity, to decline and conjugate. Do
you think he has done nothing who has got through this amount of
trouble? Therefore, we do beg a month's assistance from you, tacitly
hoping you will give us three, though ashamed to ask it; and if that
cannot be, we have a good hope that some one else will meantime be
found, who may build on your foundations. If that hope should fail
us, still such is our student's force of intellect, and such his wish to learn,
that we are confident he will by his own efforts struggle on at last to
mediocrity; and with that, perhaps, he will be content, as he is not
ambitious of being a Greek scholar, except for the purpose of studying
his Bible with greater profit and securer judgment. And after all, if
no result is obtained, what harm is done? Suppose the bishop's own
studies are not much advanced, it will still be of no little use in encouraging the minds of the young, that so distinguished a person should
be enlisted among the Grecians. And as in every kind of study, an early
initiation is important, so in the present case the bishop's age makes
me especially desirous that the business should not be put off another
day. . . .

Nichols III, pp. 254–7. Allen II, pp. 485–6

3   Reform versus Revolt: 1517–21

Erasmus spent these years in Louvain. He had reached the pinnacle of his fame
and enjoyed an international reputation. At the same time he published many
of his most quoted volumes: *Paraphrases of the New Testament* (1517–), *The
Complaint of Peace* (1517), *The Colloquies* (1518–), *The Method of True Theology*
(1518), and the *Paraclesis*, or introductory epistle to his Latin edition of the
New Testament (1519). Erasmus's publications are a blend of humanism and
the *Devotio Moderna*, and reflect the spirit of reform which he called *philosophia
Christi*. In keeping with his philosophy of Christ, Erasmus urged a thorough
reform of abuses within the Church. He even rallied to the cause of Martin
Luther, until it became clear that the 'Wittenberg Gladiator' would sever
Christendom in order to preserve the goals of the Reformation. In the end,
Erasmus withdrew from the catastrophe of violence which ensued, true to his
beliefs in non-violence and the inviolability of the Church.

Erasmus to More. Louvain, c. 10 July 1517
. . . I have learned, at last, who it was among those court people that
raised such a conflict against me. There is a certain master from Paris,

formerly a Carmelite, who in hope of an abbacy was admitted to the Benedictine order—although of all men, most given to evil speaking—and soon after became suffragan, that is, a sort of sham bishop, of Cambrai. This person has been barking loudly against me; and that not at court only; for there is no convivial meeting at which he does not declaim against Erasmus—having a special dislike for the *Moria*—a pious man forsooth, that cannot bear any attack upon St. Christopher or St. George! And yet this creature has great influence with Chièvres, who directs everything, and perhaps also with the king, whose confessor he has lately become, in place of Josse Clichtove, who was appointed to that office, and was afterwards rejected, for no better reason than this: that he was very lean and had not ten hairs on his head! The prejudice against me has been increased by [Francis] Deloin, having made a French translation of the *Moria*, which is now understood even by theologians, that is, if they happen to know French.

I stuck to Tunstall, as long as I might, and we finished the collation of the New Testament; when that was done, and I was anxiously thinking in what terms I could fitly express my thanks, he chose to add a present of fifty French crowns, which he would not allow me to decline. As I live, this age has nothing to compare with that man!

Peter Gillis' health is still unsatisfactory. He has frequent relapses and fears something, which I guess rather than know, and for which I should be very sorry. His wife has had a miscarriage since my return to England, which I attribute to her alarm about her husband's critical state.

I have removed entirely to Louvain, intending to pass some months with the theologians, who have received me kindly enough. My pension has been partly paid by the chancellor out of his pocket, that is, to the extent of two hundred florins, which he is to recover somehow or other; and I expect a hundred more, but who is to pay this, when all are gone? The chancellor, in his farewell words, bade me be of good cheer. He intended, as I understand, to give me a bishopric; in his position, it is easier to make a man a bishop than to pay a promised amount of money.

My friend Lefèvre has not treated me in a very friendly way in his last edition of the Apostolic Epistles. He maintains his own opinion with too much acrimony, carping at some things which have nothing to do with the question affecting him. I am vexed with the man and intend to answer him in a letter which I shall presently publish; but I shall keep a restraint upon myself, so that the discussion may not have the appearance of a contest. If you have any curiosity about it, read our Notes upon the Second Chapter of the Epistle to the Hebrews, and his 'Examinations' upon the same passage. But you will recognise the second edition of the work by what Lefèvre has written in the opening page.

I am staying here at Louvain with [John] Paludanus, the Orator of the University, but anything you have sent to Peter Gillis will be safe. I wrote you word that your lucubrations have been already sent to Basel; I mean the *Utopia*, the *Epigrams*, and the *Lucian*. I have told them, either not to undertake the business at all or to take pains to do it well, and have sent them a learned and industrious man as an assistant for that purpose.

I have not yet decided what residence to choose. I do not like Spain, to which I am again invited by the Cardinal of Toledo. The German stoves and their roads infested by robbers are not to my taste. Here there is snarling in abundance, without any profit; and if I wished to do so, I could not stay long. In England, I am afraid of disturbances and have a horror of slavery. If you have yourself any advice ready, please let me have it, for I simply despair of so arranging matters among my own people as to overcome the prejudices of monks and theologians; and day by day the assassins are forming a party, and only want a leader. It is well for me that the suffragan is going to Spain; and there he is pretty sure to die, being not under seventy years of age. Nevertheless there are some Friars Preachers and Carmelites, who are beginning to incite the populace to stone-throwing, a plague which is nowhere so prevalent as among our countrymen. But as yet not a word to my face, either at court or among the people! I fancy they are afraid of the lion's teeth. Indeed, they should feel some scratches, such as they deserve, if it were not that this might scarcely consist with Christian moderation! At any rate, I intend to persevere in that course by which I may advance the cause of enlightenment, so far as I am allowed to do so. . . .

Nichols II, pp. 574–6. Allen III, pp. 4–6

Erasmus to Cuthbert Tunstall. Louvain, 17 July 1517
We have removed to Louvain with all our baggage, though no accommodation quite adapted to our taste or our studies has yet been found.

Lefèvre d'Etaples has furnished us with a fresh subject of controversy. He has published a new edition of his Commentaries on St. Paul, correcting several passages in accordance with our criticism, but without any mention of our work, except in one place, that is, in the second chapter of the Epistle to the Hebrews. There he is not satisfied with maintaining his own construction but finds fault with ours in a some-what ill-natured way, while at the same time he carps at some other matters which have nothing to do with his work. In short, in dealing with a friend, indeed a very good friend, as he himself writes, he has not acted in a very friendly way, and has shown himself, not to say more, to be subject to human frailty. We shall answer, but without acrimony; not for the purpose of refuting his opinion, which in our observations we have censured without altogether rejecting it, but to show that we are not quite so stupid as he makes out. . . .

Nichols II, p. 586. Allen III, pp. 19–20

Erasmus to John Caesarius. Antwerp, 16 August 1517
I highly disapprove of the *Epistles of Obscure Men*. Their pleasantry might amuse at the first glance, if such a precedent had not been too aggressive. I have no objection to the ludicrous, provided it be without insult to any one. But it was more annoying, when in the second edition my name was mixed up in it: as if it were not enough to play the fool, without exposing us to prejudice, and in a great measure destroying the fruit obtained by so much laborious study. And even that has not been deemed sufficient; a second book, like the former one, has made its appearance, in which there is frequent mention of persons, to whom I am quite sure that tricks of this kind are anything but agreeable. How inconsiderate is the conduct of these writers, not only in their own interest but in that of all to whom literature is dear!

But of all such incidents none has given me so much annoyance, as the report (if true), which has been brought me by my servant James, that there is some sort of publication in the hands of many persons at Cologne, directed against Pope Julius, and representing him as ex-cluded by St. Peter from heaven. I had heard some time ago of some such play being acted in France, where there has always been an excessive licence with respect to nonsense of this kind, and I suppose that somebody has turned it into Latin. I wonder what people are thinking of when they waste their leisure and their labour in such a way. But I am still more surprised to find that there are persons who suspect that such signal folly has proceeded from me. I attribute this to the fact that the language used is, perhaps, not such bad Latin! I did write playfully in the *Moria*, but without drawing blood and without any mention of names, Our satire was aimed at the manners of men, not against the character of any man. But if what my servant has told me is true (as to which I am not yet satisfied), I beg you to do your best to suppress any such wicked trifles before they are printed; not that their authors deserve to have this service done them, but that it is our business to have regard to the general credit of literature, which is undeservedly tainted by such freaks. As far as I am myself concerned, every one that knows me will, I am sure, understand that dreary compositions of this kind have always been extremely displeasing to me, as unworthy of learned and honourable men. . . .

> Nichols II, pp. 610–11. Allen III, 44–5

Erasmus to John Froben. Louvain, 25 August 1517
Whatever my More has hitherto written has always been supremely delightful to me; though I have somewhat distrusted my own judgment on account of the close friendship between us. But now that I find all the learned subscribing to my opinion, and even surpassing me in their respect for his divine genius—not certainly because of a greater affection on their part, but of a clearer discernment—I applaud at this late hour my own sentence, and shall not henceforth be afraid to proclaim what I think. What indeed might not have been expected from that admirable felicity of nature, if this genius had had Italian instruction, if it had been entirely consecrated to the Muses, and had been allowed to ripen at its proper season? When he was very young, he amused himself with epigrams, most of them being written when he was still a boy. He has never left England, except once or twice, when he has had a mission for his prince in Flanders. Beside his wife and family, beside the duties of an office that he holds, and a flood of legal business, he is distracted by such a quantity of important public affairs, that you may well wonder that he finds time even to think of books.

Hence it comes that we have sent you his early exercises, as well as his *Utopia*, that, if you think fit, they may, printed with your types, be commended to the world and to posterity; since such is the authority of your press, that the learned are ready to accept any book with pleasure, if it be known to have come from the house of Froben. . . .

> Nichols III, pp. 21–2. Allen III, pp. 56–7

Erasmus to George Halewin. Louvain, 29 August 1517
. . . *Moria* was at first understood by few; until Listrius added some notes. But now that by your means she has begun to talk French, she is understood even by those who do not understand their own Psalter. I should like myself to hear my *Moria* chattering in that language; if you have not a copy by you, let me know at any rate where I can send for one.

I have removed to Louvain altogether; that is, library and all. You must know that my relations with the theologians are most peaceful and even intimate; for some scandal-mongers had spread it about that I was at war with them. They are resolved to receive me into their Order, and who would not prefer this to being admitted to the fellowship of the gods? Atensis is singularly favourable; Dorp seems heartily friendly. One or two of the poor bark at me, but only when I am away.

Nichols III, p. 25. Allen III, p. 63

Erasmus to Henry VIII. Antwerp, 9 September 1517
Illustrious king, among your numberless truly royal and heroic endowments—by which you not only recall the merits of your admirable parent, Henry, the Seventh of that name, but even surpass them—various admirers may choose different subjects for praise. For myself, I regard them all with respect; but what chiefly commands my approbation is this: that whereas being gifted with an extraordinary clearness of mind, you have no lack of wisdom yourself, you still delight in familiar converse with men of prudence and learning, and most of all with those who do not know how to flatter. It is as though you had somewhere read that verse of Sophocles, and indeed I do not doubt you have read it: kings become wise by wise companionship.

Another chief merit is this: that among so many affairs in which your kingdom, and indeed the whole world, is concerned, you scarcely let a day pass but you bestow some time upon reading, and delight in converse with those ancient sages who are anything but flatterers; while you choose especially those books, from which you may rise a better and wiser man, and more useful to your country. Thus you are far from agreeing with persons who think that princes of the highest rank ought, of all things, to keep clear of serious or philosophic study, and that, if books are taken in hand at all, nothing should be read but amusing stories, scarcely good enough for women, or mere incitements to folly and vice. The two conceptions of wisdom and of sovereignty are thus assumed to be diametrically opposed to each other; whereas they are so closely connected that if you take away one from the other, you leave nothing but the mere title of sovereign, like the cenotaphs which display on the outside the names and pedigrees of the dead, the inside being empty.

Moreover, as an intelligent and pious prince is wise, vigilant, and provident for the whole community, being one that is transacting not his own business but that of the public, so is it right that every man should endeavour to the utmost of his power to help him in his cares and anxieties; and the wider his empire, the more need has he of this kind of service. A sovereign is an exceptional being among mortals, an image of the deity; and yet he is a man. For my own part, since it is only out of my small stock of literature that I can make any payment of this duty to kings, I did some time ago turn from Greek into Latin Plutarch's little work upon the means of distinguishing a flatterer from a friend, and dedicated it to your majesty by the mediation of the cardinal, who in the government of your realm fills the same part to you as Theseus did to Hercules, or Achates to Aeneas. But being suddenly drawn at that time into the hurricane of war by a sort of fatal storm, which then fell upon all Christendom, you had no leisure—I may well suppose—to give any attention to literature, when the business in hand could only be conducted with the sword. I now, therefore, send again to your highness the same book, though it has been since communicated to the world and is now printed for the third time; and I send it with interest, having attached to it the panegyrical eulogy of Philip, King of Castile, whose memory I know you keep sacred; as one whom, when you were yourself a boy, you loved as an elder brother, and whom your excellent father had adopted as a son.

To these I have added the *Institution of a Prince*, an offering which I made not long since to Charles, the King Catholic, when he was newly initiated into sovereignty. Not that he stood in need of our admonitions; but, as in a great storm, the steersman, however skilful he may be, is contented to receive a warning from any quarter, so a sovereign, destined to rule so many kingdoms, ought not to spurn any advice that is proffered in a serious spirit, while he is resolved to follow that, which of all the plans proposed he may judge to be best. But what estuary will you anywhere find, that has such disturbing currents as the tumults that arise in extensive empires? Or who ever saw at sea such fearful tempests as those hurricanes of human affairs, which we have witnessed in these last few years? And still more dangerous storms appear to be impending, if things are not set in order by the wisdom and piety of princes. As a last consideration, having been raised to the rank of councillor, I thought it right to respond at once to my appointment by this act of duty, and not merely to give my opinion in particular cases but to show to a prince of no ordinary character, but still a boy, some of the sources, as it were, from which all counsels flow. . . .

Nichols III, pp. 45–7. Allen III, pp. 77–9

Erasmus to Willibald Pirckheimer. Louvain, 2 November 1517

I have received the pamphlet, illustrious sir, together with your letter; to which I propose to reply in few words. Torn to pieces with hard work, I just remain alive, and am staying at Louvain, having been admitted into the society of the divines here, although I have not the title of doctor in their university. This I have preferred to do, rather than accompany Prince Charles to Spain, especially when I saw the court split up into so many factions, as Spaniards, Maranians, Chièvres' party, French, Imperialists, Neapolitans, Sicilians, and what not?

Last spring when I went to England for some private business, the king, of his own accord, gave me the kindest welcome, and so did the cardinal, who is, so to speak, a second king. Beside a handsome house, they offered me six hundred florins a year; and I thanked them in such a way as neither to accept nor refuse the terms proposed. I am living here at a considerable cost to myself; nevertheless I am determined to stay for some months, partly to finish the work I have in hand and partly to see what is to be the outcome of the brilliant hopes held out to me in the prince's name, at the moment of his departure, by John Le Sauvage, Chancellor of Burgundy, who, as he is most learned himself, is also a patron of all men of letters.

My New Testament, which was hurried through the press rather than edited, at Basel, I am now remodelling in such a way that it will be a different work, and I hope to finish it within four months. I was much pleased with your pamphlet, and with your friendly defence of Reuchlin, in which you seem to me more fluent than usual—I think, because, as Fabius says, your heart has made you eloquent, and not only your intellect and erudition. But I reckon, myself, that it is calamitous to carry on warfare in any way; and further that nothing is more calamitous than to have to do with a sordid and disreputable foe. For with whom, after all, has Reuchlin to fight? It is a nest of hornets, which even the Roman pontiff is afraid to provoke, so that Pope Alexander used to say, he thought it safer to offend the mightiest of kings than any individual of those herds of mendicants, who under pretext of this abject name exert a veritable tyranny over the Christian world; though I do not think it fair to attribute to the entire Order what is committed by the fault of a few. Then again, look at the instrument employed by these false professors of true religion: a brazen-faced creature, as to whose character there can be no mistake, and who would not be pelted with the name of Half-Jew, if he had not by his acts shown himself to be a Jew and a half.

Therefore it is not only a disreputable but an empty conflict, in which learned men are engaged against such an adversary, as it is one from which, whether they conquer or are defeated, they can gain nothing but discredit. A hangman is a more suitable person to suppress such madness. It should be the care of the bishops, of the most righteous Emperor Maximilian, of the magistrates of the famous city of Cologne, not to foster so poisonous a viper, to the certain destruction of the Christian religion unless the antidote be provided that such a mischief requires. This I say from no private grudge; he has never hurt me, or if he has libelled me at all, I am not affected by it; and the matter in question does not concern me in the least. Still I am sorry that the concord of the Christian world should be so unworthily broken up by the impostures of one profane and unlearned Jew, and that with the aid of persons who profess to be supporters of the Christian religion.

But enough of these matters! Not to leave your very learned pamphlet altogether without criticism, I do not quite approve of that list of Reuchlin's supporters. For where will you find a man, religious and learned, that is not on his side? Who does not execrate that brute, unless it be one who either does not understand the matter or seeks his personal advantage to the injury of the public? Again, while you are scouring the field against dialecticians and philosophers, I should have preferred to see you give your whole attention to the matter in hand and leave other persons and other things to take care of themselves. . . .

Nichols III, pp. 113–15. Allen III, pp. 116–19

Erasmus to John Caesarius. Louvain, 3 November 1517
. . . That the learned take the part of Reuchlin is only natural kindness; but that they are entering into written controversy with that pestilent *Corn*—that trumpeter of the Furies, that mouthpiece of certain masked theologians and veritable vicar of Satan—of this, I by no means approve. Made up, as he is, of evil-speaking, he cannot be overcome by censure, and does not know what it is to blush. A brazen-faced buffoon, he glories in being introduced in any way into the books of the learned, being more ambitious of approval by the most numerous than by the best. But what if the world understood his treachery and perceived that the man under the pretext of defending the Christian faith is in fact proceeding to its subversion? He will then have earned the gratitude of his circumcised friends, to whom he will have done the same service as Zopyrus did to Darius. I would stake my life that if an anatomy could be made of him, you would not find one Jew but six hundred Jews in his breast. We must beware of an Angel of Satan

transfigured into an Angel of Light. I wish the proverb were not so true as it is: 'A bad Jew always makes a worse Christian.' And I trust that learned men will think too highly of themselves to enter into a contest with this foulest of monsters—a contest from which, whether they conquer or are defeated, they can carry off nothing but mud and poison. I wonder that our magistrates, our bishops, and our emperor do not put a stop to a plague of this sort. It is easy, indeed, to do mischief, while the people are wanting in judgment; and the least spark may give rise to a wide-spread fire. And what would be more desired by the Jews—whose cause this fellow is forwarding, while he pretends to oppose it—than such a severance of Christian concord? For my own part, provided the New Testament remain intact, I had rather that the Old should be altogether abolished than that the peace of Christendom should be broken for the sake of the books of the Jews. I wish this fellow were still entirely a Jew; and we might then use more circumspection in admitting the rest!

Nichols III, pp. 124–5. Allen III, p. 127

Erasmus to Domenico Cardinal Grimani. Louvain, 13 November 1517
. . . If thy admiration is stirred by the arches or pyramids, which are the vestiges of ancient superstition, wilt thou not be more delighted with the monuments of religion, which are handed down in the books of the Apostles. Thou admirest Hadrian's statue and the Baths of Domitian; wilt thou not welcome more readily the sacred Epistles of Peter and of Paul? If in the books of Sallust or of Livy thou art pleased with the ancient story which tells thee from what an origin thou wast lifted under thine eagle's auspices to a world-wide supremacy, destined soon to fail, shall it not be still more delightful to learn in the books of Apostles and Evangelists, from what beginnings under Christian auspices thou has attained an ecclesiastical sovereignty, which is never to cease. As with the Jews, no trace remains of their holy Temple, so thy Capitol, to which the ancient poets vainly promised eternity, has so completely disappeared, that its very locality cannot now be pointed out. If thou admirest the tongue of Cicero, of which thou canst scarcely tell whether it did more good or harm to the Commonwealth, art thou not still more delighted with the eloquence of Paul, to whom thou owest thy religion and salvation? Thou wert always greedy of praise, and thou hast indeed in him a trumpeter of thy glory as authoritative as he is renowned. What greater triumph than to be praised by the mouth of an Apostle? . . . It is thy part to see that thou degenerate not from Rome to Babylon! Jerome admits that in his time the

evidences still remained in Rome of the religion praised by Paul. 'Where else,' says he, 'do men repair in such numbers and with so much zeal to the Churches and to the tombs of Martyrs? Where does the Amen resound so like the thunder of Heaven and shake the temples from which their idols have been ejected? Not that the Christians of Rome have a different faith from that of all the churches of Christ, but that their devotion and simple readiness to believe are greater.' Magnificent, indeed, is this testimony of Jerome, but what would he now say if he could see in the same city so many churches, so many cardinals, so many bishops, if he saw how all the princes of the world are seeking responses from this one surest oracle of Christ; and what crowds are meeting here for religion's sake from the furthest corners of the world! A Christian scarcely feels himself to be such, unless he has seen Rome and saluted the Roman pontiff, as a sort of earthly deity, upon whose nod all the welfare of mortals depends! We should add, that under the Tenth Leo, he would see the Roman city free from the tempest of war, flourishing no less in learning than in religion. The place, which alone possesses so many persons pre-eminent in ecclesiastical dignity, so many men distinguished in every branch of learning, so many lights and ornaments of mankind, you might well term a world rather than a city. Nothing remains to be asked of heaven but that our pontiff should continue to respond to the praises he receives, that his piety should be no less than his felicity, his goodness exceed his majesty. This will come to pass, if he endeavours to reproduce the character and lives of Peter and of Paul, under whose auspices he rules; and their likeness cannot anywhere be found more vividly expressed than in their own Epistles.

Meantime, most holy Father, a fragment of the writings of Paul will be more readily welcomed by others, if it shall come to them from your hands; that is from the hands of one who is an admirable patron of every study—especially of those in which a knowledge of languages is required; and who is at the same time so conspicuous for moral integrity that brilliant as are the lights that surround him, his personality is still eminently bright—not in such a fashion as to throw others into the shade but on the contrary to add an excess of light and distinction to characters in themselves illustrious.

Nichols III, 141-4. Allen III, 139-40

Erasmus, Complaint of Peace (*1517*)

. . . But I am ashamed to remember for how light and vain causes Christian princes provoke the world to war. This prince doth find out or feigneth some old or corrupt title. As though it were some great matter, who should govern and rule the kingdom, so that if only the advantage and profit of the commonweal were seen unto. Another findeth a fault that some trifle—I cannot well tell you what—is omitted in the confederation and league of a hundred titles and articles. Another man is privately offended with him for his spouse deceitfully conveyed away or for some light word or merry scoff freely spoken.

And there be the which thing of all others is most criminal and wicked: that through a tyrannical deceit, because they feel and perceive their power by the concord of the people to decay and by their dissension to be established, do suborn and appoint them that of purpose shall move war, that they may divide those that be joined and the more licentiously and freely rob and spoil the unfortunate people. Others there be most villainous, the which are nourished with the damages and loss of the people, and in the time of peace have little to do in the commonweal.

What infernal furies could send in such poison into a Christian heart? Who hath taught Christian men this tyranny? The which neither any Dionysius nor any Mezentius hath known. They are rather beasts than men and only noble by tyranny, nor nowheres noble nor wise but to do hurt and mischief, nor never in accord and agreement but to oppress the commonwealth. And they that do these things are taken and accepted for Christians and, everywhere thus polluted, approach and come to the holy churches and altars. O most pestilent persons, worthy to be into the remotest islands exiled!

Paynell, pp. 30–31

Erasmus, Complaint of Peace (*1517*)
. . . If even from the heart ye do hate war, I shall counsel you how ye may defend concord. Perfect peace doth not consist in affinities nor in the confederations of men, of the which we do oftentimes perceive and see that wars do rise and spring. The fountains whence this evil doth break must be purged; evil cupidities and desires do engender these debates and tumults. And whilst every man doth serve and please his affections, the commonweal, in the mean season, is afflicted and troubled; and yet no man attaineth the things that he by evil means and ways doth desire.

Let princes be wise for the profit of the people and not for their own profit; and let them truly be wise that they may measure their majesty, their felicity, their riches, their glory with those things that truly and in deed make men great and excellent. Let them be of such a mind towards the commonweal as a father is towards his family. A king shall esteem and judge himself great and noble if he command and rule those that be good; and happy, if he makes his subjects fortunate and wealthy; and noble, if he command and govern those that are free; and rich, if he have rich subjects; and flourishing, if he have cities that flourish with perpetual peace. . . .

But if war cannot be avoided, yet let it be so conducted that the mischief thereof may fall upon their heads that gave the occasion and causes thereof. Now the princes make war in safety; the captains grow great thereby; the greatest part of the evils and losses is poured upon the husbandmen and common people, unto whom the war pertaineth not nor that gave no cause nor occasion thereof. . . .

Paynell, pp. 40, 41

Erasmus to John Fisher. Louvain c. 5 March 1518

Reverend Father, I am reluctantly preparing for a fresh journey, for the purpose of issuing an emended and more complete edition of the New Testament, being apprehensive that this business will be badly managed, unless I am on the spot myself. I beg your piety, if there is anything to which you think my attention should be directed, to let me know by letter through the bearer, who is sent partly for this purpose, and is to return to me without delay. As far as we could do so, we have made the emendations which appeared to be required; although we shall never, I suppose, succeed in obtaining the approval of all the preachers! . . .

As the journey we are now undertaking is a very long one, having to go to Venice, or at the least as far as Basel, we shall want an easy-going horse that will be capable of hard work. Should you have any such to spare, it will be a very great favour, if you will send him by the bearer.

This winter has seemed very long to me; so that partly from distaste, partly by continued study, I have almost worn myself out. What remains is the last act of our play, and, if I am not mistaken, of our life. Henceforth it is my intention to remain in seclusion and to sing a song to myself and the Muses. There is no pleasure in this constant sword-play with such a number of wranglers. I did wish to do my part, such as it might be, in the advancement of studies, and should not grudge the labour, if my wish could be accomplished. . . .

Lefèvre gives no answer at all, not even by a private letter to me; but I hear that he has taken offence at my *Apologia*, as if forsooth it were due to his authority, that after such an attack I should hold my tongue.

And yet I have put a curb upon my righteous grief and made a large concession to our old friendship, or to Christian modesty. You see how Jerome thunders against Ruffin, only because he had been cited by him in a figured way; and am I not to answer Lefèvre, who has made me 'a subverter of the prophetic intelligence,' 'contumeliously abusing the glory of Christ,' 'a partisan of the blasphemous Jews,' saying 'things most unworthy of Christ and of God,' 'adhering to the Flesh and opposing the Spirit,' writing 'things which are constantly at variance with each other,' 'things that needed more than one Anticyra,' and, while he is defending Christ's dignity, represents me as its adversary—shall I, let me ask, not answer him at all? However pious, however gentle, however friendly Lefèvre is, these expressions are found in his books, and are acknowledged by him as his own. If they are not found there, I may be accused of infatuation; if these and more than these are there, it was worthwhile to weigh, whether I had deserved any of them; if I had, let them refute what I have advanced; if not, why should they not rather be angry with Lefèvre for insidiously making so harsh an attack upon a friend, than with me, who am defending myself with a shield only; not, I repeat, with weapons of offence, as by common right I might surely have done. . . .

Nichols III, pp. 285–6. Allen III, 236–7

Erasmus to John of Louvain. Louvain, 2 January 1518
I could not but heartily welcome your so friendly, so prudent, or to describe it shortly, your so Christian counsel. As regards the *Moria* I have undertaken to satisfy the reader, partly in the Preface of the work itself, partly in the Epistle to Dorp, which is now added to the book. But what are you to do with those whom no reasons can appease, and who indeed loudly condemn what they have never read? If I had foreseen that those friends of yours would be so deeply offended, I might perhaps have suppressed the work, being of that mind, that if it is in my power to satisfy everybody, I would gladly do so, as far as it can be done without adulation. But it is of no use to regret the publication now, after the book has gone through more than twelve editions.

I should very much like to know why, of all mankind, the only persons that have taken offence are monks and theologians. Can it be that they all recognise their own likeness in my descriptions? The pope read the *Moria* through and laughed over it; he only added, 'I am glad to find our Erasmus has his own place there too!' And yet there is no set of men whom I treat with more bitterness than popes!

I have no taste for evil-speaking; but if I chose to describe theologians and monks as most of them really are, it would then be apparent with what civility they are spoken of by Folly.

That the book is read in schools, I had never heard before; though indeed I did take pains to admit nothing in it that would be corrupting to that age; for as to your fear that the reading of it might alienate them from all religion, I do not understand what that means. Is there any danger of all religion being disliked because something is said against those who are superstitiously religious? I only wish that all who are now called 'religious' were worthy of that name. Indeed, I will say more freely still, I would that priests and people were such true followers of the religion of Christ that those who are now the only persons called religious would not appear religious at all! The world is everywhere full of monasteries. I do not myself condemn any method of life; but make the estimate for yourself: how few there are in them who, beyond church services and ceremonies, have any religion at all!

I have never blackened any man's character, while I have tilted in a playful way at the common and most notorious vices of mankind. And yet for the future I intend to act with still greater moderation; and if there are some persons whom I cannot possibly satisfy, I shall console myself with the example of St. Paul, who through evil report and good report followed that which was right. At any rate I go so far as this, that if I have not the approbation of all, I have at any rate that of the greatest and the best. And perhaps the others at last will praise the same person when dead, whom they censure while he is living. . . .

Nichols III, pp. 208–10. Allen III, pp. 183–4

Erasmus to Marcus Laurinus. Louvain, 5 April 1518
I have received your letter, which is love itself; for what other sound does it utter, what other breath does it breathe? I have been no less longing for your company than you for mine, and I do hope that we shall now have that indulgence. As for the faultfinding of those detractors, who after trying their teeth upon every possible object, are not jeering at my 'inconstancy,' I did laugh, I confess, being already accustomed to that kind of babble, but my laughter was partly sardonic, for while to myself, against calumnies of that sort, a good conscience might well suffice, still who would not feel some annoyance at the obstinate and perverse ingratitude of men? No persons are more in need of my labours than those who thus bark against my studies and their own accommodation; and none bark more fiercely or savagely

than those who have never seen even the cover of my book. Do, my
dear Mark, make the experiment yourself, and you will find I speak
true; when you meet with any person of the kind, let him go on raging
against my New Testament; and when he has talked himself hoarse,
ask him whether he has read the work itself. If with unblushing fore-
head he says he has, then urge him to point out the passage with which
he finds fault; you will not meet with one of them that can do it.
But look now, how Christian this proceeding is, how worthy of their
profession as monks, to tear in tatters before an unlearned audience
the reputation of another (which they cannot repair if they wished to
do so), when all the while they know nothing at all about the matter
with which they find fault; not considering the truth of that saying of
St. Paul; evil-speakers shall not possess the kingdom of God.

There is no more infamous charge than that of heresy, and this is
the charge they bring at once against any one that offends them, even
by a nod! And then, as it is said, that among the Swiss, if one man out
of a crowd points his finger at a person, all the rest do the same, and
run up to the spoil, so, as soon as any one of this herd begins to grunt,
they are presently all grunting together and inciting the people to
throw stones; as if, forgetting their proper profession, they had no
other business but this: to cast a stain, by the virulence of their language, upon the characters of respectable men. To use the words of the
psalmist: 'they have sharpened their tongues like a serpent; adder's
poison is under their lips.' Thus those who ought to be preachers of
Christian piety have chosen to be the detractors of the piety of others,
and those who profess themselves hierophants show themselves
sycophants. . . .

As to their cavil that I am preparing a new edition because I am not
satisfied with the former one, suppose that to be the case, what fault
can they find if I am anxious to be better than myself, and to do that
which was done by Origen, by Jerome, and by Augustine, especially
when I had frankly stated in my first edition that I intended to do so,
if the occasion arose? That is not what I am doing now, but I am
adopting the same plan that has been followed in the third edition of
the *Adages*. Beside this, whereas in my former translation I had made
very sparing changes for fear of giving offence to over-sensitive minds
I have now been encouraged by the advice of learned men to venture
a little further in that direction; and I proceed to support the changes
made by a fuller citation of authorities, in order that those who are
hard of belief may have no excuse for turning back. And lastly I add
some passages which were then hastily passed over. But if meantime

any sentence should occur which may give offence to learned and pious minds, I do not hesitate to alter it; having no intention of claiming to be more than a man. The first edition may be despised, if it were not that I have explained in it a number of passages in which Thomas Aquinas went astray, not to speak of other writers. Let my critics deny this, or refute it, if they can. But if it is undeniable, they should acknowledge how much they may be benefited by our labours, by which Aquinas himself would have profited if he were living. This boast of mine should not be misconstrued as said in his dishonour, as I do not compare myself with him, even if I have made some points clear which escaped his notice. And what has been said of Thomas, they may consider to be said of Liranus, and indeed of Augustine and Hilary. They may despise my work, but they must confess that countless passages are now made plain, which were not understood before, even by persons of more than ordinary learning. I would ask finally why do they condemn a book which is not condemned by the pope, to whom it is dedicated? I sent it to him; he has accepted it, he has read it, and has thanked me for it by letter as well as by his acts.

But these wrangling critics, naturally stupid and rendered doubly blind by the malady of evil-speaking, believe, I fancy, that it has been my intention to supersede entirely the translation which we have in use, and which in several places, I myself prefer to the reading of the Greek copies; whereas all that I have done is to translate the text which I found in the Greek manuscripts, pointing out in the notes which reading I approve or disapprove. Suppose that I had done nothing but make this translation, so that the readings of the Greek manuscripts might be compared with the Vulgate, even by persons ignorant of Greek; what fault, I ask, would they find in this? As it is, I show by manifest proofs that in a multitude of passages our version is depraved, but not so far as to endanger the Faith; and I point out how Cyprian, Jerome and Ambrose agree with the Greek manuscripts. And yet those critics of yours cry out, as if some awful crime had been committed. But what avails it, my Mark, to use any arguments with those who wilfully shut their eyes that they may not see and close their ears that they may not hear. Enough satisfaction has been given them in the Apologies, if they are willing to listen; and if they are not, we endeavour in vain to satisfy those who had rather calumniate than learn.

But these stern critics find a want of steadiness in me, because they hear that I am preparing to go to Basel. As if I were going to make this journey, or had made it before, for my own amusement! I have edited

Jerome; I have edited the Greek Testament, beside many other works; and in order to be of service to the public, I have taken no account of a most dangerous journey, or of the expenses incurred in it; and I have taken no account of the labours with which a considerable part of my health and life have been worn away. What a marvellous instance of inconsistency it is, when I have not chosen to drink with them, rather than go off to Basel! They run up and down themselves, and fly over lands and seas, not at their own cost—mendicity being their profession —but with money scraped together from widows, whose heads they turn with the burden of sins, which they throw upon them; despoiling holy maidens and beguiling the genius of simple brethren for the purpose of mischief, in order to throw discredit upon men who are deserving well of the Christian commonwealth. And these forsooth are accounted steady and grave persons, while I, because at my own cost of money and of comfort, I am ministering to the public service, am convicted of inconstancy!

Let him choose, they say, some town for his residence. Do I seem then to be living here in Scythian solitude? Do these people think a man is not in existence, unless they see him constantly at their drinking parties. I hold that my home is at that place, where I have my library, and what little furniture I possess; and if it is the public service that demands a change of residence, I surely deserve praise for my devotion, not blame for my inconstancy! If the need of this journey could have been bought off with three hundred gold pieces, I would readily have paid that sum. As it was, the journey had to be made.

I have never changed my locality, unless I was either driven out by plague or compelled to move by considerations of health or some honourable business. The only journey I ever voluntarily undertook was my journey to Italy, undertaken partly that I might visit for once the sacred places, and partly that I might enjoy the libraries of that country, and some intercourse with its learned men. Of that inconstancy I have not yet repented.

I have been living here, without moving, for nearly two years. I might with the amplest expectations have accompanied the Catholic king. I have been invited with the promise of mountains of gold by the king of the French. I have been invited with the greatest kindness by the King of England and the Cardinal of York; and by Francis, Archbishop of Toledo, who has lately died. I have been invited by the Bishop of Paris, by him of Bayeux, by the Archbishop of Mainz, by the Bishops of Liège, of Trèves, of Basel and of Rochester, by the Duke of Bavaria and the Duke of Saxony. I make no false boasts; what I say is known to many, and may be proved by their own letters. Neglecting all these offers, I have persevered in the business which I had in hand and am called inconstant when I am bent upon completing the work which I had so laboriously begun.

If the merit of constancy consists in occupying the same locality for the longest period, the highest praise is due to rocks and to the stems of trees, and the next to shells and sponges! It is no fault to change one's locality, but to change it amiss is wrong. It is no merit to have lived long in the same place, but it is so to have lived laudably there. Socrates is praised for having resided all his life as an honest citizen in Athens; on the other hand no fault is found with Plato for travelling. John the Baptist never travelled out of Judea; Christ only reached the confines. On the other hand, we make no charge of inconstancy against the Apostles because their travels extended over the world. No one condemns the wanderings of Hilary because the hermit Paul never left his cavern. But why should I call these examples to the mind of those who are not constant even in the same city, but shift from time to time their fold and pasture, and move their lodging whenever they are attracted by a more luxurious or dainty kitchen. They find a lack of constancy in me because I have not been drinking with them in the same town for five and forty years—like sponges which live only to soak—have not been following loose pleasures, nor playing at dice, nor acting the part of sycophant! For my part, I much prefer my own fickleness to their constancy, and think it a far finer thing to have lived in many places, that the best men, wherever you have been, long for your return, than to have lived in the same town, I will not say disgracefully, but in such a way that it is no matter whether you have lived at all. If a man's health requires a change of locality, will they refuse permission to act on this motive? And they are now finding fault with me for setting the public advantage before other considerations. They reject the help I offer them. This they may do, if only it is accepted by the good and learned. No one is forced by me to be wiser than he chooses.

But to these people, my Mark, let us bid farewell; and with pure and Christian hearts, while we love the good, let us tolerate the bad, if they refuse to be vanquished even by kindness. The lips will some time or other find a salad to suit them; the bad knot will meet with a wedge to match it; and seeking to plant their teeth on something soft, they will find it hard. For my part I have myself neither time nor inclination to struggle with this itch! . . .

Nichols III, pp. 322–9. Allen III, pp. 263–8.

Erasmus to Paul Bombasius. Basel, 26 July 1518

. . . You know, most excellent Bombasius, how I have always shrunk from the courts of princes, judging the life which is led there to be nothing but splendid misery, with a masquerade of happiness; but also such a court as that one might well be pleased to remove, if youth could be recalled. The king, the most sensible monarch of our age, is delighted with good books, and the Queen is well instructed—not merely in comparison with her own sex—and is no less to be respected for her piety than her erudition. With such sovereigns, those persons have the greatest influence who excel in learning and in prudence. Thomas Linacre is their physician, a man whom it is needless for me to characterise, when by his published books he has made himself sufficiently known. Cuthbert Tunstall is Master of the Rolls, an office which is of the highest dignity in that country; and when I name him, you cannot believe what a world of all good qualities is implied. Thomas More is one of the council, the supreme delight, not of the Muses only, but of pleasantry and of the graces, of whose genius you have been able to gain some scent from his books. Pace, with a character near akin, is the king's secretary. William, Lord Mountjoy, is at the head of the Queen's household, and John Colet is the preacher. I have only named the chief people. John Stokesley, who beside that scholastic theology, in which he yields place to none, is also well versed in the three tongues, is one of the chaplains. A palace filled with such men may be called a temple of the Muses rather than a court. What Athens, what Porch, what Lyceum would you prefer to a Court like that?

Your congratulation about Lefèvre is as painful to me as our conflict was against my wishes. I should have been glad, indeed, if he had been more moderate in his attack. But so it is: no one is always wise; and what is amiss in the matter may be imputed to my ill-luck. For what else could I do? Lefèvre is a man of high character, learned, humane, and moreover a friend of former days—but of that happiness some evil genius appears to have been jealous—and even now my feeling for the man is such, that it will be very painful to me if anyone thinks worse of him on my account. Some persons, who find a pleasure in these duels, are spreading a rumour of recrimination; but between ourselves we are agreed, and we shall not allow so old and so sincere a friendship to be effaced by one little cloud of discord. If there was some bitterness between Barnabas and Paul, what wonder if in the relations between *us* there is some human weakness?

How much credit is attributed to my writings by learned persons where you are, I do not know. Here it is certain that more is attributed to them than I can acknowledge, although there are some who bark loudly against them; but these are for the most part people, who either do not read what I have written or will read it to no purpose, whatever it may be. Certainly if I were not encouraged by the fair judgment of so many excellent men, I should long ago have regretted the sleepless hours which I am employing to the best of my power in the furtherance of our common studies, principally of sacred subjects. . . .

Nichols III, pp. 421–3. Allen III, pp. 356–7

Erasmus to Paul Volz. Basel, 14 August 1518

. . . I do not altogether regret this work [*Enchiridion*], however, if it arouses in so many the desire for true piety. Nor do I think that every kind of reproach should be levelled against me if I fall short of my own counsels. First of all, it is a part of piety to wish truly to become pious; and I do not believe that a heart filled with such intentions should be disdained, even if at times the effort is not crowned with success. One must ever make the effort throughout life, and success on occasion comes to him who has tried again and again. But he has travelled a good part of a difficult journey who has become well acquainted with the way. Therefore I am not moved by the jests of those who scorn this little book as not being learned enough or as one which could be written by any schoolboy, because it does not discuss the questions of the Scotists. As if nothing is learned without these! Let this little book not be sharp-witted provided it be pious. Let it not prepare a person for the mental gymnastics of the Sorbonne but for Christian peace of soul. Let it not contribute to theological argument but to a theological life. What is to be gained by discussing that which everyone discusses? Who today is not occupied with theological questions? With what else are the swarms of schoolmen concerned? There are almost as many commentaries on the *Sentences* as there are theologians. What other kind or category of manual writer is there except those who blend over and again one manual with another and, in the fashion of a pharmacist, repeatedly concoct the old out of the new, the new out of the old, one out of many, and many out of one? How could the great mass of these volumes teach us to live properly when not even a lifetime is enough to read them? It is as if a doctor would prescribe to a patient seriously ill that he read the books of Jacobus a Partibus and all others of a similar character, wherein he will find the remedy to restore his health. But in the meantime the patient dies, nor will there be anyone who can be helped. . . .

Olin, pp. 110–11. Allen III, pp. 362–3

Erasmus to Antonio Pucci. Basel, 26 August 1518

. . . We had reached the period when it was time for me to think of putting the New Testament in form; and now the plague, breaking out all around, is driving us away before the completion of a work, in our zeal for which we have hitherto disregarded, not money only, but life itself; so anxious was I, that the book which I had once dedicated to the Tenth Leo might be made worthy of him. For the first edition did not satisfy me in every particular; although even that is approved by all the most accomplished and learned persons, an outcry having been raised against it only by a few sycophants, who were not men of learning, and had never read the book, and who, moreover, while they barked at it in his absence, had not a word to say against it in the presence of its compiler. It is now to go forth afresh, and, if I am not mistaken, so completed as not to appear unworthy of Leo or of posterity. It would be vain for me to tell, as none would believe, what exertions it has cost me. I trust it may be proportionately serviceable to the Christian commonwealth, this being the only object we have had in view; to which end your sublimity will be able to contribute no little assistance, if you will not deem it too much trouble to obtain some sort of Brief from the pope, testifying that the work has his approval. In this way the mouth of those few sycophants will be closed.

The two cardinals, by whom I presented the former edition to Pope Leo, had both written answers: one of which was addressed by Andrew Ammonius to this place, but was lost on its way; while the other, which Andrew kept in his own hands, has been lost with him. We have written a few days ago about this matter to Cardinal Grimani and to Paul Bombasius.

To prevent any scruple arising in your mind, I will explain in a few words the plan of my work. Having first collated several copies made by Greek scribes, we followed that which appeared to be the most genuine; and having translated this into Latin, we placed our translation by the side of the Greek text, so that the reader might readily compare the two, the translation being so made that it was our first study to preserve, as far as was permissible, the integrity of the Latin tongue without injury to the simplicity of the Apostolic language.

Our next care was to provide that any sentences which had before given trouble to the reader, either by ambiguity or obscurity of language, or by faulty or unsuitable expressions, should be explained and made clear with as little deviation as possible from the words of the original, and none from the sense; as to which we do not depend upon any dreams of our own, but seek it out of the writings of Origen,

Basil, Chrysostom, Cyril, Jerome, Cyprian, Ambrose, or Augustine. Some annotations were added (which have now been extended), wherein we inform the reader, upon whose authority this or that matter rests, relying always upon the judgment of the old authors. We do not tear up the Vulgate Edition—which is, however, of uncertain authorship, though it is ascertained not to be the work of either Cyprian or Ambrose or Hilary or Augustine or Jerome—but we point out where it is depraved, giving warning in any case of flagrant error on the part of the translator, and explaining it, where the version is involved or obscure. If it is desirable that we should have the Divine Books as free from error in their text as possible, this labour of mine not only corrects the mistakes which are found in copies of the Sacred Volumes, but prevents their being depraved in future; and if it is wished that they should be rightly understood, we have laid open more than six hundred passages, which up to this time have not been understood even by great theologians. This they admit themselves, as indeed they cannot deny it. If to that controversial theology, which is almost too prevalent in the schools, is to be added a knowledge of the original sources, it is to this result that our work especially leads. Therefore no kind of study is impeded by our labour, but all are aided.

Although we have translated throughout the reading of the Greek scribes, we still do not so approve it in every case, as not in some instances to prefer our own text, pointing out in every case where the orthodox Latin writers agree or disagree with the Greek. It may be added that the variety of readings not only does not impede the study of the Sacred Scriptures, but even assists it according to the authority of St. Augustine; neither indeed is this variety ever so important as to lead to the peril of the Christian faith.

To sum up the matter, I am either misled by the love of my work or it is destined to perform an important service to sacred studies, and to secure for the Tenth Leo no small honour in another generation, when Envy shall be still, and the utility of the result shall be recognised; which will be both fuller and more mature, if the approbation of the Supreme Shepherd is added. This approbation I desire only to show that he is pleased with the work on account of the service it may render to sacred studies; and for my dedication of the book to him I ask no further reward. Some other men might expect a present or solicit a benefice. I, who have taken so much pains to be of service, shall think that I have received an ample return if that result shall come to pass, for the sake of which I have undertaken so many watches. Your eminence will secure this object by two words, and in so doing will do what will be pleasing to Christ himself, and also to all students, and especially agreeable to Froben, who may make this claim: that there is no printing press to which Sacred Literature is more indebted than to his. . . .

Nichols III, pp. 429–32. Allen III, pp. 380–82

Erasmus to Thomas Cardinal Wolsey. Antwerp, 18 May 1519

. . . By your means all Britain is cleared of robbers and of vagabonds, so that it is now as free from noxious men as it is from poison and wild beasts. By your authority the perplexities of litigation are no less effectually untied than was the Gordian knot by the Great Alexander; the differences of noblemen are arranged; the monasteries are restored to their ancient discipline; and the clergy recalled to a more approved manner of life. Polite Letters, which were struggling against the patrons of ancient ignorance, are supported by your favour, defended by your authority and fostered by your liberality, the most learned professors being by ample salaries invited to your aid. In the purchase of libraries, rich with every good author, you vie with Ptolemy Philadelphus himself, more renowned for this possession than for his kingdom. The three tongues, without which learning is incomplete, are recalled at your command; for by the benefaction, which is now conferred upon the famous school of Oxford, I judge all Britain to be obliged; and, indeed, I trust that this brilliant example will, before long, awaken the minds of our princes also. I see, I see a truly golden age arising, if that temper of yours shall prevail with some proportion of our sovereigns! These most holy efforts will receive a due reward from Him, under whose auspices they are made; neither will posterity be ungrateful, when in a distant age that generous heart, born for the benefit of humanity, will still be celebrated alike by Latin and Greek eloquence.

For, myself, rejoicing as I do, in the general felicity, I am not sorry that my own name is cast into the shade by more recent lights, when I see those around me, compared with whom I appear no wiser than a child. Enough for me to claim this praise, if indeed I can fairly do so, to be described as one of those who have done their best to drive out of this part of the world that barbarous ignorance of languages, with which Italy was wont to reproach us. How far I have been successful in this, I know not; that I have striven to do so I know, and striven not without some of that jealousy, which accompanies and pursues exceptional efforts, as the shadow follows the light. But the majority is now more kind; only a few still hold out, too old to hope, too stupid to learn, or too arrogant to wish to know better!

These people see only too plainly that their own authority will fall to the ground if we have the Sacred Books accessible in an amended form, and seek their meaning at the fountain-head. And so high a value do they set upon their own importance that they had rather have many things unknown, many things misread and cited amiss from the Divine Books, than appear to be ignorant themselves of any point. But inasmuch as they are conscious of their own inferiority in argument and aware that, if they deal with books, they do nothing but betray their own ignorance and folly, making themselves a laughing-stock to the learned, they have given up open fighting and have recourse to stratagems, loading with their slanders literature and its defenders, and me above all, whom they judge to have had some influence in the revival of these studies. Whatever writing of an invidious nature may be published, they fasten it upon Erasmus; and here you will detect the very genius of calumny at work, when the cause of Good Letters is mixed up with the affairs of Reuchlin or of Luther, whereas they have no proper connection with each other.

For my own part, I never had any fancy for the Cabala or the Talmud; and as for Reuchlin himself, I have only once met him at Frankfort, when nothing passed between us, except such friendly civilities as are usual between scholars. Not that I am ashamed to have joined in friendly correspondence with him. He has a letter of mine in which, before I knew him by sight, I advised him to abstain from those plain terms of abuse of his opponents, in which after the German fashion he indulges in his Apology; so far is it from the truth, that I have ever encouraged writings affecting any one's good name!

Luther is no more known to me than to any stranger he might meet; and as for the man's books, I have not had time to turn over more than one or two pages. And yet it is pretended—so I am told—that he has had my help in this work! If he has written aright, no credit is due to me; and if the reverse, I deserve no blame, seeing that in all his lucubrations, not a tittle is mine. Any one who cares to investigate the matter will find this to be quite true. The man's life is by a wide and general consent approved; and it is no small presumption in his favour, that his moral character is such that even his foes can find no fault with it. If I had had ample leisure to read his works, I do not claim so much authority as to pass judgment upon the writings of so important a person; although in these days you find boys everywhere pronouncing with the greatest temerity, that this proposition is erroneous, and that heretical. And, indeed, we were at one time all the more inclined to find fault with Luther, for fear of a prejudice that might arise against literature, upon which I did not wish a further burden to be laid. For I saw plainly enough how invidious an act it is to disturb the stability of things from which a rich harvest is reaped by priests or monks.

The first of these writings which came out were several propositions concerning papal pardons. These were followed by one or two pamphlets about confession and penance; and when I became aware that some persons were intent upon their publication, I did my best to discourage it, that they might not strengthen the prejudice against Good Letters. This circumstance will be shown by the evidence even of those who are Luther's well-wishers. At last a whole swarm of pamphlets came out; no one saw me reading them; no one heard me give any opinion either for or against them. I am not so rash as to approve that which I have not read, nor such a sycophant as to condemn that which I do not know; although in these days this is commonly done by those who have least excuse for doing so.

Germany has now many young men who afford the greatest promise both of erudition and of eloquence, and by whose means she may some time be able to make the same boast as is now fairly made by Britain. None of them are personally known to me, except Eobanus, Hutten, and Beatus. These, with all the weapons they have at command, are waging war against the enemies of the languages and of Good Letters. The freedom which they claim I might myself admit to be intolerable, did I not know how atrociously they are attacked both publicly and privately. Their assailants, in their sermons, in their schools, in their convivial parties, allow the most odious and indeed seditious appeals to be made of the ignorant multitude, but they judge it to be an intolerable offence, if any of their victims venture to murmur, when even the little bees have their sting, with which they may wound an assailant, and the mice have teeth to use in their own defence. Whence comes this new race of Gods, fixing the character of heretic on whomsoever they choose and mingling earth and sky, if any one calls them sycophants? And while they do not hesitate to find a name for what even Orestes is ashamed to mention, they demand of us not to be named themselves without some honourable preface—such confidence have they in the stupidity of the multitude, not to say of our princes!

For myself, little as I have been able to do in the pursuit of Good Letters, I have always loved them; and I give my support to their adherents who are everywhere in favour with out nobility, if we except a few Midases, whom some one will some time take an opportunity of describing! And yet my favour only extends so far, that I support that which is in alliance with Virtue; and if anyone will consider with what faults those authors were saturated who mainly assisted in the old revival of literature in Italy and France, he cannot fail to give his approval to the writers of our own time, whose moral character is such that they should rather be objects of imitation than of blame to their theological censors. And whatever they produce is suspected to be mine, even among you in England, if we may believe what is told us by the merchants who come to this country from yours! For my part I will frankly confess that I cannot fail to admire literary genius, while I disapprove any licence of the pen, whoever the author may be.

Some time since, [Ulrich] Hutten amused with a book, the title of which was *Nemo*. Everybody knows that the subject is a ludicrous one; and the theologians of Louvain, who think themselves more sharp-sighted than Lynxes, insisted that it was mine! Presently there came out another publication, called 'Fever,' and that was mine too, when the whole character of the book, as well as its whole phraseology, is quite different from my work! . . .

I have advised by letter all those young German writers to control their excessive freedom of language, and certainly to abstain from any attack upon persons of authority in the Church—lest they should prejudice against literature those by whose patronage they might be able to stand up against their foes. What more am I to do? I can advise, but have no power to compel. I may temper my own style, but to control the pen of another is not in my power. The absurdest thing of all is, that the work which was lately written by the Bishop of Rochester against Lefèvre was suspected to be mine, when there is so great a difference of style—and indeed I have no pretensions to the erudition of that divine prelate. There were also persons to be found who ascribed More's *Utopia* to my authorship—everything new, whether I like it or not, being attributed to me!

Several months ago an ill-starred and ridiculous booklet came out, the subject of which sufficiently shows that it was written upon the last vacancy of the papal See, but by what writer is not known, save that its contents show that, whoever it was, his sympathies were with the French. The suspicion of its authorship goes the round of many different persons, especially among the Germans, the work being current among them under various titles. When I met with it here myself some years ago, circulated in a furtive way, and had some taste of its contents—for I galloped through it rather than read it—many persons can bear witness how hateful it was to me, and what pains I took, that it should be hidden in eternal darkness—a thing that has been done by me more than once in the case of other publications, as many persons will admit. The facts are shown in a letter written by me to John Caesarius, which was published at Cologne from a copy furtively obtained. And I am told that there are some people in your parts, who are trying to fix upon me the suspicion of being the author of this publication; so unwilling are those persons who regret the revival of learning and of better studies, to leave anything untried that may help to carry out their purpose. The sole argument they rely upon is that of the style, which nevertheless is not much like mine, unless that is little known to myself. And yet what wonder would there be, if some expressions here and there agreed with my phraseology; when in these days my lucubrations pass through so many hands that even in the books of those who are writing against me, I often recognise my own style, and have the sensation of being struck by a shaft winged with my own feathers. I have not hitherto composed, and do not intend to compose, any work to which I do not prefix my name. We did some fencing long ago in the *Moria*, but without drawing blood, though perhaps with more freedom than enough. At any rate I have taken every precaution that nothing should proceed from me, which would either corrupt the young by obscenity or in any way hinder piety; give rise to sedition; or draw a black line across any one's character. Whatever exertions I have hitherto made have been made for the assistance of honourable studies and the advancement of the Christian religion; and all persons on every side are thankful for what has so been done, except a few theologians and monks, who have no wish to be wiser or better than they are. May I lose the favour of Christ if I do not desire that whatever I have of talent or of eloquence should be wholly dedicated to His glory, to the Catholic Church, and to sacred studies.

But of this personal matter I have said more than enough, and was going to write nothing at all, if a British merchant, on arriving here from home, had not persistently asserted that some persons had endeavoured to impose this utterly false suspicion upon your eminence, whose singular prudence, nevertheless, makes me quite confident that you will not listen or give any attention to such impudent calumnies. Indeed, if you will deign some time or other to try the experiment in a personal interview, you will find Erasmus devoted to the dignity of the Roman See, especially under the Tenth Leo, to whose piety he recognises how much he owes, and also heartily attached to those persons who lend their services to the cause of letters and of religion, among whom your eminence holds a principal place. . . .

Nichols III, pp. 379–86. Allen III, pp. 587–93

Erasmus to Martin Luther. Louvain, 30 May 1519

. . . Your letter was most pleasing to me, showing as it does the keen-
ness of your mind and your Christian spirit. I can hardly tell you in
words what commotion your writings have occasioned here. So far,
I have been unable to pluck that most unfounded suspicion from the
minds of some that your works have been written with my assistance,
and that I am the ringleader of your faction, as they style it. They
deemed this a good excuse for stifling good literature which they
regard with a deadly hatred as something which might detract from
the majesty of theology; for of this they make more account than they
do of Christ, and at the same time make it an opportunity to assail
me whom they regard as influential in advancing the cause of learning.
The whole movement is carried on by clamour, brazenness, trickery,
detraction, and calumny, so that had I myself not seen it, nay, felt it
myself, I should never have believed anyone who said theologians
could become so insane. You might say that it was a deadly pestilence.
And yet this poisonous thing, though springing from a few, has crept
into many, so that a great part of this crowded university is infected
with the malady.

I have asserted that you are the veriest stranger to me, that I have
not yet read your books, and that as a consequence I have neither
censured nor approved anything that may be in them. I have only
advised some not to be so spitefully vehement in public about books
which they have not read, but to leave the decision to those whose
judgment is of the most value. And I have warned them to reflect
whether it was expedient to bring before promiscuous assemblies such
matters as these which could be better refuted in books or discussed
among scholars, especially when with unanimous consent the author's
personal character was commended. But it was all to no purpose,
for up to the present they rant and rave with their one-sided and
notorious disputes. How often has peace been agreed upon between us!
How often have they on the most groundless suspicion excited fresh
disturbances! And they think they are theologians. Those who are
attached to the court here hate these theologians, and that is blamed
upon me. All the bishops are well disposed towards me. They [the
theologians] place no trust in books; their only hope of victory lies
in their calumnies, which I disregard, relying on the consciousness of
my own rectitude. Towards you they are becoming a little milder.
They fear my pen, a fact which is indicative of their evil consciences,
for I would certainly paint them in their native hues, and serve them
right, did not the teaching and example of Christ restrain me. Wild

beasts are made gentle by kindness; these men are rendered savage by good deeds. . . .

Mangan II, pp. 116–17. Allen III, pp. 605–7

Erasmus to Albert of Brandenburg. Louvain, 19 October 1519

. . . About those propositions of Luther's to which they object. I make no question at present; what I do question, however, are the method and the occasion adopted. Luther has dared to cast doubts on *indulgences*; but others before him have made exceedingly rash statements about them. He has had the temerity to speak somewhat moderately about the power of the Roman pontiff, but others had previously written of it in extravagant terms, of whom the principal writers were the three Dominicans: Alvarus, Sylvester, and the Cardinal of St. Sixtus. He has been so bold as to contemn the conclusions of St. Thomas, which, however, the Dominicans esteem almost more than the four Gospels. He has presumed to raise some scruples about the matter of confession, a subject which the monks use perpetually for entangling the consciences of men. He has not hesitated in a measure to cast aside the judgments of the Schoolmen, to which these latter attach too much importance, although they are not in exact accord about them; for they change them eventually, introducing new ones to take the place of the old.

It has distressed pious minds to hear in the universities scarcely a single discourse about the doctrine of the Gospel; to see those sacred authors, so long approved by the Church, now considered antiquated; to hear in sermons very little about Christ but a great deal about the power of the Pope, and the opinions of recent writers thereon. Every discourse openly manifests self-interest, flattery, ambition, and pretence. Even though Luther has written somewhat intemperately, I think that the blame should rest on these very happenings. Whoever favours the doctrine of the Gospel favours the Roman pontiff, who is the chief herald thereof, although the rest of the bishops are also likewise heralds. All the bishops act in the place of Christ, but among these the Roman pontiff is pre-eminent. Of him we must have this feeling: that he desires nothing but the glory of Christ, whose servant he glories in being. They merit very little consideration who ascribe to him through flattery what he himself does not claim and what is not necessary for his Christian flock. And yet some who are causing these tumults are not doing it from zeal for the pontiff, but are abusing his power for their own enrichment and unjust domination. We have, in my opinion, a pious pontiff; but in these tempestuous times there are many things

of which he is not aware; many things also which even if he wished
to do so he could not control. . . .

Mangan II, pp. 152–3. Allen IV, pp. 103–4

Erasmus to Georg Spalatin. Louvain, 6 July 1520
. . . I have written recently to Philipp Melanchthon, but in such a manner
that I feel as if I had written to Luther by that same letter. I pray that
Christ the Almighty will so temper the pen and mind of Luther that
he will procure for evangelical piety the greatest possible amount of
good, and that he will give to certain people a better understanding—
people who seek their own glory by the ignominy of Christ and follow
their own profit by abandoning Him. In the camp of those who oppose
Luther I perceive many who smack of the world more than of Christ.
And yet there are faults on both sides. Would that Hutten, whose
talents I much esteem, would moderate his writing! I should prefer
Luther to refrain from these contentions for a little while, and to
expound the Gospel simply, without admixture of personal feelings:
perhaps his undertaking would succeed better. Just now he is exposing
even good literature to an ill-will which is ruinous to us and unprofitable to himself. And there is danger that the corruption of public
morality, which all declare requires a public remedy, may, like a
pestilence that is stirred up afresh, wax ever more strongly. Not always
is the truth to be put forth. And it makes a wide difference in what
manner it is put forth. . . .

Mangan II, pp. 156. Allen IV, p. 298

Erasmus to Leo X. Louvain, 13 September 1520
I trust your Holiness will not listen to the calumnies against me and
Reuchlin. We are charged with being in confederacy with Luther.
I have always protested against this. Neither of us has anything to do
with Luther. I do not know him. I have not read his writings; I have
barely glanced at a few pages. I gather from what I have seen that
Luther rejects the modern hairsplitting and superfluous subtleties in
the explanation of Scripture and inclines to the mysticism of the early
Fathers. I supported him so far as I thought him right, but I was the
first to scent danger. I warned Froben, the printer, against publishing
his works. I wrote to Luther's friends. I bade them caution Luther
himself against disturbing the peace of the Church. I did tell him in
a letter, which your Holiness has seen, that he had friends in Louvain,
but that he must moderate his style if he wished to keep them. I thought
the knowledge might have a useful influence on him. This was two

years ago, before the quarrel was so much embittered. But if anyone can prove that even in table-talk I have defended his opinions then let me, if men so please, be called a Lutheran. I have not written against him as I have been asked to do: first, because to reply to him I must first have studied what he has said attentively, and for this I have no leisure; and next, because it would be a work beyond my powers or knowledge—the universities had taken up the subject, and it was not for me to anticipate their verdict; and thirdly, I confess, because I hesitated to attack an eminent man when I had not been ordered to interfere. I trust, therefore, that I may rely on your Holiness' protection. I dare not oppose even my own diocesan. I am not so mad as to fly in the face of the Vicar of Christ. I did not defend Luther when I might lawfully have done so. When I said I disapproved of the character of the attacks on him, I was thinking less of the man himself than of the overbearing attitude of the theologians. Their asssaults on him were carried on with malicious acerbity and dangerous appeals to popular passion, and the effect was only to give importance to his writings and provoke the world to read them. If they had first answered and confuted him they might then have burnt his books, and himself too if he had deserved it. But the minds of a free, generous nation cannot be driven. It would have been better for the theologians themselves if they had taken my advice and attended to it. . . .

Froude, pp. 263–4. Allen IV, pp. 344–5

Erasmus to Lorenzo Campeggio. Louvain, 6 December 1520

. . . Jerome, who was himself a monk, was the most effective painter of monastic vices, and sketches with satiric salt the lives of the brothers and sisters. The scene is shifted, the actors are changed, but the play is the same. When the Reuchlin storm was over came these writings of Luther, and they snatched at them to finish Reuchlin, Erasmus, and learning all together. They cried that learning was producing heresies, schisms and Antichrist, and they published my private letters to the Archbishop of Mainz and to Luther. As to Luther himself, I perceived that the better a man was the less he was Luther's enemy. The world was sick of teaching which gave it nothing but glosses and formulas, and was thirsting after the water of life from the Gospels and Epistles. I approved of what seemed good in his work. I told him in a letter that if he would moderate his language he might be a shining light, and that the Pope, I did not doubt, would be his friend. What was there in this to cry out against? I gave him the truest and kindest advice. I had never seen him; I have not seen him at all. I had read little that he had written, nor had matters taken their present form. A few persons only were clamouring at him in alarm for their own pockets. They called on me to pronounce against him. The same persons had said before that I was nothing but a grammarian. How was a grammarian to decide a point of heresy? I said I could not do it till I had examined his authorities. He had taken his opinions from the early Fathers, and if he had quoted them by name, he could hardly have been censured. I said I had no leisure for it, nor could I indeed properly meddle when great persons were busy in replying to him. They accused me of encouraging him by telling him that he had friends in England. I told him so to induce him to listen to advice. Not a creature hitherto has given him any friendly counsel at all. No one has yet answered him or pointed out his faults. They have merely howled out heresy and Antichrist. . . .

I have myself simply protested against his being condemned before he has been heard in his defence. The penalty for heresy used to be only excommunication. No crime now is more cruelly punished. But how, while there are persons calling themselves bishops and professing to be guardians of the truth, whose moral character is abominable, can it be right to persecute a man of unblemished life, in whose writings distinguished and excellent persons have found so much to admire? The object has been simply to destroy him and his books out of mind and memory, and it can only be done when he is proved wrong by argument and Scripture before a respectable commission that can be trusted. Doubtless, the pope's authority is vast, but the vaster it is, the less it ought to be influenced by private affections. The opinions of pious, learned men should receive attention, and the pope has no worse enemies than his foolish defenders. He can crush any man if he pleases, but empires based only on terror do not last, and the weightier the pope's judgment and the graver the charge, the greater caution should be used. Every sensible man, secular or spiritual, even among the Dominicans themselves, thinks as I do about this. Those who wish Luther condemned disapprove of the methods now pursued against him, and what I am here saying is more for the good of the pope and theology than in the interest of Luther. If the decrees of the Holy See and of the Doctors of the Church are to carry weight, they must come from men of irreproachable character, whose judgment we can feel sure will not be influenced by worldly motives. . . .

If we want truth, every man ought to be free to say what he thinks without fear. If the advocates of one side are to be rewarded with mitres and the advocates of the other with rope or stake, truth will not be heard. Out of the many universities in Europe, two have condemned certain propositions of Luther; but even these two did not agree. Then came the terrible Bull, with the pope's name upon it. Luther's books were to be burnt, and he himself was denounced to the world as a heretic. Nothing could have been more invidious or unwise. The Bull itself was unlike Leo X, and those who were sent to publish it only made matters worse. It is dangerous, however, for secular princes to oppose the papacy, and I am not likely to be braver than princes, especially when I can do nothing. The corruptions of the Roman Court may require reform, extensive and immediate, but I and the like of me are not called on to take a work like that upon ourselves. I would rather see things left as they are than to see a revolution which may lead to one knows not what. Others may be martyrs if they like. I aspire to no such honour. Some hate me for being a Lutheran; some for not being a Lutheran. You may assure yourself that Erasmus has been, and always will be, a faithful subject of the Roman See. But I think, and many think with me, that there would be better chance of a settlement if there was less ferocity, if the arrangement was placed in the hands of men of weight and learning, if the pope would follow his own disposition and would not let himself be influenced by others. . . .

Froude, pp. 269–72. Allen IV, pp. 402–9

Erasmus to Aloysius Marlianus. Louvain, 25 March 1521
. . . You caution me against entangling myself with Luther. I have taken your advice and have done my utmost to keep things quiet. Luther's party have urged me to join him and Luther's enemies have done their best to drive me to it by their furious attacks on me in their sermons. Neither have succeeded. Christ I know: Luther I know not. The Roman Church I know, and death will not part me from it till the Church departs from Christ. I abhor sedition. Would that Luther and the Germans abhorred it equally. It is strange to see how the two factions goad each other on, as if they were in collusion. Luther has hurt himself more than he has hurt his opponents by his last effusions, while the attacks on him are so absurd that many think the pope wrong in spite of themselves. I approve of those who stand by the pope, but I could wish them to be wiser than they are. They would devour Luther offhand. They may eat him, boiled or roast, for all that I care, but they mistake in linking him and me together, and they can finish him more easily without me than with me. I am surprised at Aleander; we were once friends. He was instructed to conciliate when he was

sent over—the pope wishing not to push matters to extremity. He would have done better to act with me. He would have found me with him, and not against him, on the pope's prerogative.

They pretend that Luther has borrowed from me. No lie can be more impudent. He may have borrowed from me as heretics borrow from Evangelists and Apostles, but not a syllable else. I beseech you, protect me from such calumnies. Let my letters be examined. I may have written unguardedly, but that is all. Inquire into my conversation. You will find that I have said nothing except that Luther ought to be answered and not crushed.

Even now I would prefer that things should be quietly considered and not embittered by platform railing. I would have the Church purified of evil, lest the good in it suffer by connection with what is indefensible; but in avoiding the Scylla of Luther I would have us also avoid Charybdis. If this be sin, then I own my guilt. I have sought to save the dignity of the Roman Pontiff, the honour of Catholic theology, and the welfare of Christendom. I have not defended Luther even in jest. In common with all reasonable men I have blamed the noisy bellowings of persons whom I will not name, whose real object is to prevent the spread of knowledge and to recover their own influence. Their numbers are not great but their power is enormous. But be assured of this, if any movement is in progress injurious to the Christian religion, or dangerous to the public peace or to the supremacy of the Holy See, it does not proceed from Erasmus. Time will show it. I have not deviated in what I have written one hair's breadth from the Church's teaching. We must bear almost anything rather than throw the world into confusion. There are seasons when we must even conceal the truth. The actual facts of things are not to be blurted out at all times and places, and in all companies. But every wise man knows that doctrines and usages have been introduced into the Church which have no real sanction, partly by custom, partly through obsequious canonists, partly by scholastic definitions, partly by the tricks and arts of secular sovereigns. Such excrescences must be removed, though the medicine must be administered cautiously, lest it make the disorder worse and the patient die. Plato says that men in general cannot appreciate reasoning, and may be deceived for their good. I know not whether this be right or wrong. For myself I prefer to be silent and introduce no novelties into religion. Many great persons have entreated me to support Luther. I have answered always that I will support him when he is on the Catholic side. They have asked me to draw up a formula of faith. I reply that I know of none, save the creed of the

Catholic Church, and I advise everyone who consults me to submit to the pope. I was the first to oppose the publication of Luther's books. I recommended Luther himself to publish nothing revolutionary. I feared always that revolution would be the end, and I would have done more had I not been afraid that I might be found fighting against the Spirit of God.

I caution everyone against reading libellous or anonymous books, books meant only to irritate; but I can advise only. I cannot compel. The world is full of poetasters and orators, and printing presses are at work everywhere. . . .

Froude, pp. 253–5. Allen IV, pp. 459–61

Erasmus to Peter Barbirius. Bruges, 13 August 1521
. . . The Louvain friars will not be reconciled to me, and they catch at anything, true or false, to bring me into odium. True, my tongue runs away with me. I jest too much, and measure other men by myself. Why should an edition of the New Testament infuriate them so? I settled at Louvain, as you know, at the Emperor's order. We set up our colleges for the three languages [Greek, Latin, and Hebrew]. The Carmelites did not like it, and would have stopped us had not Cardinal Adrian [later Pope Adrian VI] interfered. I did my best with the New Testament, but it provoked endless quarrels, Edward Lee pretended to have discovered 300 errors. They appointed a commission, which professed to have found bushels of them. Every dinner table rang with the blunders of Erasmus. I required particulars, and could not have them. At length a truce was patched up. They were to admit that my work had merit. I was to stop the wits who were mocking at Louvain theology. Then out came Luther's business. It grew hot. I was accused on one side from the pulpits of being in a conspiracy with Luther; on the other I was entreated to join him. I saw the peril of neutrality, but I cannot and will not be a rebel. Luther's friends quote, 'I came not to send peace on earth, but a sword.' Of course the Church requires reform, but violence is not the way to it. Both parties behaved like maniacs. You may ask me why I have not written against Luther. Because I had no leisure, because I was not qualified, because I would sooner face the lances of the Switzers than the pens of enraged theologians. There are plenty to do it besides me: bishops, cardinals, kings, with stakes and edicts as many as they please. Besides, it is not true that I have done nothing. Luther's friends (who were once mine also) do not think so. They have deserted me and call me a Pelagian. But if severity is to be the course, someone else, and not I, must use

the rod. God will provide a Nebuchadnezzar to scourge us if we need scourging.

It would be well for us if we thought less of our dogmas and more about the Gospel; but whatever is done ought to be done quietly, with no appeals to passion. The opinions of the leading men should be given in writing and under seal. The point is to learn the cause of all these disturbances, and stop the stream at the fountain. The princes must begin, and then I will try what I can do. My position at present is odious. In Flanders I am abused as a Lutheran. In Germany I am cried out against as an anti-Lutheran. I would forfeit life, fame, and all to find a means to compose the strife. . . .

Froude, pp. 287–8. Allen IV, p. 554

Erasmus to Archbishop William Warham. Bruges, 23 August 1521.
. . . The condition of things is extremely dangerous. I have to steer my own course, so as not to desert the truth of Christ through fear of man, and to avoid unnecessary risks. Luther has been sent into the world by the genius of discord. Every corner of it has been disturbed by him. All admit that the corruptions of the Church required a drastic medicine. But drugs wrongly given make the sick man worse. I said this to the King of Denmark lately. He laughed, and answered that small doses would be of no use. The whole system needed purging. For myself I am a man of peace, and hate quarrels. Luther's movement was not connected with learning, but it has brought learning into ill-repute, and the lean and barren dogmatists, who used to be my enemies, have now fastened on Luther, like the Greeks on Hector. I suppose I must write something about him. I will read his books, and see what can be done. . . .

Froude, pp. 288–91. Allen IV, pp. 567–8

PART III *The Watershed 1521–9*

Erasmus returned to Basel in November of 1521, and for eight years he acted as the general editor of John Froben's press. The years in Basel afforded Erasmus an opportunity to recast some of his earlier works. This is especially true of the *Adages* (1523, 1526, 1528) and *The Colloquies* which had begun as a set of exercises for teaching Latin composition, and soon became an instrument for reform. Erasmus issued new and enlarged editions of the *Colloquies* in 1522, 1523, 1524, 1526, 1527 and 1529. These delightfully witty conversations offered the reader a running commentary on contemporary events and magnified Erasmus' deep concern for social and religious reform. Erasmus' concept of Christianity was offended by pilgrimages and public processions. Such hollow displays of religious fervour seemed hopelessly out of step with the image of the historical Christ. Erasmus pleaded for more belief but fewer beliefs.

Erasmus also devoted considerable time to a new edition of the New Testament (in 1527) and new editions of *The Paraphrases on the New Testament* and of his *Epistles* (1521, 1528, 1529). Moreover, he edited and published editions of the following Church Fathers: Hilary (1523), Jerome (1524), Irenaeus (1526), Ambrose (1527), Augustine (1528–9), and Lactantius (1529). He also composed a number of popular religious treatises: *A Devout Treatise upon the Pater Noster* (1523), *A Method of Praying to God* (1524), and *The Christian Path* (1529). Finally, he defended unaffected Latin rhetoric against the blind imitators of Cicero (*Ciceronianus*, 1528). For Erasmus, what one said was far more important than how one said it.

But by far the most important work of Erasmus in this period was his *Discourse on Free Will* (*De Libero Arbitrio*) which appeared in 1524. Erasmus, appealing to reason and common sense, defended man's free will. He argued that the Christian, who was justified by faith in Christ's redemption, co-operated with God's grace to effect his salvation. In effect, Erasmus denounced predestination. Luther replied in 1525 (*De Servo Arbitrio*) that salvation depended exclusively on God's saving grace. Man was a wholly dependent creature. After 1525 it was certain that the two leaders of the Reformation had adopted uncompromising stances. What had begun as a friendly exchange of views, now hardened into vituperation and alienation. Erasmus reiterated his motto, 'I yield to none', as Luther clung to 'Here I stand'.

A   THE STORM CLOUDS

The years 1521 to 1524 prepared Erasmus for a more active role in the cause of the Reformation. He defended, albeit indirectly, the Hebraic studies of John Reuchlin against conservative opponents, going so far as to number Reuchlin among the saints in his *Colloquies*. However, the real danger to Erasmus' philosophy of Christ came not from the opponents of Reuchlin, but from the pen of a scriptural scholar who offered the faithful three intractable pamphlets in 1520: *On the Babylonian Captivity of the Church*, *An Appeal to the Nobility of the German Nation*, and *The Liberty of a Christian Man*. These treatises of Luther lit the fuse which ignited a revolution.

Erasmus to Bishop John Fisher. Basel, 1 September 1522
Reverend Father, your letter has greatly comforted me in such calamities. I am worn out in fact, not so much by my studies, failing which I could hardly live, as by recurring diseases: first there was an infectious cold, along with fever, and shortly after, the gravel. At each assault, that is to say, almost every fourth day, I am ready to die with pain. At the latest labours, the most tearing of all, my stomach was so upheaved that my system has not recovered. The weakness subsists and a touch of fever has set in. My poor body slowly declines from day to day with dysentery. I think it is some kind of senile phthisis.

My illness is in no small way aggravated by the relentless intrigues of a number of stupid people. The last act of the tragedy is now being performed in Rome. There is a certain Stuñica [Jacobus Lopis], a Spaniard, a raving impudent braggart, who is roused against me by the Preachers. It is now for the new Pope [Adrian VI] to settle the case. I know what he was at one time; what he will be in his high office, I do not know. The only thing I know is that he is a thorough scholastic, and not altogether up to good learning. His friendship and faithfulness I acknowledge and remember.

We had been considering for some days the work in hand, when your letter was delivered to us. I shall really set to work in earnest when settled. For I have been compelled through bad health to change my quarters. Many letters invite me to go to Rome.

I have been twice offered a pension of five hundred ducats a year, not counting the money for the journey, by the Reverend Bishop of Sion. But the thought of the Alps and the Apennines terrifies me: I wonder whether so weak a body as mine could be safely trusted there.

Besides, I am also expected in France. The King has kindly sent a safe-conduct. But I would rather see peace restored between the monarchs. In Brabant, they are stirring up great commotions about Luther. The whole matter is led by men who hate me—and that, through no fault of his—even more than Luther himself, though I am not Lutheran.

I loathe dissension. Meanwhile, whatever I choose to do, I must accomplish without further delay. Anyway, I shall let you know my decision.

There was no place where I could have found better accommodation for the winter than here, where I want for nothing. But the wines of the country disagree with me.

. . . [Johann] Reuchlin has gone before us to the Powers above. I numbered him among the saints in the *Colloquies* printed last summer. . . .

Rouschausse, pp. 79–81. Allen V, pp. 123–4

Erasmus to Adrian VI. Basel, 22 December 1522
. . . This is no ordinary storm. Earth and air are convulsed: arms, opinions, authorities, factions, hatreds, jarring one against the other. If your Holiness would hear from me what I think you should do to make a real cure, I will tell you in a secret letter. If you approve my advice you can adopt it. If not, let it remain private between you and me. We common men see and hear things which escape the ears of the great. But, above all, let no private animosities or private interests influence your judgment. We little dreamt when we jested together in our early years what times were coming. With the Faith itself in peril, we must beware of personal affections. I am sorry to be a prophet of evil but I see worse perils approaching than I like to think of, or than anyone seems to look for. . . .

Froude, p. 309. Allen V, p. 155

Erasmus to Marcus Laurinus. Basel, 1 February 1523
. . . Again, there are among those who favour Luther some who gnash their teeth and are furious because out of timidity of mind, as they

put it, I am deserting the evangelical cause, and not only deserting it, but also attempting to strengthen that of the popes, or, as they say, the papist cause. Now I have often enough already answered others on this point, but I will very willingly discuss the subject with any Lutheran whatsoever, provided he have a regard for justice; and I opine that I shall be able to prove my case from the points which he shall grant me. For firstly I shall ask him what he thinks of Luther. Undoubtedly he will declare him to be a holy and evangelical man, and a restorer of Christian piety. Then I shall ask him whether those who are devoted to him resemble him in this. Without doubt he will assert that to be so. Then I shall ask him whether it be in accord with the Gospel to drag anyone into their sect by force and artifice, especially when they know that the profession of such a belief as theirs is no less dangerous than was the profession of a Christian in the early days. It was the practice of the Jews to scour land and sea in order to entrap one proselyte into the net of the law. The Apostles attracted none by human artifices, and concealed the identity of those who had professed the name of Christ until the moment of acknowledging their faith was at hand.

I could say the same thing if the profession of the Lutheran faction were only a profession of evangelical belief, and if anyone could make that profession secretly amongst them at any time. Now I leave to others to decide as to what kind of a profession of faith theirs is. Whatever it is, it originated without my knowledge and progressed in spite of my warnings, even to the extent that a great part of the world began to applaud the spectacle. Then came the *Captivity of Babylon*, the *Abrogation of the Mass*, the defence of the entire doctrine of [John] Huss; besides other things which their being written in the Saxon tongue prevented me from reading. And yet, although so far I have pronounced no verdict on the dogmas of Luther, for many reasons, but principally because I perceived the matter to lie beyond the scope of my comprehension, yet I have given evidence in many of my letters that I am entirely averse to any association with the followers of Luther, and that I desire a little more Christian moderation in those of his writings which I have happened to read, and wish for less bitterness. Here I shall again call on my Lutheran friend to say whether or not he deems that an excellent and praiseworthy deed which he performs at great risk of his own life and serious risk to the lives of others. He will reply, I suppose, that it is truly apostolic, and worthy of eternal remembrance. Well, now, with your permission, who would not deem me the most arrogant of living mortals were I to arrogate so much praise to myself, when I did not deserve the least little bit? Nay, who would not think me more insane than ever Orestes was, if I were to angle for a most empty glory purchased at the risk of my life? Long since, many monarchs and church dignitaries have felt persuaded that I was the source, the originator, the defender, and the supporter of the entire teaching of Luther, and that, moreover, the books which are in circulation under his name are really mine. Ought I in silence to suffer such glory to be given to me? St. John the Baptist cries out 'I am not the Christ!' and does it become me to remain silent? But they will say, 'You have given too much proof of this in many epistles.' Nay, so far, in so many epistles, I have yet been hardly able to persuade some people, so deeply infixed was this impudent lie in the minds of the many.

With respect to moderation and abuse, again shall I question my Lutheran friend whether or not he deems it expedient to spread the teaching of Luther as widely as possible throughout the world, and to make it commendable to both the highest and the lowest. Of a surety he will answer that it is especially expedient. Why then are some of them angry with Erasmus for desiring to see removed from his books two things which particularly destroy confidence and alienate the minds of all good men?—I allude to his arrogance and his uncontrolled abuse. And yet these things are so remarkably manifest that those who defend him most warmly have no excuse which they may offer save that my sins have so deserved, so that I am scourged as with scorpions by this harsh scolder. The first thing that made me suspicious about the spirit of Luther was the ferocity of his pen and his ever-ready abuse; and I have no doubt . . . that others have had the same experience. . . .

I should like here again to summon my Lutheran friend, whom I have chosen as a rather just judge. The causes of indignation are of this sort. I appeared in some letters of mine, I know not where, to offer a hope that, if I were allowed, and had the leisure, I should write in behalf of the peace of the Christian world and of the dignity of the Apostolic See. Now how does such a promise adversely affect Luther? But they pretend that I have written against him something, I know not what, which is certainly not true so far, although all the rest of the world is preparing to write against him. Why should they be angry with me alone if I bestir myself in the same direction, having been ordered to do so by those whom it were scarcely safe to refuse? But I think my critic will concede me this: that Luther is not so perversely unjust as to be angry if one dissents from him in anything, since he permits himself to differ, not only from all the Doctors of the Church, but also from the decrees of the Councils; or consider himself injured, if someone, abstaining from abuse, search out the truth by the testimony of the Scriptures (to which he attributes prime importance) and by solid reasoning. For he summons all, and the Roman pontiff summons all no less insistently than Luther, to argue out the case by means of solid reasonings and by the testimony of the Scriptures. Hence it was not just for them to threaten me, before they had seen with what reasoning and with what moderation I would write.

Let us hear then the rest of my offences. 'He still esteems highly and acknowledges the Roman Church,' they say. 'He still demands that the Roman pontiff be honoured, and he writes that no good man has ever withdrawn himself from that jurisdiction.' These and many other things of the same sort appear in their letters. Of jurisdiction I have never written. At times I have written that all pious men respect the dignity of the pope. For who would not respect the dignity of him who represents for us by his evangelical virtues Christ himself? And I add the following whenever I defer to the dignity of the pope: nobody knows in what the true dignity of the pope consists; nor is this stated in one place in my lucubrations. But I have learned from the Gospels and the Apostolic Epistles that honour is to be given to even heathen kings, unless they command us to do what is plainly impious. By that rule I deem no bishop's dignity should be contemned. And is it not impious to despise a good bishop? But they paint for themselves those whom they wish to contemn. 'And who is the Roman pontiff?' they exclaim. 'Is he not a burner of the Gospel, an enemy of God, a seducer of all Christian people?' If they are speaking of such a pontiff as that, he would never be approved by me. And yet, even if there were such, it is not for me to hurl them from their throne, for Christ still lives, and holds in His hand the whip to scourge such from His temple.

'But there is no hope,' they say, 'that a better one than Leo will follow.' Now I am not the judge of Leo; he has his own judge by whom he stands or falls. If so many good ones precede him, why may there not be the hope that popes similar to those early ones may follow? But of that I allege nothing, lest I may seem to flatter. When adjured to do so by the impious high-priest, Christ himself made answer; nor was he wholly silent when ordered to speak by Pilate. How did Paul plead his cause before Festus, Felix, and Agrippa? Did he not call them tyrants, servants of the devil, slaves of sin, and enemies of God, who were presently to be sentenced to eternal fire? Now, see what those people would have replied to anyone who would excuse me for my forbearance. 'That is the way Erasmus should speak,' my critic says: 'Pope, thou art Antichrist; bishops, you are seducers; your See of Rome is abominable to God'; and many other even more detestable things of the same tenor. They do not approve of the forbearance of Erasmus, unless they preface their praise with such things as those, so evangelically, forsooth. This first I shall enquire from my critic, whether he thinks such demands which he makes of me are just? and then whether he considers them useful in this Lutheran affair? If I were to write such things as those against good popes, would I not appear somewhat unjust? If I were to rage in that manner against bad popes, what else should I do than stir up hornets' nests to sting myself and many others? . . .

There remains still to be discussed my very greatest offence. In my *Paraphrase*, in which I explain the ninth chapter of the Apostle St. Paul to the Romans, I attribute a small degree of efficacy to Freewill, following therein Origen and Jerome. Now, since my Paraphrase is a sort of commentary, and since I profess in many passages that I am following the approved and early interpreters, what crime do I commit if I follow here and there Origen and Jerome, writers in my estimation who are not to be contemned in the matter of the Scriptures? Moreover, my book appeared before Luther had promulgated his dogma, or rather that of Wickliffe, that whatever we do either of good or evil is of absolute necessity. For my *Paraphrase* was printed at Louvain in 1517, and existed some months in manuscript at Antwerp previous to being printed, and a certain person was called quite Erasmian because he believed as I do about Freewill, and differed from Luther. But they pardoned him for it on the ground that he was a young man with a bright future, who would in a short time feel differently about the matter.

Here again I call on my fair-minded critic, and ask him why I should be brought to book as the author of this opinion, when I had written it before Luther had promulgated his dogma, all the theologians, both ancient and modern, Origen, Jerome, Chrysostom, Hilary, Arnobius, Scotus, and Thomas, being in agreement with me on the point; and why anyone who dissents from Luther should be called Erasmian rather than Hilarian or Jeronymite, especially since I did not undertake to treat the matter at any length in my *Paraphrase*, but casually passed over it, just as did St. Paul, who did not deign to there respond to an insincere questioner. And yet observe, dear reader, how much less weight I there attribute to Freewill than do either the ancient writers or the later universities. I suspect that these are the words in the ninth chapter by which they are offended. When I propounded that monstrous question which is put to God, and by which some endeavour to fasten on him an injustice, 'No,' I say, 'there is something [which] resides in our own will and our own effort, but it is so little that, compared with the gratuitous beneficence of God, it seems to be nothing at all. No one is damned except by his own fault; no one is saved unless by the grace of God. Therefore He deems those worthy whom he wishes, but in such a way that it is a reason for you to be grateful, not to complain.' Those words appear in my *Paraphrase*.

I saw herein the peril of Scylla on the one hand drawing us to a trust in works, which I confess to be the greatest pest of religion; on the other hand I beheld a Charybdis, an evil still more formidable by which many are now held, saying: 'We will follow our inclinations; for whether we torment ourselves or indulge our will, yet what God has once decreed for us will happen.' Thus I so qualified my pronouncement on the matter as to allow some little weight to Freewill, lest I should open a window to so capital a stupidity that, throwing away all effort towards a better life, everybody should do as he pleased. And yet I wrote this quite unaware that there was anyone who wished to remove entirely all power of Freewill, a dogma such that, even if it struck me as being true, yet should I hesitate to spread it in naked words among the populace. Everyone knows that before the days of Christ philosophers disputed about fate; and from them have come down to us insoluble questions about foreknowledge, predestination by God, Freewill of man, and of what is to happen to us hereafter; in all of which questions I deem it the very best policy not to bother oneself too anxiously, since they form for us an impenetrable abyss. . . .

Mangan II, pp. 210-15. Allen V, pp. 221-7

Erasmus to Pope Adrian VI. Basel, 22 March 1523
. . . Would that I possessed the ability which you attribute to me, that I might put an end to this dissension; for I would not hesitate to heal these public evils even at the cost of my own life. In the first place, there are many who wield a more facile pen than myself, and this affair is not to be settled by writing. My learning is far beneath mediocrity, and what I may have is derived from the ancient writers and is fitter for the pulpit than for the arena. As for my power to influence, of what avail would be the authority of such a humble individual as myself? Could Erasmus influence those whom so many universities, so many monarchs, and even the sovereign pontiff himself have failed to move? If I ever enjoyed their personal regard, it has either grown

so cold now that it no longer exists, or it has entirely perished, or, finally, it has been changed to hatred. I, who was formerly described in a myriad of letters as 'the thrice-greatest hero,' 'the king of letters,' 'the star of Germany,' 'the sun of learning,' 'the mainstay of literature,' 'the champion of a more genuine theology,' am now passed over in silence, or depicted in far different colours.

I care nothing for such empty titles, which were only a burden to me; but see the epithets they launch at my head, the vicious pamphlets with which they attack me, and the threats they hold out against me! There were not lacking some who threatened me with death if I stirred. . . .

You will say, 'So far I hear nothing but complaints; I am waiting to hear your plan.' Now what I had said is a part of my plan; however, I will come to that now. I observe it to be favoured by many that this evil should be remedied by severity, but I fear that the event may hereafter prove this to have been an unwise counsel. I see a greater chance than I could wish that the matter may end in an atrocious slaughter. I am not now discussing what these people deserve, but what will further the interests of public tranquillity. The malady has spread too deeply to be cured either by knife or cautery. I admit that formerly among the English the faction of Wickliffe was thus stifled by the power of the kings, but that the sect was really stifled rather than eradicated. And yet I know not whether what was feasible in that kingdom, which was under the sway of one king, would be possible in so vast an empire as ours, cut up as it is into so many kingdoms. It is evident that there will be no need of my advice should there be a decision to overcome the evil by imprisonment, scourgings, confiscation, exiles, rigorous penalties, and death. However, I perceive that a different line of treatment is most pleasing to your gentle nature, that you would rather cure than punish. This would not be very difficult if all were of the same mind as yourself, and, laying aside their private inclinations, would, as you write, sincerely seek the glory of Christ and the salvation of Christians. But if each one is intent on his own private profit, if theologians insist that their authority bolstered up on every side shall be supported, if the monks allow nothing to be taken away from their privileges, if the kings cling to their rights with tenacity, it will be most difficult to act for the benefit of everybody.

Our first duty will be to find out the sources whence this evil revives so often, and before all to apply the remedy to those. Then it will be very useful if pardon is again extended to those who have erred by the persuasion or by the urging of others; or rather a sort of amnesty for all their former misdeeds which seem to have occurred by some fatality. If God deals thus with us day after day, forgetting our offences as often as the sinner is sincerely sorry, why should not the Vicar of God do the same? And yet, meanwhile, many innovations are repressed by ruler and magistrates which are little aids to piety, but great helps to sedition. I could wish, if it were possible, that the privilege of publishing pamphlets were limited to some extent. Let there also be given to the world the hope of having certain things remedied of which it justly complains. At the sweet name of liberty all will breathe again. We must aim at this in every possible way as far as it can be done without damage to religion; and we must aim at relieving the consciences of men as far as that is consonant with the dignity of princes and bishops. But this dignity must be estimated by those things in which their dignity truly consists, just as the liberty of the people is to be estimated. . . .

Mangan II, pp. 206, 207–8. Allen V, pp. 258–61

Erasmus to Paul Bombasius, 19 January 1524
. . . At Rome they make me out to be a Lutheran, but in Germany I am held as an extreme anti-Lutheran . . . I suppose you are aware of the defamatory pamphlet which Hutten got out against me. Besides him many others have books in preparation, and are ready to launch them on the first occasion that I shall write against Luther. And yet, urged as I am on all sides by kings and my own friends, I have assumed that task, although I know that I shall bring about nothing but a renewal of these tumults. For there is nothing more pertinacious than these people; and you would hardly believe how numerous they are. Meanwhile, during the interregnum, Stuñica at Rome has returned to his miserable work, as I hear. Such is the bad luck of Erasmus. Of this present pontiff my mind has very happy presentiments, and I will crawl thither if I can, even though only half alive. . . .

Mangan II, p. 235. Allen V, p. 385

Erasmus to Clement VII. 13 February 1524
. . . If your Holiness could only know with what fidelity, with what constancy, I have behaved in this affair [of Luther], and that neither the solicitations of mighty princes nor the machinations of learned friends, nor again the hatred of certain theologians and monks who, by reason of my services to the study of the languages and good literature, hate me even worse than they hate Luther, have been able to force me to associate myself with the promoters of this seditious under-

taking, or to conspire against the dignity of your See. And because on this account I am enduring so much hostility and menaces from the Germans, your Holiness will deem it unfair that Stuñica should so often and with such impunity rage at me with his furious and much-talked-of screeds, which bring disgrace on Rome and hatred on the name of the pontiff. For he everywhere boasts that he is voicing the sentiment of your beloved city of Rome, although it is a fact that he is acting contrary to the commands of the cardinals and contrary to the orders of Leo and Adrian. Believe me, most Holy Father, those persons who are prompting this comedian to whom such calumnies come naturally are serving very poorly either the pontifical dignity or the interests of public tranquillity, but are yielding to their own private animosities in this thing, as well as manifesting a strange sort of insanity.

He has collected from all the books which I issued before the name of Luther was heard of, a few bits and scraps which he corrupts and interprets in the worse sense possible, but in such a manner that, even without anyone replying to him, any reader with the slightest sense of fairness will execrate the mind of such a fellow. If it be proper to calumniate people in that way, I will find you many things in the works of Jerome and Bernard. When I wrote I never in the least suspected that these times were at hand, for, had I known it, I should have passed over many of these matters in silence, or I should have written them otherwise; not that they are impious, but that the evil-minded lay hold of everything which suits their purpose. . . .

I have always submitted myself and my works to the judgment of the Roman Church, and will not object even if she pass upon me an adverse decision, for I will endure everything rather than become seditious. But my confidence is very firm that your Holiness's sense of justice will not allow me to be given up to the insane hatreds of a few people.

As a pledge of my intentions towards you, I am sending you my *Paraphrase on the Acts of the Apostles*, which by chance has been just now issued from the press. I had destined it for the Cardinal of York, whose most loving patronage I enjoy for a long time past; but I have changed my mind, and will dedicate to him the book *On Freewill* against Luther which I now have in hand, and which I think will be more acceptable to him. The emperor and Margaret [the emperor's aunt] are inviting me back to Brabant; and the French king is enticing me with mountains of gold to go to his court. But nothing shall tear me away from Rome, only death, or the gravel, more cruel still, provided I shall feel that your sense of justice will be my future protection against my calumniators. I do not expect that my teachings will be approved by all, but I do trust that my fidelity and sincerity of conscience will speak in my behalf with all good and fair-minded men. . . .

Mangan II, pp. 233-4. Allen V, pp. 398-9

Erasmus to Martin Luther. Basel, 8 May 1524
I do not admit that you love evangelical sincerity more than I do, for there is nothing that I will not endure in its behalf, and up to the present moment I have sought every occasion to make the Gospel common to all. Moreover, what you style my weakness or my ignorance is partly conscience, partly good judgment. In reading your works I greatly fear that Satan in some way is deluding your mind, while other things of yours so captivate me that I wish my fears to be false. I am unwilling to profess what I am not yet persuaded of, much less that which I do not understand. So far I have helped the interests of the Gospel much better than many who boast that they are Evangelicals. I perceive arising many abandoned and seditious men on account of all this. I observe a decline of literature and the sciences. I remark a severing of friendships, and fear that this tumult may turn out to be a bloody one. If your mind is sincere, I pray God that he will favour what you are doing. For myself nothing shall so corrupt me that I shall knowingly betray the Gospel for human reasons.

I have written nothing so far against you that I did not see could be done without injury to the Gospel, although by writing I could have won great applause from princes. I have been opposed to those only who endeavoured to persuade the rulers that there was a compact between you and me, that we agreed in everything, and that whatever you taught was in my works. This opinion can scarcely even now be torn from the minds of some of them. Whatever you write against me gives me no great concern. When I consider the world, nothing could fall out more happily for me. I desire to render this soul of mine to Christ pure, and I want every one to be of the same frame of mind. If you are prepared to give a reason to all for the faith that is in you, why do you take it in bad part that any one should dispute with you for the sake of learning better? Perhaps, Erasmus by writing against you may do more good to the cause of the Gospel than some foolish scribblers of your own party who will not suffer a man to be a quiet spectator of these contentions; and oh! that they may not have a tragical issue. But they drive me to the direct opposite of your course, even if our monarchs did not demand it. Their wickedness renders the

Gospel hateful to those who are inclined to be prudent, and compels their rulers to crush their tumults. Now that cannot be done without injuring the innocent. They listen to no one, not even to you. They fill the world with crazy books, for sake of which they deem it proper to contemn the orthodox Fathers.

But it would take too long to write about such matters. I pray that the Lord may turn all things to His glory. You cry for moderation in my *Spongia*, when in that work I said not a word about Hutten's life, his luxury, his mistresses, his most abandoned methods of gambling, his vainglorious boastings which had become intolerable to even his most patient friends, his wastefulness, his extortion of money from the Carthusians, his cutting off the ears of two Dominican monks, his assault and robbery of three abbots on the public thoroughfare, on account of which one of his servants was decapitated, as well as other well-known villainies. And while he was never provoked to it by a word from me, he broke friendship with me in favour of a most abandoned rascal, and charged me with such a load of false crimes as no buffoon would charge another with. I do make mention of his most perfidiously making public my letter to [Albert of] Mainz with the suppression of his name; but I say not a word about another perfidious act which he perpetrated on me. He induced me to commend him to the emperor's court by many letters, although he had already conspired against the emperor, desiring only to abuse the name of the emperor in order to get a wife. Under such provocation by him whom I had befriended, was I not within my rights to express myself thereon? And yet I am called immoderate. Why is Otto [Brunfels] standing with Hutten? I never by a single word offended him for which he should now rage at me. And you call such men like to me? I do not consider them men but rather furies, so far am I from admitting them like to me. Is it by such monsters as these, forsooth, that the Church shall be restored? Has the newborn Church such columns as these? Shall I entangle myself in such a compact? . . .

Mangan II, pp. 239–40. Allen V, pp. 451–3

B 'ON THE FREEDOM OF THE WILL' (1524)

Erasmus published *On the Freedom of the Will* to protest against Luther's extreme views. He was angry with Luther but he mollified his displeasure. In offering a gentle rebuke, Erasmus disarmed his critics. Indeed, his scholarly examination of the scriptural evidence for and against the doctrine of Free Will brought denunciations from both the left and the right. But Erasmus was clearly his own man. He steadfastly refused to join either camp.

Erasmus to Duke George of Saxony. Basel, 6 September 1524

... That hitherto I have not obeyed the exhortations of your highness arose from many reasons, but from two in particular. First, because I felt that on account of my years and my disposition I was unequal to such a very risky business, and, secondly, because, from some strange trait of my nature, I have always shrunk from gladiatorial contests of this nature. For what is accomplished by the screeds which are now flying around everywhere, other than what is usually done in the gladiatorial arena? Moreover, whatever Luther's doctrine may be, I have always regarded himself as a necessary evil in these universally corrupt phases of the Church's condition; and I was in hopes that from him, as from a somewhat bitter and violent remedy, something of health-giving efficacy might be developed in the body of Christian people. But now, since I find that many take my moderation for a collusion with Luther, with whom I have never had any private understanding; and since I see that under the pretext of the Gospel there is being brought forth a new sort of characters who are shameless, insolent, and ungovernable, who, in a word, are such that not even Luther himself can endure them; and yet with the same recklessness with which they contemn bishops and rulers, they contemn even Luther himself. I enter the arena at almost the same age at which Publius the actor entered on the stage; and how happy the issue of it is to be, I know not, though I certainly trust that it may be profitable and beneficial to the republic of Christ.

I am sending to your majesty my book *On Freewill*, concerning which I saw your most erudite epistle some time ago. I have been spurred on in this matter by the letter of his serene majesty of England, and by that of Clement VII, but far more forcibly by the wickedness of some of those brawlers, who will destroy the Gospel and learning together unless they are restrained. I desired the tyranny of the Pharisees to be destroyed, not changed; but, if it is to be preserved, I would prefer the popes and bishops just as they are, rather than some of those sordid Phalarises who are the most intolerable of all. I await the judgment of your highness, for whom I desire every good. . . .

Mangan II, pp. 245–6, Allen V, pp. 543–4

Erasmus to Philipp Melanchthon. Basel, 10 December 1524

. . . The pope's advocates have been the pope's worst friends, and the extravagant Lutherans have most hurt Luther. I would have held aloof had it been possible. I am no judge of other men's beliefs. There are actors enough on the stage, and none can say how all will end. I do not object generally to the evangelical doctrines, but there is much in Luther's teachings which I dislike. He runs everything which he touches into extravagance. True, Christendom is corrupt and needs the rod, but it would be better, in my opinion, if we could have the pope and the princes on our side. [Lorenzo] Campeggio was gentle enough, but could do nothing. Clement was not opposed to reform, but when I urged that we should meet him half-way nobody listened. The violent party carries all before it. They tear the hoods off monks who might as well have been left in their cells. Priests are married, and images are torn down. I would have had religion purified without destroying authority. Licence need not be given to sin. Practices grown corrupt by long usage might be gradually corrected without throwing everything into confusion. Luther sees certain things to be wrong, and in flying blindly at them causes them more harm than he cures. Order human things as you will, there will still be faults enough, and there are remedies worse than the disease. Is it so great a thing to have removed images and changed the canon of the Mass? What good is done by telling foolish lads that the pope is Antichrist, that confession carries the plague, that they cannot do right if they try, that good works and merits are a vain imagination, that free will is an illusion, that all things hold together by necessity, and that man can do nothing of himself? Such things are said. You will tell me that Luther does not say them—that only idiots say them. Yes, but Luther encourages men who say them, and if I had a contract to make I would rather deal with a papist than with some evangelicals that I have known. It is not always safe to remove the Camarinas of this world, and Plato says you cannot guide the multitude without deceiving them. Christians must not lie, but they need not tell the whole truth. Would that Luther had tried as hard to improve popes and princes as to expose their faults. He speaks bitterly of me. He may say what he pleases. [Andreas] Carlstadt has been here. He has published a book in German maintaining that the Eucharist is only a sign. All Berne has been in an uproar, and the printer imprisoned. . . .

You are anxious that Luther shall answer me with moderation. Unless he writes in his own style, the world will say we are in connivance. Do not fear that I shall oppose evangelical truth. I left many faults in him unnoticed lest I should injure the Gospel. I hope mankind will be the better for the acrid medicines with which he has dosed them. Perhaps we needed a surgeon who would use knife and cautery. Carlstadt and he are going so fast that Luther himself may come to regret popes and bishops. His genius is vehement. We recognise in him the *Pelidae stomachum cedere nescii*. The devil is a clever fellow. Success like Luther's might spoil the most modest of men.

Froude, pp. 327-8. Allen V, pp. 593-6; 596-8

Erasmus to Duke George of Saxony. Basel, 12 December 1524
. . . When Luther first spoke the whole world applauded, and your highness among the rest. Divines who are now his bitterest opponents were then on his side. Cardinals, even monks, encouraged him. He had taken up an excellent cause. He was attacking practices which every honest man condemned, and contending with a set of harpies, under whose tyranny Christendom was groaning. Who could then dream how far the movement would go? Had Daniel foretold it to me, I would not have believed him. Luther himself never expected to produce such an effect. After his theses had come out I persuaded him to go no further. I doubted if he had learning enough. I was afraid of riots. I urged the printers to set in type no more books of his. He wrote to me. I cautioned him to be moderate. The emperor was then well inclined to him. He had no enemies save a few monks and papal commissioners, whose trade he had spoilt. These people, fools that they were, kindled a fire, and it was then said to be all my fault—I ought to have silenced Luther! I thought no one could be less fit. My old enemies took up the cry, and told the emperor that I was the person to do it. They only wanted to throw me among the wolves. What could I have done? They required me to revoke what I had said at first in Luther's favour. A pretty condition! I was to lie against my own soul, make myself the hangman of a set of prostitute wretches, and draw the hatred on myself of all Luther's supporters. I have or had some popularity in Europe. I should have lost it all, and have been left naked to be torn in pieces by the wild beasts. You say the emperor

and the pope will stand up for me. How can the emperor and the pope help me when they can hardly help themselves? To call on me to put myself forward is to saddle an ox or overload a broken-down horse. I am to sacrifice myself for the Catholic Faith! It is not for everyone to uphold the Ark. Even Jerome, when he attacks heresy, becomes almost a heretic. I do it! Are there no bishops, no college dignitaries, no hosts of divines? Surely among so many there were fitter persons than I. Some really tried. Great persons declared war. The pope put out a Bull, the emperor put out an edict, and there were prisons, faggots, and burnings. Yet all was in vain. The mischief only grew. What could a pigmy like Erasmus do against a champion who had beaten so many giants? There were men of intellect on Luther's side to whom I had looked up with respect. I wondered what they found in him to impress them; but so it was. I thought I must be growing blind. I did see, however, that the world was besotted with ritual. Scandalous monks were ensnaring and strangling consciences. Theology had become sophistry. Dogmatism had grown to madness, and, besides, there were the unspeakable priests, and bishops, and Roman officials. Perhaps I thought that such disorders required the surgeon, and that God was using Luther as he used Pharaoh and Nebuchadnezzar. Luther could not have succeeded so signally if God had not been with him, especially when he had such a crew of admirers behind him. I considered that it was a case for compromise and agreement. Had I been at Worms, I believe I could have brought it to that. The emperor was not unwilling. Adrian, Clement, Campeggio have not been unwilling. The difficulty lay elsewhere. Luther's patrons were stubborn and would not yield a step. The Catholic divines breathed only fire and fury. If that was to be the way, there was no need of me. I conceived, moreover, that if it was fit and right to burn a man for contradicting articles decreed by the Church, there was no law to burn him for holding mistaken opinions on other subjects, as long as he defended them quietly and was otherwise of blameless life. The Paris divines do not think on the papal power as the Italian divines think, but they do not burn each other. Thomists and Scotists differ, but they can work in the same schools. Stakes and prisons are vulgar remedies. Two poor creatures have been burnt at Brussels, and the whole city has turned Lutheran. If the infection had touched only a few it might be stamped out, but it has gone so far that kings may catch it. I do not say let it alone, but do not make it worse by bad treatment. Fear will alter nothing, and spasmodic severity exasperates. If you put the fire out by force, it will burst up again. I trust, I hope that Luther will make a few concessions and that pope and princes may still consent to peace.

May Christ's dove come among us, or else Minerva's owl. Luther has administered an acrid dose to a diseased body. God grant it prove salutary. Your highness would not have written as you have done if you knew all that I could tell you. The pope, the emperor, his brother Ferdinand, the King of England, wrote to me in a far different tone. Your freedom does not offend me. It rises only out of your zeal for the Faith. I risked the loss of my best friends by refusing to join Luther, but I did not break off my connection with them because they did join him; and Adrian and Campeggio, and the King of England, and the Cardinal of York all say that I did right. I vex Luther more by continuing my intimacy with them than I could do with the most violent abuse. . . .

Froude, pp. 329-31. Allen V, pp. 602-7

Erasmus to Martin Luther. Basel, 11 April 1526
Your letter has been delivered too late; but had it arrived in the best of time, it would not have moved me one whit. I am not so simple as to be appeased by one or two pleasantries or soothed by flattery after receiving so many more than mortal wounds. Your nature is by now known to all the world, but you have so tempered your pen that never have you written against anyone so frenziedly; nay, what is more abominable, so maliciously. Now it occurs to you that you are a weak sinner, whereas at other times you insist almost on being taken for God. You are a man, as you write, of violent temperament, and you take pleasure in this remarkable argument. Why then did you not pour forth this marvellous piece of invective on the Bishop of Rochester [John Fisher] or on John Dobneck of Wendelstein? They attack you personally and provoke you with insults, while my *Diatribe* was a courteous disputation. And what has all this to do with the subject— all this facetious abuse, these slanderous lies, charging me with atheism, Epicureanism, scepticism in articles of the Christian profession, blasphemy, and what not—besides many other points on which I [in the *De Libero Arbitrio*, 1524] am silent? I take these charges the less hardly, because in all this there is nothing to make my conscience disturb me. If I did not think as a Christian of God and the Holy Scriptures, I could not wish my life prolonged even until tomorrow. If you had conducted your case with your usual vehemence, without frenzied abuse, you would have provoked fewer men against you. As things are, you have been pleased to fill more than a third part of the volume with such

abuse, giving free rein to your feelings. How far you have given way to me the facts themselves show—so many palpable crimes do you fasten on me; while my *Diatribe* was not even intended to stir up those matters which the world itself knows of.

You imagine, I suppose, that Erasmus has no supporters. More than you think. But it does not matter what happens to us two, least of all to myself who must shortly go hence, even if the whole world were applauding us: it is *this* that distresses me, and all the best spirits with me, that with that arrogant, impudent, seditious temperament of yours you are shattering the whole globe in ruinous discord, exposing good men and lovers of good learning to certain frenzied Pharisees, arming for revolt the wicked and the revolutionary, and in short so carrying on the cause of the Gospel as to throw all things sacred and profane into chaos; as if you were eager to prevent this storm from turning at last to a happy issue; I have ever striven towards such an opportunity. What you owe me, and in what coin you have repaid me—I do not go into that. All that is a private matter; it is the public disaster which distresses me, and the irremediable confusion of everything, for which we have to thank only your uncontrolled nature, that will not be guided by the wise counsel of friends, but easily turns to any excess at the prompting of certain inconstant swindlers. I know not whom you have saved from the power of darkness; but you should have drawn the sword of your pen against those ungrateful wretches and not against a temperate disputation. I would have wished you a better mind, were you not so delighted with your own. Wish me what you will, only not your mind, unless God has changed it for you. . . .

. . . I confess that it is right that the authority of Holy Writ of itself shall weigh more than all the opinions of the whole of mankind. But this is not a controversy about the Scriptures. Both of us receive and venerate the selfsame Scriptures, but the trouble is about the sense of the Scriptures. . . . 'What is the need of an interpreter, when the Scripture is so plain?' But, if it is so plain, why have so many excellent men groped blindly for so many centuries, and this in a matter so important that they themselves earnestly desire it to seem clear? If the Scriptures contain nothing obscure, what need was there for prophecy in the times of the Apostles? They exclaim that this was the gift of the Holy Ghost. . . . Well, then to whom did this gift pass after the death of the Apostles? If it passed to everybody, then every interpretation of ours is uncertain. If it passed to nobody, then every interpretation of our is uncertain today when so many obscurities are puzzling the erudite. If it passed to those who succeeded the

Apostles, then someone may cry out that for many centuries the successors of the Apostles had not the Apostolic spirit. And yet of these men we may assume very probably, other things being equal, that God infused His spirit into them when He gave them their mission, just as we believe it more probable that He gave grace to the one who was baptised than to the one who was not baptised.

But [he says] Holy Writ cannot be at variance with itself, since all of it proceeds from the same spirit. . . . Now I understand freewill to be that quality of the human will by which a man is able to apply himself to those things which lead to eternal salvation or to turn away from them. . . . *Ecclesiasticus*, Chapter XV, says: 'God made man from the beginning, and left him in the hand of his own counsel. He added His commandments and precepts. If thou wilt keep the commandments and perform acceptable fidelity forever, they shall preserve thee. He hath set water and fire before thee; stretch forth thy hand to which thou wilt. Before man is life and death, good and evil; that which he shall choose shall be given him.' . . .

I am pleased with the opinion of those who contribute something to freewill, but very much more to grace. You must not avoid the Scylla of arrogance in such a way that you may be cast on the Charybdis of despair and inaction. . . .

'Why,' you may say, 'should anything be granted to freewill?' That there may be something which may deservedly be charged to the wicked who have willingly failed to respond to the grace of God; that the calumnious charge of cruelty and injustice on the part of God may be removed; that despair on our part may be avoided; that excessive security may be shunned; and that we may be stimulated to endeavour. For these causes freewill has been laid down as a dogma by almost all men, but of no avail without the grace of God, lest we might arrogate anything to ourselves. But some one may say, 'Of what avail is freewill if it works nothing?' I reply, of what avail is man at all, if God works in him just as the potter in his clay, and just as He would in a stone? Now, if this matter has been sufficiently demonstrated to be such that it is not expedient, as far as piety is concerned, to scrutinise it too closely, especially among the uneducated; if I have shown that this opinion is based on more numerous and more evident passages of Scripture than the other; if it is plain that Holy Writ is in many passages obscure and figurative, or even at first glance seems to be in disagreement with itself and that, on that account, whether we wish it or not, we must depart from it verbally and literally somewhat, and must modify the sense by interpretation; and if finally there is set forth the

many inconveniences, I will not say absurdities, which would follow
if freewill were once entirely taken away, and if it were openly brought
to pass, by the accepting of this judgment of which I have spoken,
that nothing of those things would perish of which Luther piously
and in a Christian manner has discussed—about supreme love for God,
about abolishing trust in our merits, our works, our endeavours, and
about transferring such to God and His promises—I would now desire
the reader to weigh this and say whether he would think it just to
condemn this judgment of so many of the Doctors of the Church which
the consent of so many ages and peoples has approved, and to take in
its place certain erroneous opinions on account of which the Christian
world is now convulsed? If these latter are true, I candidly confess
the dullness of my mind in not being able to understand them. Of a
certainty I will not knowingly resist the truth; I sincerely favour the
freedom which is truly of the Gospel, and I detest whatever is opposed
to the Gospel. I do not herein play the part of a judge, as I have already
said, but of one who would thresh out the matter thoroughly; and
yet I am truly able to affirm this, that in discussing this matter I have
preserved that religious point of view which was in the olden days
demanded of the judges appointed for the consideration of these
capital cases. Old a man as I am, it will not shame me or be irksome
to learn from a young man, provided he teaches me what is more
satisfactory to my judgment, and does it with the gentleness of the
Gospel. Here I am sure someone will say, 'Let Erasmus learn to know
Christ and be strong; let him dismiss his human prudence, for no one
understands such things as these who has not the Spirit of God.' If I do
not yet understand what Christ is, I have hitherto certainly wandered
far afield; still I would surely like to learn what spirit has guided so
many Doctors and Christian people; for it is probable that the people
understood what the bishops, who do not understand this new doctrine,
used to teach them for now nearly thirteen centuries. I have finished:
let others judge. . . .

                                        Huizinga, pp. 240–42. Allen VI, pp. 306–7

Erasmus to Charles V. Basel, 2 September 1527
. . . Relying on the protection of popes and princes, but especially on
your Majesty, I have drawn on my head with great danger to my life
the whole Lutheran faction, which I would were not so widely spread.
If proof of this is needed, the *Servum arbitrium,* which Luther in a
more than hostile manner wrote against me, will testify, as will the two
books of the *Hyperaspistes* in which I reply to him. Now, after this

movement of Luther has begun to decline, and this partly from my efforts and trials, there are arising there [in Spain] certain people who, under a feigned pretext of religious zeal, are looking out for the interests of their bellies and their desire for power. I am fighting for Christ, not for the interests of men, while they are rendering Spain, that most fortunate country for many reasons, a land of unrest by these unsettled tumults. From preludes of this sort we shall see at length the greatest tempests arise; for, as a fact, this Lutheran movement sprang from much slighter causes. As far as I am concerned, I shall not cease to the last breath of my life to cherish the cause of Christian piety; and it will be the part of your Majesty's kindness constantly and continually to favour those who sincerely and stoutly defend the Church of God. Under the banners of Christ and your own I fight, and under them will I die; but I will die with a more satisfied mind if I may be first permitted to see tranquillity restored to the Church and to the whole of Christendom by your power, your wisdom, and your good fortune. I shall never cease to pray that God will grant us this through your efforts, and may He preserve your Majesty and prosper you always. . . .

Mangan II, pp. 274-5. Allen VII, pp. 159-60

Erasmus to a Monk. Basel, 15 October 1527

. . . I am afraid that you may be imposed upon by the specious deceptions of certain persons who are boasting in splendid phrases of the Gospel liberty of today. Believe me, if you understood more of this movement from close observation, you would not be tired of that life you are leading. I see a class of men coming forth from whom my soul earnestly shrinks. I see no one becoming better, but, as many as I have known, they are surely worse, so that I sincerely grieve that formerly in my works I advocated spiritual freedom, though I did it with good intentions, never suspecting that such people would arise. It was my desire that something of ceremony might be abated, so that true piety might thereby benefit. Now the ceremonies are abandoned in such a way that instead of spiritual liberty there has succeeded an uncontrolled licence of the flesh. Some towns of Germany are filled with vagabonds, monks who have run away from their monasteries, priests who have married, most of them hungry and naked. There is nothing going on amongst them but dancing, eating, drinking, and fornication. They neither teach nor study, and there is no sobriety nor sincerity of life. Wherever they are, all good order ceases together with piety. I would write you more about these matters if it were safe to commit it to paper. You have lived worthily for so many years in that community of yours, and now, as you say yourself, your life is verging towards its evening, although you are perhaps eight or nine years younger than I. You dwell in a most commodious locality, in a fine climate, where the conversation of learned men brings to you much of solace, where there is an abundance of books, where there is intelligence. What in this life can be sweeter than to spend your leisure in meadows of this sort? There, tasting in advance, as it were, the felicity of celestial existence, especially in an age like the present, than which nothing can be depicted more turbulent or calamitous. I have known several of those who, having been deceived by the empty hope of liberty, have deserted their monasteries. Having changed their habit, they married; but, poverty-stricken and exiles, they became detestable to those to whom they were previously dear, and finally came to that state that, although there were those who wished to help them, it was not safe to do so. How their conscience troubles them, only the Lord knows; and how in their hearts their new surroundings suit them, is for them to see. What kind of liberty is that where it is not allowable to say prayers, where it is not permitted to say Mass, where it is not proper to fast, where it is not licit to abstain from meat? Think what could be more wretched than such things, even in these times? If a man be young and rich, he may for a few years enjoy the pleasures of this world, if indeed there be such here. But to seek to enjoy them when he is already advanced in years indicates insanity rather than mere folly. But you will say the rules and regulations are onerous, not to mention the jealousies and things of a similar nature. Whatever of such sort there may be present, it is the merest trifle to bear, provided that your disposition be good. In the world you would have to endure harsher things. So may God grant better sentiments to those people who by their wonderful tales are disturbing the tranquillity of your mind. May I die if I should not prefer to dwell with you there than to be the highest bishop in the palace of the emperor, provided that this poor, weak body of mine had strength to live there. But you are not aware either of the happiness you are enjoying or the misery of the times. . . . Hence, my dearest brother in the Lord, through our long and ancient friendship, and in the name of Christ, I beg, beseech, and entreat you to banish this weariness from your mind, and not to give ear to the deadly talk of men who will assist you not at all, but who will laugh at you rather when they have enticed you into the pit. If with all your heart you will despise the false attractions of this world, if you will give yourself entirely to Christ, if you will devote yourself to sacred literature and to meditating on the heavenly life, believe me, you will find more than abundant solace, and this little weariness of which you speak will vanish like smoke. If you take my advice and afterwards find that what I say is not true, then reproach me accordingly. And now, my dearest friend and brother in the Lord, may that same Lord fill your heart with every spiritual consolation. . . .

                                    Mangan II, pp. 275-7. Allen VII, pp. 199-201

Erasmus to Martin Bucer. Basel, 11 November 1527

. . . You assemble a number of conjectures as to why I have not joined your church. But you must know that the first and most important of all the reasons which withheld me from associating myself with it was my conscience. If my conscience could have been persuaded that this movement proceeded from God, I should have been now long since a soldier in your camp. The second reason is that I see many in your group who are strangers to all Evangelical soundness. I make no mention of rumours and suspicions. I speak of things learned from experience, nay, learned to my own injury; things experienced not merely from the mob, but from men who appear to be of some worth, not to mention the leading men. It is not for me to judge of what I know not; the world is wide. I know some as excellent men before they became devotees of your faith; what they are now like I do not know. At all events I have learned that several of them have become worse and none better, so far as human judgment can discern.

The third thing which deterred me is the intense discord between the leaders of the movement. Not to mention the Prophets and the Anabaptists, what embittered pamphlets Zwingli, Luther and Osiander write against each other! I have never approved the ferocity of the leaders, but it is provoked by the behaviour of certain persons; when they ought to have made the Gospel acceptable by holy and forbearing conduct, if you really had what you boast of. Not to speak of the others, of what use was it for Luther to indulge in buffoonery in that fashion against the King of England, when he has undertaken a task so arduous with the general approval? Was he not reflecting as to the role he was sustaining? Did he not realise that the whole world had its eyes turned on him alone? And this is the chief of this movement. I am not particularly angry with him for treating me so scurrilously; but his betrayal of the cause of the Gospel, his letting loose princes, bishops, pseudo-monks and pseudo-theologians against good men, his having made doubly hard our slavery, which is already intolerable

—that is what tortures my mind. And I seem to see a cruel and bloody century ahead, if the provoked section gets its breath again, which it is certainly now doing. You will say that there is no crowd without an admixture of wicked men. Certainly it was the duty of the principal men to exercise special care in matters of conduct, and not be even on speaking terms with liars, perjurers, drunkards and fornicators. As it is I hear and almost see, that these things are far otherwise. If the husband had found his wife more amenable, the teacher his pupil more obedient, the magistrate the citizen more tractable, the employer his workman more trustworthy, the buyer the seller less deceitful, it would have been great recommendation for the Gospels. As things are, the behaviour of certain persons has had the effect of cooling the zeal of those who at first, owing to their love of piety and abhorrence of Pharisaism, looked with favour on this movement; and the princes, seeing a disorderly host springing up in its wake made up of vagabonds, fugitives, bankrupts, naked, wretched, and for the most part even wicked men, are cursing, even those who in the beginning had been hopeful.

It is not without deep sorrow that I speak of all this, not only because I foresee that a business wrongly handled will go from bad to worse, but also because at last I shall myself have to suffer for it. Certain rascals say that my writings are to blame for the fact that the scholastic theologians and monks are in several places becoming less esteemed than they would like, that ceremonies are neglected, and that the supremacy of the Roman Pontiff is disregarded; when it is quite clear from what source this evil has sprung. They were stretching too tight the rope which is now breaking. They almost set the pope's authority above Christ's; they measured all piety by ceremonies, and tightened the hold of the confession to an enormous extent, while the monks lorded it without fear of punishment, by now meditating open tyranny. As a result 'the stretched string snapped,' as the proverb has it; it could not be otherwise. But I sorely fear that the same will happen one day to the princes, if they too continue to stretch their rope too tightly. Again, the other side having commenced the action of their drama as they did, no different ending was possible. May we not live to see worse horrors!

However, it was the duty of the leaders of this movement, if Christ was their goal, to refrain not only from vice, but even from every appearance of evil; and to offer not the slightest stumbling block to the Gospel, studiously avoiding even practices which, although allowed, are yet not expedient. Above all they should have guarded against all sedition. If they had handled the matter with sincerity and moderation, they would have won the support of the princes and bishops; for they have not all been given up for lost. And they should not have heedlessly wrecked anything without having something better ready to put in its place. As it is, those who have abandoned the Hours do not pray at all. Many who have put off pharisaical clothing are worse in other matters than they were before. Those who disdain the episcopal regulations do not even obey the commandments of God. Those who disregard the careful choice of foods indulge in greed and gluttony. It is a long-drawn-out tragedy, which every day we partly hear ourselves and partly learn of from others. I never approved of the abolition of the Mass, even though I have always disliked these mean and money-grabbing Mass-priests. There were other things also which could have been altered without causing riots. As things are, certain persons are not satisfied with any of the accepted practices; as if a new world could be built of a sudden. There will always be things which the pious must endure. If anyone thinks that Mass ought to be abolished because many misuse it, then the Sermon should be abolished also, which is almost the only custom accepted by your party. I feel the same about the invocation of the saints and about images.

Your letter demanded a lengthy reply, but even this letter is very long, with all that I have to do. I am told that you have a splendid gift for preaching the Word of the Gospel, and that you conduct yourself more courteously than do many. So I could wish that with your good sense you would strive to the end that this movement, however it began, may through firmness and moderation in doctrine and integrity of conduct be brought to a conclusion worthy of the Gospel. To this end I shall help you to the best of my ability. As it is although the host of monks and certain theologians assail me with all their artifices, nothing will induce me wittingly to cast away my soul. You will have the good sense not to circulate this letter, lest it cause any disturbance. We would have more discussions if we could meet. . . .

Huizinga, pp. 244-6. Allen VII, pp. 231-3

Erasmus to Thomas More. Basel, 29 February 1528

. . . In the numerous difficulties with which I am surrounded, the letter of the king, couched as it was in the kindliest terms, inviting me to England and promising everything worthy of such a benign prince, afforded me the greatest solace. He reminded me of what I had formerly written to him, that I had selected England as an abode for my old age. But now, my dear More, things are in such a state that I ought rather to be looking around for a place to lay my bones where it will be permissible for me to repose in death, since I perceive that such is not possible for me anywhere while I live. All men predict that a great revolt is upon us. The heretical sect of the Anabaptists, which is more widely spread than anyone thinks, is meditating an eruption. You will learn of my own troubles from my messenger Quirinus, a youth of tried reliability, whom I have decided to send to England because he knows all my affairs, so that I might arrange with my friends there as to what could be done, or what was best to be done. I would have rendered thanks to the king for his kindness, but, half-dead as I am from so many toils, and having no leisure, I preferred not to write at all to such a monarch than in a perfunctory way. If you will be so good, you can declare to him my gratitude, and that I am not ignorant or unmindful of the exceeding generosity which he has so often manifested in my behalf, though I feel I merit it not at all. I trust that you, and all those who are most dear to you, are well. . . .

Mangan II, p. 279. Allen VIII, p. 338

Erasmus to Hermann von Wied, Archbishop of Cologne. Basel, 19 March 1528
. . . Affairs of *bonae literae* were going along famously, except that the violent factiousness of certain people, trying to give us a new world all at once, has virtually ripped apart the fabric of the state with discordant views and contentious dogmas, and has shattered the harmony of the whole Church. And here, indeed, has vanished my fruit and recompense for so many sleepless nights, so much toil, so many years spent.

Personal loss, however, would matter little if it were compensated for with public good, especially, of course, the glory of Christ, who ought to be the only goal of all our actions. There can be nothing felicitous and prosperous in human affairs except what Christ performs in us so that, with our human passions subdued, our will may serve His will. . . .

Although I am deeply distressed by this tempest of the world I still have some hope that Divine Providence will change these tumults ultimately for the good. Prudent moderation on the part of leaders will be most conducive towards this end, a moderation which shuns factious impiety in such a way as to always have an understanding of true righteousness, plucking up weeds, that is, in such way as not to damage the wheat. This would be done more readily if, purging ourselves of private interests, we all fixed our sights on one target, the glory of Christ. . . .

Allen VII, pp. 362, 364. Himelick II, pp. 192, 193

C CONCEDO NULLI: 'I YIELD TO NONE'

Having offered neither support nor solace to the Lutherans and the Roman Catholics, Erasmus opened himself up to personal attacks. The so-called 'pillars of the Church' accused him of intolerable arrogance and pointed to his seal, *concedo nulli*, as proof of their assertion. Erasmus replied that this motto meant something else to him: 'I seized on the omen and interpreted it as a warning that the end of my existence was not far off . . . exhorting me to correct my life.' He devoted the remaining years in Basel to the study of Sacred Scripture and the Church Fathers.

Erasmus to Alfonso Valdés. Basel, 1 August 1528
I have learned very plainly from other men's letters what you indicate very discreetly, as is your way—that there are some who seek to make Terminus, the seal on my ring, an occasion for slander, protesting that the addition of the device 'Concedo nulli' [I yield to none] shows intolerable arrogance. What is this but some fatal malady, consisting in misrepresenting everything? Momus [Greek god of ridicule] is ridiculed for criticising Venus's slipper; but those men outdo Momus himself, finding something to carp at in a ring. I would have called them Momuses, but Momus carps at nothing but what he has first carefully inspected. These fault-finders, or rather false accusers, criticise with their eyes shut what they neither see nor understand: so violent is the disease. And their stupidity combined with a malice no less extreme, when they are already more notorious than they should be. They are dreaming if they think it is Erasmus who says *Concedo nulli*. But if they read my writings they would see that there is none so humble that I rank myself above him, being more liable to yield to all than to none.

Now those who know me intimately from close association will attribute any vice to me sooner than arrogance, and will acknowledge that I am closer to the Socratic utterance, 'This alone I know, that I know nothing,' than to this, 'I yield to none.' But if they imagine that I have so insolent a mind as to put myself before all others, do they also think me such a fool as to profess this in a device? If they had any Christian feeling they would understand those words either as not mine or as bearing another meaning. They see there a sculptured figure, in its lower part a stone, in its upper part a youth with flying hair. Does this look like Erasmus in any respect? If this is not enough, they see written on the stone itself *Terminus*: if one takes this as the last word, that will make an iambic dimeter acatalectic, *Concedo nulli Terminus*; if one begins with this word, it will be a trochaic dimeter acatalectic, *Terminus concedo nulli*. What if I had painted a lion and added as a device 'Flee, unless you prefer to be torn to pieces?' Would they attribute these words to me instead of the lion? But what they are doing now is just as foolish; for if I mistake not, I am more like a lion than a stone.

They will argue: 'We did not notice that it was verse, and we know nothing about Terminus.' Is it then to be a crime henceforward to have written verse, because they have not learned the theory of metre? At least, as they knew that in devices of this kind one actually aims at a certain degree of obscurity in order to exercise the guessing powers of those who look at them, if they did not know of Terminus—although they could have learned of him from the books of Augustine or Ambrose—they should have inquired of experts in this kind of matter. In former times field boundaries were marked with some sign. This was a stone projecting above the earth, which the laws of the ancients ordered never to be moved; here belongs the Platonic utterance: 'Remove not what thou hast not planted.' The law was reinforced by a religious awe, the better to deter the ignorant multitude from daring to remove the stone, by making it believe that to violate the stone was to violate a god in it, whom the Romans call Terminus, and to him there was also dedicated a shrine and a festival, the Terminalia. This god Terminus, as the Roman historian has it, was alone in refusing to yield to Jupiter because 'while the birds allowed the deconsecration of all the other sanctuaries, in the shrine of Terminus alone they were unpropitious.' Livy tells this story in the first book of his *History*, and again in Book 5 he narrates how 'when after the taking of auguries the Capitol was being cleared, Juventas [Youth] and Terminus would not allow themselves to be moved.' This omen was welcomed with universal rejoicing, for they believed that it portended an eternal empire. The youth is useful for war, and Terminus is fixed.

Here they will exclaim perchance: 'What have you to do with a mythical god?' He came to me; I did not adopt him. When I was called to Rome, and Alexander, titular Archbishop of St. Andrews, was summoned home from Siena by his father, King James of Scotland, as a grateful and affectionate pupil he gave me several rings for a memento of our time together. Among these was one which had *Terminus* engraved on the jewel; an Italian interested in antiquities had pointed this out, which I had not known before. I seized on the omen and interpreted it as a warning that the term of my existence was not far off—at that time I was in about my fortieth year. To keep this thought in my mind I began to seal my letters with this sign. I added the verse, as I said before. And so from a heathen god I made myself a device, exhorting me to correct my life. For Death is truly a boundary which knows no yielding to any. But in the medal there is added in Greek, Ορα τέλος μακροῦ βίου, that is 'Consider the end of a long life'; in Latin Mors ultima linea rerum. They will say: 'You could have carved on it a dead man's skull.' Perhaps, I should have accepted that, if it had come my way; but this pleased me, because it came to me by chance, and then because it had a double charm for me; from the allusion to an ancient and famous story, and from its obscurity, a quality specially belonging to devices.

There is my defence on Terminus, or better say on hair-splitting. And if only they would at last set a term to their misrepresentations! I will gladly come to an agreement with them to change my device, if they will change their malady. Indeed by so doing they would be doing more for their own authority, which they complain is being undermined by the lovers of good learning. I myself am assuredly so far from desiring to injure their reputation that I am deeply pained at their delivering themselves over to the ridicule of the whole world by these stupid tricks, and not blushing to find themselves confuted with mockery on every occasion.

Huizinga, pp. 246-9. Allen VII, pp. 430-32

Erasmus to Bernard von Cles. Basel, 24 February 1529
Reverend Bishop. I hope that this much-spoken-of Council [Diet of Spires: 15 March 1529] will procure for us the long-hoped-for tranquillity against this tempest, with the Lord's assistance, which Council, his serene highness, the King of Hungary and Bohemia, with what I consider pious zeal, is attempting to bring about. Your lordship will easily guess in what a coil I am here, not that I fear anything from the city council, but there is a great rabble of all kinds in this city. I have many enemies and some friends, but the influence of the latter is not of great weight in the present state of affairs. I should very much like my friends to bring it about that his most serene highness King Ferdinand should invite me hence by letter, as if he needed to use me in some matter. I trust I shall be at liberty to depart hence, not that I am accountable to anyone, but in that way I may make my departure more safely. There is no place I should prefer to Spires, but I fear that

my very infirm health would be poorly calculated to withstand the clamorous bickerings of the princes. Freiburg is my next choice, but it is a very petty town, and I hear that the townspeople are somewhat superstitious. For a long time the eating of fish has so disagreed with me that, if I even touch it, I am in danger of my life. Although I have the best of reasons, and although I have a papal dispensation covering all cases, yet the ignorant populace would exclaim at me, erring no less by their superstition than the opposite side errs by its wilful disobedience. For it is a graver matter to condemn your neighbour who, compelled by the greatest necessity and authorised by the supreme pontiff's permission, eats meat, than if he ate it without necessity. This very thing has kept me here for quite a time, for perhaps I should not have minded moving in the winter season. Hence I beg of you, that of your wonderful kindness you will give me your advice and help in this matter; and may you ever enjoy the best of health. I am sending you the proof-sheets of my work, *On the Christian Widow*, which I have, at the request of a certain person, dedicated to her most serene highness Maria, former Queen of Hungary, whose brother I have been unwilling to interrupt with correspondence, occupied as I deem he must be by such a multitude of affairs. His majesty has always had and ever will have my most willing service as long as my life lasts. . . .

Mangan II, pp. 310–11. Allen VIII, pp. 65–6

Erasmus to Louis Ber. Basel, 2 March 1529
. . . How safe it may be for me to remain here I know not. Murmurings and threats, not at all evangelical, of a few are brought to my notice, and I know well that wherever I go it will be at the risk of my life, although that is only a trifle, since even a change of wine or of clothing is a source of peril to me. But whatever the result, I must go away somewhere. . . .

Mangan II, p. 311. Allen VIII, p. 73

Erasmus to Francisco Vergara. Basel, 17 March 1529
. . . There is also that species of enemies who have lately begun to spring out of ambush. They feel put out that good literature should treat of Christ, as if nothing could be elegant but what is pagan. To their ears Jupiter Best and Greatest sounds better than Jesus Christ the Redeemer of the world, and Conscript Fathers than the Holy Apostles. They extol with praise Pontanus to the skies, while they turn up their noses at Augustine and Jerome. But I would rather have one ode of Prudentius hymning Jesus than a whole shipload of the poems of Pontanus,

whose learning and eloquence in other directions I do not at all despise. Among these people it is almost more disgraceful not to be a Ciceronian than not to be a Christian; just as if, were Cicero now alive, he would not speak differently about Christian matters than he did in his own day, when it was the main part of eloquence to speak to the point at issue. No one denies that Cicero excelled in the art of speaking, although not every kind of eloquence is suitable to particular persons or subjects. What means this odious boasting about the term *Ciceronian*? Let me whisper what I think about it in a few words. Under this pretence they hide their paganism, which is dearer to them than the glory of Christ. It will not much grieve me to be blotted from the list of *Ciceronians*, provided I shall be inscribed in the ranks of Christians. . . .

Mangan II, pp. 294-5. Allen VIII, p. 89

Erasmus to Louis Ber. Basel, 30 March 1529
. . . When will there be an end of these screeds by which I am being battered, and of the rage of those whose teeth are piercing arrows, on whose lips is the poison of serpents, and whose tongues are sharp swords? When will their villainy cease? From such outrageous conduct neither shame nor conscience, nor the authority of their rulers, nor the fruitlessness of their efforts so often cast in their face, restrains them from doing their nefarious work at meals, in private conversations, in secret confession, in sermons, in public lectures, in the palaces of kings, in travelling by land and sea. . . . And they are everywhere and speak all tongues. . . . And so they make themselves prevail, even though their cause, as they say, is barren. Now I speak only Latin; but had I a hundred tongues, of what avail am I alone against so many banded phalanxes, particularly when I have to fight not only against the forces of the enemy but also those of my own side? There is not one of these sects which does not hate me mortally, but especially that one whose members are trying to take away the Real Presence from us, and yet I am traduced to certain bishops and princes of being, as it were, in collusion with such as those.

. . . In such a flood of evils there is no quiet harbour of refuge throwing out a comforting light for my old age, now that I am fit neither for the tables of the lowly nor the halls of princes, except on condition that I associate myself with some one of these sects, a thing which I would surely have done had I been able to convince myself that everything they taught was right. Because I have not in any way been able to do this in the past, nor even now. I have resolved to fight with six

hundred sects rather than depart from the fold of the Catholic
Church.

It is not obscure for what frivolous reasons these people first attacked
me. To the great advantage of theology I cultivated languages and
polite literature, which they now pretend to admire, although more
than forty years ago they left no stone unturned to destroy and uproot
them when they were just beginning to spring up. And that was the
seed of this present tragedy. I exhorted the theologians that, leaving
aside their little questions which have more of ostentation than of
piety, they should betake themselves to the very sources of the Scriptures and to the ancient Fathers of the Church. Moreover, I did not
wish that scholastic theology should be abolished, but that it should be
purer and more serious. That, unless I am mistaken, is to favour, not
to hurt it. I exhorted the monks to be what they said they were, namely,
dead to the world, to trust less to external ceremonial, and to embrace
rather true piety of soul. Is this wishing well or ill to the monks?
I have noticed a few who take vows on themselves rashly, others who
seek to entrap untutored youth in their net; but I have never approved
of those who, without grave reasons, or without the authority of the
popes, desert their order. Nay I have even counselled and strengthened
many who were in doubt on this point. . . . Never have I contemned
the constitutions and rites of the Church, nor taught that they were to
be contemned; but I have given preference to the precepts of God;
I have shown the progression from ceremonies to better things; and,
if by the negligence of man anything foreign to them has crept in,
I have indicated how such might be corrected, a thing which the
Church has often done. There is no sacrament of the Church which I
have not always venerated, although I perceive that the ancient Fathers
entertained differing ideas concerning matrimony. Regarding sacra-
mental confession I have never doubted, but have considered it to be
religiously observed as if coming down to us from the spirit of Christ
and I have never dared, nor would I now dare, to approach the table
of Christ to depart this life, without confessing to a priest what has
been troubling my conscience. It is only that I have had my doubts
whether the sort of confession now in use has been handed down to us
by Christ himself; but my doubts have been only such that I should
favour it strongly if anyone were to prove it by unanswerable arguments.
I have never dreamed of abrogating the Mass. Concerning the Eucharist
I see no end of arguing; yet I have never been able to persuade myself,
nor shall I, that Christ who is truth, who is love, would have permitted
his beloved Spouse to remain so long in such an abominable error,

and suffer her to adore a fragment of bread instead of Himself. Touching the words with which we consecrate, I confess that at times I have desired to be more fully instructed; but regarding such scruples I easily allow myself to acquiesce in the judgment of the Catholic Church. The teaching by which certain persons attribute to everybody the power of consecrating, absolving, and ordaining, I have always held to be manifest insanity. I have always shrunk from sects and schisms, nor have I hitherto associated myself with any faction, although many reasons pushed me in that direction; nor have I ever collected any disciples, or, if I obtained any, I handed them over to Christ. . . . It was not necessary for anyone, on account of the wicked morals of some, to depart from the pious dogmas of the Church; but it is the duty of Christian prudence to extirpate once and for all both root and branch of these evils so that they may not easily spring up again. My own private misfortune I bear with more resignation because I know it cannot last very long. Already I am declining, and I recognise that my last hour is near; but indeed I cannot contemplate the open ruin of the Church without grieving. If this storm affected only those who are responsible for it, things would be more bearable. Now how many pious priests, how many upright monks, how many holy virgins, are being treated with indignity in various ways? and, if we regard the beginning of this affair, more atrocious things seem to threaten us, unless the goodness of a propitious Deity shall deign to avert them, the which I trust will not be lacking to us if with sincere hearts we have recourse thereto. In this goodness, my dearest lord and friend in Christ, let your heart and the hearts of all the afflicted find consolation. . . .

Mangan II, pp. 311-14. Allen VIII, pp. 117-22

Erasmus to Anthony Fugger. Basel, 5 April 1529
. . . I am accustomed for so many years to this nest, and to transplant an old tree is frowned upon even by a proverb of the Greeks. All the same, it is not safe for me to remain here, not that anyone commands me to go, but that those who wish me ill and who spread calumnies about me on every occasion will, if I stay here any longer, take it to indicate that I approve of whatever is going on here. . . . Also, since I must leave Basel, I prefer to get somewhere far away from it. . . .

Mangan II, p. 314. Allen VIII, pp. 132-3

PART IV *The Harvest (1529–36)*

The acceptance of the Zwinglian Reformation in Basel forced Erasmus, in 1529, to settle in Freiburg. Here he lived for six years, complaining of 'the dirt, bad food and fleas'. During these years he completed a treatise on *The Art of Preaching* (*Ecclesiastes*, 1535), which he dedicated to the martyred Bishop of Rochester, John Fisher. In June of 1535, Erasmus left Freiburg for Basel in order to supervise the publication of his *Ecclesiastes* and to edit the works of Origen. He lived in the home of Jerome Froben, the son of his old friend, surrounded by admirers. Having declined the offer of a Cardinal's hat from Paul III, Erasmus chose to live out the last year of his life in seclusion. His body ached with pain and his spirit grieved over the loss of Sir Thomas More and Bishop Fisher. 'I am a man who lives from day to day and every day expecting death, often longing for it, so horrible are the pains.'

A FREIBURG: THE 'BARKINGS OF THE HOUNDS' PERSIST

At the invitation of the town council, Erasmus moved to Freiburg. He was anxious to get to work, and within a few months, he completed his edition of St. Augustine (1529). He also turned to the question of reunion and published a collection of paraphrases on the Psalms in 1533, which he aptly titled *On Restoring Concord in the Church* (*De ecclesiae concordia*). This work was a call to fellowship and peace, but it fell on prejudiced ears. The 'barkings of the hounds' drowned out all such pleas for unity. Erasmus became the scapegoat, the object of derision and criticism from Lutherans and Catholics alike.

Erasmus to Aemilius de Aemiliis. Freiburg, 17 May 1529

. . . All grows wilder and wilder. Men talk of heresy and orthodoxy, of Antichrists and Catholics, but none speak of Christ. The world is in labour. Good may come if Christ directs the birth. There is no help else. Paganism comes to life again; Pharisees fight against the Gospel; in such a monstrous tempest we need skilful pilots. Christ has been sleeping so far. I trust the prayers of the faithful will wake Him. He may then command sea and waves, and they will obey Him. The monks have howled. The theologians have made articles on belief. We have had prisons, informations, bulls, and burnings; and what has come of them? Outcries enough; but no crying to Christ. Christ will not wake till we call to Him in sincerity of heart. Then He will arise and bid the sea be still, and there will be a great calm. . . .

Froude, p. 362. Allen VIII, p. 176

Erasmus to John Botzheim. Freiburg, 13 August 1529

. . . In such times as ours it is better to call on the Lord than to trust in princes and armies. We must pray to Him to shorten these days. Alas! Christianity has sunk so low that scarce a man knows now what calling on the Lord means. One looks to cardinals and bishops, another to kings, another to the black battalions of monks and divines. What do they want? What do they expect from protectors, who care nothing for Catholic piety, and care only to recover their old power and enjoyments? We were drunk or asleep, and God has sent these stern schoolmasters to wake us up. The rope has been overstrained. It might have stood if they had slackened it a little, but they would rather have it break than save it by concession. The pope is head of the Church, and as such deserves to be honoured. He stretched his authority too far, and so the first strand of the rope parted. Pardons and indulgences were tolerable within limits. Monks and commissaries filled the world with them to line their own pockets. In every Church were the red boxes and the crosses and the papal arms, and the people were forced to buy. So the second strand went. Then there was the invocation of saints. The images in churches at first served for ornaments and examples. By-and-by the walls were covered with scandalous pictures. The cult ran to idolatry; so parted a third. The singing of hymns was an ancient and pious custom, but when music was introduced fitter for weddings and banquets than for God's service, and the sacred words were lost in affected introductions, so that no word in the Liturgy was spoken plainly, away went another. What is more solemn than the Mass? But when stupid vagabond priests learn up two or three Masses and repeat them over and over as a cobbler makes shoes; when notorious profligates officiate at the Lord's table, and the sacredest of mysteries is sold for money—well, this strand is almost gone too. Secret confession may be useful; but when it is employed to extort money out of the terrors of fools, when an institution designed as medicine for the soul is made an instrument of priestly villainy, this part of the cord will not last much longer either.

Priests who are loose in their lives and yet demand to be honoured as superior beings have brought their order into contempt. Careless of purity, careless what they do or how they live, the monks have trusted to their wealth and numbers to crush those whom they can no longer deceive. They pretend that their clothes would work miracles, that they could bring good luck into houses and keep the devil out. How is it at present? They used to be thought gods. They are now scarcely thought honest men.

I do not say that practices good in themselves should be condemned because they are abused. But I do say that we have ourselves given the occasion. We have no right to be surprised or angry, and we ought to consider quietly how best to meet the storm. As things go now there will be no improvement; let the dice fall which way they will. The Gospellers go for anarchy; the Catholics, instead of repenting of their sins, pile superstition on superstition; while Luther's disciples, if such they be, neglect prayers, neglect the fasts of the Church, and eat more on fast days than on common days. Papal constitutions, clerical privileges, are scorned and trampled on; and our wonderful champions of the Church do more than anyone to bring the Holy See into contempt. There are rumours of peace. God grant they prove true. If the emperor, the pope, and the kings of France and England can compose their differences and agree on some common course of action, evangelical religion may be restored. But we must deserve our blessings if we are to enjoy them. When princes go mad, the fault is often in ourselves.

Froude, pp. 363–5. Allen VIII, pp. 253–5

Erasmus to Cuthbert Tunstall. Freiburg, 31 January 1530
. . . So far the battle has been fought with books and pamphlets. We are coming now to guns and halberds. If I cared less for my soul than my body I would rather be with the Lutherans; but I will not forsake the one Church with death now close on me in the shape of a stone in my bladder. Were Augustine to preach here now as he preached in Africa, he would be as ill-spoken of as Erasmus. I could find 600

passages in Augustine, and quite as many in St. Paul, which would now be called heretical. I am but a sheep; but a sheep may bleat when the Gospel is being destroyed. Theologians, schoolmen, and monks fancy that in what they are doing they strengthen the Church. They are mistaken. Fire is not quenched by fire. The tyranny of the Court of Rome and a set of scandalous friars set the pile alight, and they are pouring on oil to put it out. As to More, I am pleased to hear of his promotion. I do not congratulate him personally, but I congratulate Britain and, indirectly, myself. It is hoped that the emperor's authority will end the German schism. I trust, at any rate, that there will be no bloodshed, that the victory will be to Christ's honour, and that we shall not have papal officials and monks in power again. The clergy are thinking only of revenge, and not the least of amending their lives. . . .

Froude, p. 374. Allen VIII, pp. 343-4

Erasmus to Christopher Mesia. Freiburg, 30 March 1530
. . . Great lords, bishops, abbots, learned men of whom I have never heard, write daily to me, to say nothing of kings and princes and high prelates who are known to all mankind. With their communications come magnificent presents. To the Emperor Charles I owe the best part of my fortune, and his loving letters are more precious than his gifts. His brother Ferdinand writes equally often to me and with equal warmth. The French king invites me to Paris. The King of England writes to me often also. The Bishops of Durham and Lincoln send me gems of epistles, so do other bishops and archbishops and princes and dukes. Anthony Fugger sent me a hundred gold florins when he heard that I was leaving Basel, and promised me as much more annually if I would settle at Augsburg. Only a few days since the Bishop of Augsburg brought me two hundred florins and two princely drinking cups.

I have a room full of letters from men of learning, nobles, princes, and cardinals. I have a chest full of gold and silver plate, cups, clocks, and rings which have been presented to me, and I had many more which I have given away to other students. Of the givers, some are sages; some are saints, like the Archbishop of Canterbury and the Bishops of London and Rochester. I have not sought their liberality; I have always said that I had enough; yet if I had no pension from the emperor these alone would suffice for my support. Some call me, as you say, a sower of heresies, and deny that I have been of service to literature. If this be so, how came I by the favours of so many dis-

tinguished men? Compare the world as it was thirty years ago with the
world as it is now, and then ask what it owes to Erasmus. Then, not
a prince would spend a farthing on his son's education; now every one
of them has a paid tutor in his family. The elder theologians were
against me always, but the younger are on my side. Even among the
monks, some who began with cursing are now taking my part; and
finally here is yourself championing me against those impertinent
Franciscans. But, my dear friend, do not make the monks your enemies.
They are Dodona's cauldrons; if you stir one you stir all. I am sorry
the Observants have so degenerated. These two loquacious lads would
not have ventured so far without encouragement from their elders.
The problem before us is how to heal this fatal schism without rivers
of blood; and these youths are spreading the fire. Such as they are past
mending. Let them alone. I have still confidence in the emperor; he
has authority; he is pious and wise; he has even genius of a certain
kind, and an imperial objection to cruelty. . .

Froude, pp. 377–8. Allen VIII, pp. 403–4

Erasmus to Jacopo Sadoleto. Freiburg, c. 14 May 1530

. . . It seems to have displeased you that in my writings I have attacked
the Orders or the members thereof who are preeminent in dignity,
unless my memory is defective, for your remarks which I read cur-
sorily I do not exactly recall. What may have escaped me at times I
know not; but certainly it was never my intention to injure in my
writings any class of people, or any Order, unless, perchance, it hurts an
Order to be admonished about those matters which add to the welfare
of any Order, and increase both its authority and dignity. For instance,
the dignity of the Theological Order consists in seriously and reverently
treating the Sacred Scriptures, leaving all frivolous claptrap aside, and
in having their manners accord with their profession. The dignity of
the Monastic Order consists in excelling the rest of the multitude by
a sincere piety, after having truly mortified their human affections.
The dignity of princes consists in this, that they keep themselves as
free as possible from the exercise of every kind of tyranny. The dignity
of bishops is, that they approach as nearly as possible the virtues of
Christ and the Apostles. He who admonishes as to these things by
assailing those who disgrace their profession so little injures an Order
that, in my opinion, he is earnestly promoting the honour and profit
of the Order. And, lest what is at times said against the degenerate
ones might be taken as condemnation of all, I frequently entreat the
reader not to consider that what is spoken against the wicked few

appertains to all. But perhaps I err in this, that I entreat the reader too frequently or too vehemently. . . . .

Mangan II, pp. 324-5. Allen VIII, p. 433

Erasmus to Wolfgang Rem. Freiburg, 2 January 1531
. . . I could not have gone there [Augsburg] without the greatest risk to my life, and I preferred to live. Then, too, I plainly saw that if I went there I should only bring new tragedies on my head instead of calming these long-standing dissensions. I was well aware on whose judgment the emperor would rely, nor was I blind to the fact that there were there present the kind of theologians that would set any man down to be worse than a Lutheran who should dare to open his mouth for the promotion of piety. And I am by nature impatient of pretence and somewhat free of speech; and if I had attuned myself to the sentiments of certain people I should have to say many things that were contrary to my conscience. So that, in a way, I am not sorry that I was sick, since on that account I had a good reason to absent myself. But the Lord will not suffer His barque to be buried by the waves, no matter how this sea may rage. . . .

Mangan II, p. 330. Allen IX, p. 104

Erasmus to Augustine Cardinal Trivulzio. Freiburg, 12 April 1531
. . . I have done my best to stop these German troubles. I have sacrificed my popularity and broken my health, and small thanks I have met with from those whose part I have taken. The Lutherans had some right to be angry with me, but I did not look to be so venomously libelled by the Catholics. I had ill-friends at Rome who tried to set the pope against me. Happily, they did not succeed. If the pope knew all he would see that Erasmus had been his truest adviser. Tell the pope from me that I have encountered trials for Christ's sake which I would not have faced to be created pope myself. I have made enemies of all the men of learning who were once warmly attached to me, and old friends are the most dangerous of foes, because they know our secrets. . . .

Froude, pp. 395-6. Allen IX, pp. 255-6

Erasmus to Audomarus Edingus. Freiburg, 16 April 1531
. . . Now for the first time I am sick to surfeit of Germany. I know whom I ought to avoid, but whom I ought to follow I fail to see. Flanders comes into my mind often, but I doubt that it would be safe for me on account of the mendicant tyrants. Maria, former Queen of

Hungary, who has taken Princess Margaret's place, as I hear, is well disposed towards me. But if she were to do anything which, I will not say the Catholics but the zealots, did not like, they would say that I had instilled something into her ear, even if I had been dissuading her from it. Nor could she protect me from those who are armed with the authority of both the pope and the emperor. I hope that you are not experiencing the same sort of things that some of the other states are, where the disturbance of so many sects destroys all tranquillity; or where all things are permitted to the Evangelicals, while others are compelled to do things which they do not approve of. Certainly force is not Evangelical. I plainly fear that, while some are Lutherans, others Zwinglians, and still more Anabaptists, we shall all become Turks when fighting with the Turks, though I hope this prophecy may prove vain. I pray for you a tranquil life; but, for myself, I must fall in this gladiatorial arena into which some of my friends have thrust me in spite of myself. . . .

Mangan II, p. 334. Allen IX, pp. 258-9

Erasmus to the Senate of Besançon. Freiburg, 26 July 1531

Magnificent and most honourable masters. When the alteration in affairs at Basel compelled me to leave that old and hence pleasing refuge, I was reflecting about migrating to Besançon, having experienced on occasion the kindness of your body and that of the canons. The canons informed me that at that moment there was some disturbance there of what kind I know not, and that it would be better for me to defer my coming for a while. This I did, and at the written request and with the approbation of King Ferdinand, I betook myself to Freiburg near at hand, where now for two years I have lived in friendly relations with all, but particularly with the University. Nor have I been a burden to anyone, maintaining myself at my own cost. But now that I perceive all things to be in a state of suspense, with forebodings of war and tumults (which I trust will not eventuate), I should prefer to be anywhere rather than at Freiburg in case anything should happen. For to this town have come, and are still coming, all who have left Basel from hatred of the sects for the reason that they have been suspected by the latter of instigating several monarchs to have recourse to arms for a settlement of the religious question. The town itself is elegant and pleasant, but there is a scarcity of goods; and, moreover, my aged frame and poor state of health require many luxuries, particularly Burgundy wine, since these German wines disagree with my stomach terribly. When, however, I have it imported here in spite of the great expense, they either send me what I have not ordered, or it is spoiled by the carters. I trust indeed that all things will remain tranquil; but if anything disagreeable should occur, I should like to make use for a time of the hospitality of your town. No one will be put to inconvenience by me, for I have, thanks to the supernal powers, enough to care for my little wants. I have no connection with any sect, and I have no followers, except in common with Christ, nor shall I have, please God. I have said things about the vices of men which have offended certain morose individuals, when it were better that they had corrected their faults rather than criticise me for a well-meant warning. All I seek is a refuge and place of quietness for my declining years. I have been, and am still, invited to other places with splendid attractions, but it is not my intention to pass beyond the boundaries of the dominion of the emperor, whose remarkable favour has stood by me hitherto against the endeavours of my enemies. If in your wisdom you deem it of importance, I can most readily obtain, both from the emperor and King Ferdinand, commendatory letters, although such is your kindness that I do not think there is need either of their letters or my own. Yet on account of the varying opinions of men, and their different feelings, I thought it wise to do nothing in the matter without first ascertaining your sentiments, for without your approbation I know not whether or not I should be able to find in your town a quiet abode. . . .

Mangan II, pp. 336–7. Allen IX, pp. 307–8

Erasmus to Julius von Pflug. Freiburg, 20 August 1531
. . . Never was so wild an age as ours; one would think six hundred Furies had broken loose from hell. Laity and clergy are all mad together. I have not the power you think. I can work no miracles. I do not know what the pope intends. As burning heretics at the stake has failed, the priests now wish to try the sword. It is not for me to say if they are right. The Turks perhaps will not leave them leisure for the experiment. The better way would be to restore the Gospel as a rule of life, and then choose a hundred and fifty learned men from all parts of Christendom to settle the points in dispute. Opinions on special subjects need not be made Articles of Faith. Some laws of the Church may require to be changed, and clergy should be appointed fitter for their duties. At present the revenues of the Church go to support a parcel of satraps, and the people are left to the new teachers, who would abolish the whole Church organisation. Had Adrian lived and reigned ten years, Rome might perhaps have been purified. He sought my

advice. I gave it, but received no answer. I suppose it did not please
him. Melanchthon is a man of gentle nature. Even his enemies speak
well of him. He tried your plan at Augsburg, and had my health
allowed I would have been there to support him. You know what came
of it. Excellent eminent men were denounced as heretics merely for
having spoken to him. Suppose that he and I were to compose a
scheme of agreement, neither side would accept it—leaders or
followers. Remember Monk John in the theatre. John, being country-
bred, had never seen a theatre. Two prize-fighters were showing
off on the boards. John rushed in to part them, and was of course
killed. . . .

Froude, pp. 397–8. Allen IX, pp. 321–2

Erasmus to Conrad Goclen. Freiburg, 14 December 1531
. . . I have now replied to the censures of the Sorbonne, and the book
of which I send you a taste is almost entirely printed. And yet I had
already replied to most of them. They are mostly Beda's propositions.
I was well aware of what that sworn brotherhood deserved; but I
restrained my pen lest, being irritated beyond moderation, they might
burn my books, which they would deem a good and proper proceeding, since Beda, with a few of his conspiring friends, rules them, and
has the president of the Parliament in his favour, as I am informed.
The censures would not have appeared had not some of them wished to
add oil to the flame. [John] Eck was in Paris, and I assume [Girolamo]
Aleander as well, whom I suspect to have gone thither principally for
the purpose of attempting Erasmus' destruction; for I know just as
well as I know I am living that he was the author of that book of
Julius Scaliger's. However, I must pretend not to know this, lest he
rage worse against me on being found out. Beda's friends, I am sure,
will never cease. And yet Beda, hostile as he is, has not approved of the
publishing of this furious balderdash of Scaliger's. . . . Even now
certain Evangelicals, of whom the ringleader is that abandoned Guel-
drian, are striving with wonderful artifices to excite the minds of the
Emperor and Ferdinand against me. At Strassburg they have printed a
book in German against his imperial majesty, and they cite the authority
of Erasmus in many passages, taken, as I suspect, from my adage
The Scarab and the Eagle, and from my preface to *Suetonius*. I have no
doubt that it is [Wolfgang] Capito and Bucer who are doing this,
secretly aided perhaps by [Henry von] Eppendorff. I have not yet seen
the book, but I learned of the affair today from a letter of the Cardinal
of Trent, who presides over Ferdinand's Privy Council, and who is

very friendly towards me. No one at Strassburg ever attempted anything against me until Noviomagus [Gerard Geldenhauer] had moved to that city. He is now at Augsburg, where he is the professor of poetry at a salary, they say, of sixty florins. It is a good thing that two of the [Evangelical] leaders have perished, Zwingli in battle and Oecolampadius shortly afterwards, of fever and abscess, for if the god of battle had favoured them it would have been all over with us. . . .

Mangan II, pp. 338-9. Allen IX, p. 406

Erasmus to John of Heemstede. Freiburg, 28 February 1533
. . . For who does not love those men who, being truly dead to the world, have dedicated themselves to God; men whose life, whose conversation, is such that no one can depart from their presence and society without being the better for it; from whom one never fears trouble or deceit, from those who hold money as rubbish and give what they have to the poor; who, according to the Gospel, pray not for revenge on their persecutors, but love those who hate them, return good for evil; who are not a source of danger to the modesty of anyone because they themselves are clean of heart and body; who, on account of their singular humility, prefer themselves to none, envy none, despise none, but the nearer they approach to the summit of perfection, the more they deem themselves most unworthy; and, although they are the true jewels and flowers of the Church, yet call themselves but scum, minimise the lapses of others or interpret them favourably, while at the same time they are severe censors of their own acts; generously enlarge on the good deeds of others, but modestly make little of their own; flatter no one nor wound him with insulting words, and never slander the absent; from whose mouth nothing is heard except what is in the heart, namely, words of love, of consolation, of friendly admonition, and of thanksgiving? Theirs is a courtesy which is not counterfeit, but springs for a good conscience. Succinctly, they remind us of the celestial city, and represent, in a way, the choirs of angels, either because they continually chant the praises of God, or because, changed into spirits, they have no commerce with carnal affections; or because they live in complete concord; or because, acting as messengers between God and men, just as the angels do, they commend the aspirations of the people to Him, and, by their assiduous prayers, obtain the greatest amount of good from Him, not for themselves alone, but for others. Furthermore, what if to these virtues is added the gift of prophecy, so that freely, purely, and without taint they may instruct the people, either by their spoken word or by their writings,

or by both? What, I say, if, crucifying their flesh by fasting, by midnight watches, and by toil, as far as they are able, they supplement those things which Christ's sufferings lack, and, as you wish evil to those men who, while you are drunk and snoring, keep their midnight watches and fast for you; and, while you are provoking the wrath of God by your gambling, your lechery, and your other crimes, are beseeching Him in your behalf; and, while you are speaking ill of them before men, are speaking well of you before God? What man will not love and venerate such semi-supernal beings as these, divinely granted to us, as it were, for the benefit of all, even though he himself be a wretch? For distinguished virtue forces even its enemies to admire it. Those who merit well of no one are yet by a natural instinct reverent towards those who pour out their benefactions equally on the good and the bad. Therefore, what sort of perversity is it that some display who despise a man because he is a monk? When you mention the name monk you are speaking of one who is the sum of all the heroic virtues, one who merits benevolence and favour from the good, and wrests it from the wicked. If the name alone displeases, instead of a monk call him an upright and solitary man, if that seems better. Now solitude is not estimated by the number of people who live together, but by their retirement from bad passions; otherwise not even the Carthusians would be solitaries. Where such solitude is present there is indeed the closest companionship. He is happily solitary who is corrupted by no wicked company, who has in his heart no tumultuous passions striving with each other out of harmony with God. Such a man may be a monk in the courts of kings, in the halls of government, or in the marts of men. What sort of perversity is it then to hate a monk simply because he is a monk? Do you profess yourself to be a Christian, yet turn away from those who are most like Christ? You will say at once, I know, that many of them differ from this description. But we shall set the seal of our approval on no kind of life whatever if we hate the good members on account of the wicked ones. What is left then? What, but to love men, to make the best of them, to shut our eyes to their lighter failings, to endeavour to remedy their graver ones rather than to make them worse, and to venerate their Order itself and its rule? And if to their courteousness as ordinary men they add that of monks who devote themselves whole-heartedly and industriously to what belongs to true religion, easily would they regain their pristine popularity with the world, and easily would they silence the tongues of the slanderers. And the result would be that, not only would they be pleasing to God and acceptable to men, but they would live here in joy and happiness. For none live more quietly and sweetly than those who are really monks; none more miserably than those who are not so from the bottom of their hearts. To the former a monastery is a paradise, to the latter a drudgery. But it is in every man's power, in great measure, to change his drudgery into a paradise. . . .

Mangan II, pp. 345-7. Allen X, pp. 163-4

Erasmus to Damian de Goes. Freiburg, 25 July 1533

. . . You ask me, my dear Damian, what you are to answer to those who accuse me. Answer that their teeth are spears and arrows, and their tongue a sharp sword. No mortal ever heard me speak against the divorce[1] or for it. I have said it was unfortunate that a prince otherwise so happy should have been entangled in such a labyrinth, and should have been estranged from the Emperor when their friendship was of such importance to the world. But I should have been mad to volunteer an opinion on a subject where learned prelates and legates could not see their way to a decision. I love the King, who has been always good to me. I love the Queen, too, as all good men do, and as the King, I think, also does. The Emperor is my sovereign. I am sworn of his council, and if I forgot my duty to him I should be the most ungrateful of mankind. How, then, could I thrust myself unasked into a dispute so invidious? Had I been consulted, I should have endeavoured not to answer; but neither the Emperor nor Ferdinand ever did consult me. Two years ago two gentlemen from the Imperial Court came to me and asked me what I thought. I said I had not given my mind to the subject and could therefore say nothing; the most learned men disagreed; I could tell them, if they liked, what I wished; but to say what human or divine law would permit or forbid in such a matter required more knowledge than I possessed. They assured me that they had come of their own accord, and had no commission from the Emperor; and except these, no mortal has ever questioned me on the subject. The fools you speak of have told an impudent lie. It is true that many years ago I dedicated the twenty-second Psalm to the new lady's father[2] at his own request. He is one of the most accomplished peers in England, and is a man of wisdom and judgment. But this is nothing to the divorce, which I hear he has neither advised nor approves. . . .

Froude, pp. 407-8. Allen X, pp. 272-3

[1] The 'divorce' of Catherine of Aragon by Henry VIII in 1533.
[2] Sir Thomas Boleyn, father of Anne Boleyn.

Erasmus to John Choler. Freiburg, 19 February 1534

. . . Would that I might have more joyful news to write you about my health; but this pain in my feet, or in my hands, or over my whole body, attacking as it does every limb, darts away to a new spot when it has sufficiently scourged the old haunt, the unbearable pain thereof lasting generally about four days; then, when the swelling appears, it becomes less painful, but, after the manner of generals, takes many fortresses and, leaving behind a garrison therein, proceeds to take another, there fighting with renewed fury, returning on the slightest provocation to the original spot of onset, which it makes worse than ever. It will not bear even the lightest touch, so that you might call it a thistle, which the Greek proverb warns you not to handle. I am beginning to fear that this little old body of mine, tortured by so much suffering and distress, may not long hold out. . . .

Mangan II, p. 352. Allen X, p. 359

B BASEL: FINAL REFLECTIONS

Erasmus spent the year 1535 to 1536 in Basel, bravely striving to finish his edition of Origen. His was an uphill battle, for he suffered from a fatal illness and hostile critics. In the course of fifteen years, Erasmus lived to see his programme of reform, *Philosophia Christi*, shattered and his reputation tarnished by extremists. He found comfort only in study and prayer. Erasmus died on 12 July 1536.

Erasmus to Bartholomew Latomus. Basel, 24 August 1535

. . . I have spent a long life, counting in years; but were I to calculate the time spent in wrestling with fever, the stone and the gout, I have not lived long. But we must patiently bear whatever the Lord has sent upon us, Whose will no one can resist, and Who alone knows what is good for us. . . . The glory [of an immortal name] moves me not at all, I am not anxious over the applause of posterity. My one concern and desire is to depart hence with Christ's favour.

Many French nobles have fled here for fear of the winter storm, after having been recalled. 'The lion shall roar, who shall not fear?' says the Prophet [Amos]. A like terror has seized the English, from an unlike cause. Certain monks have been beheaded and among them a monk of the Order of St. Bridget [Richard Reynolds] was dragged along the ground, then hanged, and finally drawn and quartered. There is a firm and probable rumour here that the news of the Bishop of Rochester [John Fisher] having been co-opted by Paul III as a cardinal caused the king [of England] to hasten his being dragged out of prison and beheaded—his method of conferring the scarlet hat. It is all too true that Thomas More has been long in prison and his fortune confiscated. It was being said that he too had been executed, but I have no certain news as yet. Would that he had never embroiled himself in this perilous business and had left the theological cause to the theologians. The other friends who from time to time honoured me with letters and gifts now send nothing and write nothing from fear, and accept nothing from anyone, as if under every stone there slept a scorpion.

It seems that the pope is seriously thinking of a council here. But I do not see how it is to meet in the midst of such dissension between princes and lands. The whole of Lower Germany is astonishingly infected with Anabaptists: in Upper Germany they pretend not to notice them. They are pouring in here in droves; some are on their way to Italy. The emperor is besieging La Goulette, in my opinion there is more danger from the Anabaptists.

I do not think that France is entirely free of this plague; but they are silent there for fear of the cudgel. . . .

Now I must tell you something about my position which will amuse you. I had written to Paul III at the instance of Louis Ber, the distinguished theologian. Before unsealing the letter he spoke of me with great respect. And as he had to make several scholars cardinals for the coming Council, the name of Erasmus was proposed among others. But obstacles were mentioned, my health, not strong enough for the duties, and my low income; for they say there is a decree which excludes from this office those whose annual income is less than 3,000 ducats. Now they are busy heaping benefices on me, so that I can acquire the proper income from these and receive the red hat. The proverbial cat in court dress. I have a friend in Rome who is particularly active in the business; in vain have I warned him more than once by letter that I want no cures or pensions, that I am a man who lives from day to day, and every day expecting death, often longing for it, so horrible sometimes are the pains. It is hardly safe for me to put a foot outside my bedroom, and even the merest trifle upsets me. With my peculiar, emaciated body I can stand only warm air. And in this condition they want to push me forward as a candidate for benefices and

cardinal's hats! But meanwhile I am gratified by the supreme pontiff's
delusions about me and his feelings towards me. . . .

Huizinga, pp. 252-3. Allen XI, pp. 215-17

Erasmus to Conrad Goclen. Basel, 28 June 1536
. . . A Certain Spaniard has by letter commended me to the heroine of
Nassau [Juliana of Stolberg?] who is coming hither. You request me to
write to her, but I know not where she is to be found, for you intimated
that she was about to leave there. If you had really known how things
were with me here, you would have answered her in my behalf that
I had been compelled to leave Freiburg on account of my health, and
with the object in view that, after seeing my *Ecclesiastes* through the
press, I was going to betake myself to Besançon in order not to be
outside the emperor's dominions, but that my health becoming worse
I was obliged to pass the winter here. Although I am here amongst
friends that are most sincere, and such as I had not at Freiburg, yet on
account of the dissensions about doctrines I would prefer to end my
days elsewhere. Would that Brabant were nearer! . . .

Mangan II, p. 376. Allen XI, p. 337

Erasmus, 'Dedication,' Ecclesiastes (or The Art of the Preacher), 1536
. . . I have found out by experience, friend Christopher [Stadius,
Bishop of Augsburg], ornament of the bishops of this age, that it was
no vain saying of the ancient oracles that trouble followed a promise.
Many years ago I promised some sort of a work on preaching, but,
to tell the truth, I was not really in earnest about it. When afterwards
I was seriously asked to make good this not seriously meant promise,
but had no time to put into effect what was being demanded of me,
I began to jot down here and there on pieces of paper notes for future
use, if perchance I might feel the will and capacity to undertake the
matter. But I did not exercise much care or order [in the selection of
my material], but seized it as opportunity offered it. The demand
becoming more urgent, I began to gather my scraps together, all
topsy-turvy as they were, some of them even being torn and stained
with dirt. When these were examined, more and more I shrank from
the task, just as I had always done previously, from some unexplain-
able feeling of my mind. I saw that the subject was as varied as it was
vast, and would make an immense volume if it were to be rightly
treated, and would also attract considerable hostility in the present
condition of the times. When at last there was a continuous demand
for it, and that I might not seem entirely false to my promise, I put

pen to paper, but with reluctance. I kept rejecting what I had written, for nothing seemed to please me. Again and again I laid it down, only to take it up again after some interval if my mind should warm to it; and I bound myself to the task with chains as tenacious as those with which Vergil tells us Aristaeus bound Proteus. Success, however, crowned his efforts, but mine did not succeed. Meanwhile I entertained the hope that, by my delaying, someone would arise who would assume the undertaking, especially among such a number of fortunate geniuses as this age has produced, who are so eager to publish new works. Since no one appeared to undertake it, and day by day I was being more vigorously urged, both personally and by letter, even to the extent of incurring abuse in the matter, I approached the distasteful business, raw and undigested as the material was, so that I might at least show my desire to fulfil my promise provided that my ability was equal to this desire. Nor was I able to work at it continuously; for at times my enfeebled health, and at times my other intervening labours, compelled me to lay aside the task I had assumed, so that it was only at long intervals that I could resume my work on it. That is why the learned reader may perhaps observe certain gaps, certain incomplete sentences, certain repetitions, certain things said in an unsuitable place. Someone may say, 'Why did you not correct later what displeased you?' Not to use deceit, it irked me to go over such a vast work, when what I had already done of it had been accomplished in spite of increasing infirmities. No one can easily imagine how piti-fully my mind longs to retire from such toils, and to rest tranquilly during what remains to me of life, little as it must be, and to be able to speak alone with Him who long ago exclaimed, and is still exclaim-ing, 'Come to me all you that labour and are heavy laden, and I will refresh you.' Hence it is that in such a turbulent, not to say, insane, age, amid so many anxieties which these times publicly, and my age and infirm health privately, bring on me, I find nothing in which my mind more willingly reposes than in this mystical colloquy. Therefore, I trust all the more that the just reader will take in good part what I here offer him, and take it as it is. . . .

Mangan II, pp. 366–7

Beatus Rhenanus, 'Preface to Erasmus' Ecclesiastes.' Schlettstadt, 1536
. . . Erasmus had returned from Freiburg to Basel in the previous year so that he might be present while his *Ecclesiastes*, or *Method of Preaching*, was passing through the press of Froben; and might also finish it there, for a part of the conclusion was still lacking; also for the purpose

of improving by change of air the bad health from which he had begun to suffer at Freiburg. He had not left as if he were never to return, for he had lived there most agreeably under Ferdinand, King of the Romans, of Hungary, and of Bohemia, who by personal letter had earnestly recommended to the authorities of that town Erasmus' importance; and there for seven years he had not only been beloved by all the members of the University, but was also highly esteemed and regarded by the town council and the citizens. After he had been repeatedly invited to her court of Brabant by Maria, the illustrious Queen of Hungary, who had even sent him money for travelling expenses, wishing to fulfil the promise he had more than once made her of returning to Lower Germany, he arranged to have all his belongings transferred from Freiburg to Basel and thence down the Rhine to Brabant when navigation should be favourable. After he had done this and the good season of the year was fast approaching, the arthritis, with which he had been afflicted at Freiburg, so confined him to his bed until nearly the following autumn that he rarely left his chamber, and only once was he outside of his room. And yet in such torturing of his limbs he never ceased to write whenever he felt the least respite, as is proved by his little commentary *On the Purity of the Christian Church*, and this present revision of Origen. But his powers diminishing little by little, for he had suffered almost a month with dysentery, he at length perceived that his end was near; and so, surrounded as ever by those visible and eminent testimonies to his Christian patience and his devout mind by which he witnessed that he had fixed his hope on Christ, crying out constantly, 'Mercy, O Jesus, Lord deliver me, Lord make an end, Lord have mercy on me,' and in the German language, 'Lieber Gott,' that is, 'Dear God,' on the twelfth of July near midnight, he died. No other words did he utter, although having full use of his reason to the very last breath. . . . How general was the regret for him was indicated by the crowds that came to view the remains. He was carried on the shoulders of the students to the Cathedral and there honourably buried near the steps that lead to the choir, as it is called, on the left side of the edifice where there was a little chapel dedicated to the Blessed Virgin. In the funeral procession were seen not only the Governor, but most of the Senators, and not a single one of the professors and students was absent. He was quite liberal during his life towards students in want and others who were worthy of help, as often as any came his way. The last wishes of this man did not differ from his usual goodness, for he made a will confirmed by the authority of Pope Clement, of the Emperor Charles, and of the Magistracy of

Basel, in which he charged his heir, the most illustrious jurisconsul Boniface Amerbach, with the duty of distributing his goods to those who were poor or infirm, to maidens of marriageable age that their virtue might be protected, to young students of good promise, and to anyone of this sort whomsoever he should find worthy of help; and he added to him two executors, Jerome Froben and Nicholas Episcopius. What could be more saintly than such a will, or more Christian? Others dedicate their property to the building and adorning of basilicas; Erasmus preferred to bestow on the living temples of God what remained of his goods after his death. . . .

Mangan II, pp. 377–9

BIOGRAPHICAL REGISTER

Adrian VI (d. 1523), pope

Aemilius de Aemiliis (d. 1531), of Brescia, alias Migli

Albert of Brandenburg (d. 1545), abp. of Magdeburg and Mainz

Aleander, Girolamo Cardinal (d. 1542), of Friuli

Alvarus, Juan (d. 1557), alias Alvarez

Amerbach, Boniface (d. 1562), of Basel

Amerbach, John (d. 1513), of Amorbach

Ammonius, Andreas (d. 1517), of Lucca

Andrelinus, Faustus (d. 1518), of Forli

Atensis, John, of Louvain

Badius, Josse (d. 1535), of Assche

Barbirius, Nicolas, of Arras

Barbirius, Peter (d. 1551), of Arras, dean of Tournai

Batt, James (d. 1502), of Bergen

Beda, Noel, theologian at Paris

Bembo, Peter (d. 1547), of Venice

Benserad, Nicolas, alias Bensrott, of Ueffeln

Ber, Louis (d. 1554), alias Baer

Bergen, Anthony of (d. 1532), abbot of St. Bertin

Bergen, Henry of (d. 1502), bp. of Cambrai

Blount, William (d. 1534), fourth Lord Mountjoy

Boerio, Giovanni B. (of Genoa), physician to Henry VII

Bombasius, Paul (d. 1527), of Bologna

Borsselen, Anne (d. 1518), of Veer

Bostius, Arnold (d. 1499) of Ghent

Botzheim, John (d. 1535), of Sasbach

Brunfels, Otto (d. 1534), of Mainz

Bucer, Martin (d. 1551), of Sélestat

Budé, William (d. 1540)

Busleiden, Francis (d. 1502), bp. of Besançon

Caesarius, John (d. 1550), of Jülich

Caminadus (i.e. Augustine Vincent), of Kamin

Campeggio, Lorenzo, Cardinal (d. 1539)

Capito, Wolfgang (d. 1541), of Hagenau

Carlstadt, Andreas (d. 1541)

Charnock, Richard, prior of St. Mary's College, Oxford

Chièvres (d. 1521), alias William Cardinal de Croy, abp. of Toledo

Choler, John, provost of Chur

Clement VII (d. 1534), pope (Giulio de' Medici)

Cles, Bernard von (d. 1539), bp. of Trent

Clichtove, Josse van (d. 1543), of Nieuwpoort

Colet, John (d. 1519), dean of St. Paul's

Cop, William (d. 1532), of Basel

Deloin, Francis (d. 1524)

Dobneck, John (d. 1552), of Wendelstein, alias Cochlaeus

Dorp, Martin (d. 1525), of Naaldwijk

Eck, John (d. 1543)

Edingus, Audomarus (d. 1542), of Op-Hasselt, alias Enghien

Edmund, Friar, of Saint-Omer

Egnatius, Baptista (d. 1553), of Venice

Eppendorf, Henry von (d. 1551)

Ferdinand I (d. 1564), King of Bohemia and Hungary

Fisher, Christopher (d. 1511), bp. of Elphin

Fisher, John (d. 1535), bp. of Rochester

Fisher, Robert, kinsman of the bp. of Rochester

Foxe, Richard (d. 1528), bp. of Winchester

Froben, John (d. 1527), of Hammelburg, printer

Froben, John (d. 1549), son of the above

Fugger, Anthony (d. 1560), of Augsburg

Gallinarius, Joannes, of Heidelberg, alias Henner

Gaza, Theodore (d. 1475), of Salonika

Goldenhauer, Gerard (d. 1542), of Nijmegen

George of Saxony (d. 1539), duke

Gillis, Peter (d. 1533), of Antwerp

Goclen, Conrad (d. 1539), of Mengeringhausen

Goes, Damian de (d. 1574), of Portugal

Goudanus, Cornelius, of Gouda, alias Gerard

Greveradus (known simply as *advocatus*)

Grey, Thomas, student of Erasmus

Grimani, Domenico, Cardinal (d. 1523)

Grocyn, William (d. 1519)

Grunnius, Lambert, imaginary papal secretary

Halewin, George (d. 1536), viscount of Nieuwpoort

Heemstede, John of, Carthusian at Louvain

Herman, William (d. 1510), of Gouda

Hutten, Ulrich von (d. 1523)

James V (d. 1542), King of Scotland

John, Cardinal of Lorraine (Jean de Lorraine)

John of Louvain, Franciscan from Amsterdam

Julius II (d. 1513), pope

Lange, John (d. 1567), of Freistadt

Lascaris, John (d. 1535), of Rhyndacus

Latimer, William (d. 1545)

Latomus, Bartholomew (d. 1570), of Arlon

Latomus, Jacob (d. 1544), of Cambron, alias Masson

Laurinus, Marcus (d. 1546), dean of St. Donation, Bruges

Lee, Edward (d. 1544), abp. of York

Lefèvre d'Etaples, Jacques (d. 1536)

Leo X (d. 1521), pope (Giovanni de' Medici)

Leonicenus, Nicolas (d. 1524), of Vicenzia

Le Sauvage, John (d. 1518)

Linacre, Thomas (d. 1524)

Lipsius, Martin (d. 1555) of Brussels

Luxembourg, Antony of, steward at St. Bertin, Saint-Omer

Manius, Peter, Dominican friar

Manutius, Aldus (d. 1574), of Venice

Marlianus, Aloysius, bp. of Tuda

Marsilius of Padua (d. 1342)

Maximilian I (d. 1519), Holy Roman Emperor

Melanchthon, Philipp (d. 1560)

Mesia, Christopher, of Seville

More, Sir Thomas (d. 1535)

Musurus, Marcus (d. 1517), of Crete

Oecolampadius, John (d. 1531), of Weinsberg, alias Hussgen

Osiander, Andreas (d. 1552), of Nuremberg

Pace, Richard (d. 1536)

Paludanus, John (d. 1525), of Cassel, alias Desmarez

Paul III (d. 1549), pope (Alexander Farnese)

Pflug, Julius von (d. 1564), bp. of Naumburg

Pico della Mirandola (d. 1533)

Pio, Albert (d. 1531), of Carpi

Pirckheimer, Willibald (d. 1530), of Eichstadt

SELECTED READING

Though one is tempted to question the interpretations of all the biographies of Desiderius Erasmus, three of them deserve careful reading: Johann Huizinga, *Erasmus of Rotterdam* (New York, 1924), Margaret M. Phillips, *Erasmus and the Northern Renaissance* (London, 1949), and Roland H. Bainton, *Erasmus of Christendom* (New York, 1969). These biographers write with enormous persuasion and grace. Yet one is likely to find the most satisfying interpretation of Erasmus' place in Early Modern Europe in the biography by Bainton. There are a number of other sources of information on more specialised topics. See, for example, the dated but penetrating lectures of Percy S. Allen, *The Age of Erasmus: Lectures Delivered in the Universities of Oxford and London* (Oxford, 1914); the masterly account of Erasmus from 1469 to 1495, based on primary sources, by Albert Hyma, *The Youth of Erasmus* (Ann Arbor, 1930), Margaret M. Phillip's excellent study of *The Adages of Erasmus*, which traces their origin and impact (Cambridge, 1964), Craig R. Thompson's useful notes in *The Colloquies of Erasmus* (Chicago, 1965), and Margaret E. Aston's probing analysis of Erasmus as the spokesman of a generation, 'Erasmus and the Northern Renaissance,' in *The Meaning of the Renaissance and Reformation*, ed. Richard L. DeMolen (Boston, 1973), Chapter 3. Finally, for a recent interpretative summary of the life and influence of Erasmus, read *Erasmus of Rotterdam: A Quincentennial Symposium*, ed. Richard L. DeMolen (New York, 1971).